The **100**
Best Investments
for Your Retirement

The 100

Best Investments
for Your Retirement

J.W. Dicks • Charles C. Smith, Jr.
James L. Paris

ADAMS MEDIA CORPORATION
Holbrook, Massachusetts

Published by Adams Media Corporation
260 Center Street, Holbrook, MA 02343

ISBN: 1-55850-609-8

Printed in Canada

J I H G F E D C B A

Library of Congress Cataloging-in-Publication Data
Dicks, J. W. (Jack William), 1949–
The 100 best investments for your retirement / J. W. Dicks,
Charles C. Smith, Jr., James L. Paris.
p.   cm.
ISBN 1-55850-609-8 (pb)
1. Investments—United States—Handbooks, manuals, etc. 2. Retirement
income—United States—Planning—Handbooks, manuals, etc. I. Smith,
Charles, 1948–   . II. Paris, James L., 1965–   . III. Title.
HG4527.D53   1996
332.6—dc20   96–14666
CIP

This publication is designed to provide accurate and authoritative information
with regard to the subject matter covered. It is sold with the understanding that
the publisher is not engaged in rendering legal, accounting, or other professional
advice. If legal advice or other expert assistance is required, the services of a
competent professional person should be sought.
    — From a *Declaration of Principles* jointly adopted by a Committee of the
American Bar Association and a Committee of Publishers and Associations

This book is available at quantity discounts for bulk purchases.
For information, call 1-800-872-5627 (in Massachusetts, 617-767-8100).

Visit our home page at http://www.adamsmedia.com

To my children, Joy, Jimmy, and Faith. For your understanding and patience with your busy Dad.
— JIM PARIS

To the memory and honor of my Daddy, Charles C. Smith, Sr.
— CHARLES C. SMITH, JR.

To Dorothy and David Edmunds, happily retired and going strong. Thanks for making me part of your family.
— J. W. DICKS

Contents

Chapter One

Retirement Account Overview 11

Individual Retirement Account (IRA) **12**

Simplified Employee Pension Plan (SEP-IRA) **14**

Keogh **15**

401(k), 403(b), and 457 Plan **17**

Annuity **18**

Chapter Two

How to Select Your Retirement Investments 23

Definition of a Successful Retirement **23**

Where Are You Now? **24**

Asset Allocation Models **27**

Where Do You Want to Go? **29**

What to Do When Time Is Running Out **31**

Passive Versus Active Investing **33**

Chapter Three

Investing in Mutual Funds 37

What Is a Mutual Fund? **37**

Mutual Fund Advantages **38**

Mutual Fund Costs **40**

How We Picked the Funds for This Book **42**

Chapter Four

The 65 Best Mutual Funds for Retirement 49
Growth and Income Funds   49
International Funds   75
Growth Funds   102
Balanced Funds   128
Bond Funds   154
The Best of the Rest   178

Chapter Five

Selecting Stocks for Retirement 199
Are Individual Stocks Appropriate for
    Retirement Investors?   201
Choosing the Type of Stock That's Best for You   202
How We Selected Stocks for This Book   206

Chapter Six

The 30 Best Growth Stocks to Own
for Retirement 209

Chapter Seven

Why Annuities Are Excellent
Retirement Vehicles 241
Fixed Versus Variable Annuities   243
Are Annuities Really Insurance Products at All?   244
How We Picked the Annuities for This Book   245

Chapter Eight

The 5 Best Annuities to Own for Retirement 249

Chapter Nine

Treasury Securities for a Secure Retirement 259
Who Should Invest in Treasuries?   260
The Case for Treasuries   263
The Case Against Treasuries   263
How to Buy Treasuries   264

Index 267

Acknowledgments

The authors would like to extend their special thanks to Robert Yetman for his work in the production of this book.

Additionally, our thanks to Dick Staron for his ideas, encouragement, and commitment to the project.

CHAPTER ONE
Retirement Account Overview

There are several important steps to take in planning for a successful retirement, but certainly one of the most important has to be the selection of an appropriate retirement account. Hopefully, most of you reading this book are doing well in advance of your actual retirement and thus will have the opportunity to truly benefit from our discussion on what's available. If not, don't be too disheartened. The fact is, it's never too late (or too early) to begin retirement planning. The strategies you use, however, will differ depending on where you are on the retirement time line. In Chapter 2, we'll discuss more fully the strategies that late starters must utilize, as well as just how retirement investing differs for someone who is already retired.

OK. Here's the situation: You've got several years to go until you retire, and you insist on getting the absolute most from your money (as well you should). The actual investments you select will play a major role in just what that amount ends up being—that's obvious. What may not be so obvious, however, is the extent to which the actual retirement plan "umbrella" you choose affects that figure. It's imperative that you understand all of the plan options that are available to you so that you may make the smartest overall decision.

You'll notice that we referred to retirement plans as "umbrellas" above. "Umbrella" is actually a good metaphor for "retirement plan," because that, in essence, is what it really is. Honest-to-goodness retirement plans act as *tax-deferred* umbrellas, sheltering you from current-year tax liabilities while the accounts are growing. This raises an important point—namely, that retirement plans are not investments. An IRA, for example, is not an investment in itself. What it *is* is an account, an umbrella, under which individual investments are placed. That misunderstanding is common, and we have to be sure it's cleared up before we go any further. You do not make a decision, for instance, to invest either in an IRA *or* a mutual fund; that's comparing apples and oranges. The IRA is the plan, the umbrella, and the mutual fund is the specific investment that you place *under* the IRA. We hope that's clear.

There are many different types of retirement plans out there, and it's important that you learn how to tell them apart. For our purposes, we'll keep our focus on the more common types of plan that are available to you. Specifically, we'll look at Individual Retirement Accounts (IRAs), Simplified Employee Pension plans (SEP-IRAs), Keoghs, company-sponsored plans—401(k)s, 403(b)s, and 457s—, and annuities. You *will* be eligible for at least *one* of these umbrellas, and the shrewd retirement planner will learn how he or she can utilize two or more of them at the same time. By the way, all of the plans we'll look at, except for annuities, must be funded with earned income. This means that you must have earned through employment *at least* the amount of your plan contribution in a given year. Now, without further delay, let's take a look at what's available to you.

INDIVIDUAL RETIREMENT ACCOUNT (IRA)

This is perhaps the best known of the nonprivate retirement plans, probably because anyone who works may open one.

Any employed person may contribute up to $2,000 of earned income each year to an IRA. A working *couple* may deposit a total of up to $4,000 each year ($2,000 apiece into respective plans), while a married couple with only one working spouse may deposit a total of $2,250 each year between a regular IRA and a spousal IRA.

Those are the basic rules that govern contributions. As you may know, IRA contributions may be tax-deductible, and there are important rules you should know regarding that feature as well. The full amount of your $2,000 IRA contribution can be deducted on your income tax return *if* your adjusted gross income is $25,000 or less (single) or $40,000 or less (married couple filing jointly). If you're single and earn between $25,000 and $35,000 you will be entitled to a partial deduction; if married and earning between $40,000 and $50,000, same thing. You may still have an IRA if you exceed those limits altogether, but no part of your contribution will be deductible. Finally, if you or your spouse is covered by a retirement plan at work, that will also severely limit the deductibility of your contribution. You would be well-advised to consult a knowledgeable tax adviser if you have questions about your own situation.

IRAs can be set up just about anywhere. You may have an IRA through a bank, as many people do. You may also have your IRA trusteed at a mutual fund company, or at a regular securities brokerage house. Really, any type of major financial institution will have the ability to serve as the custodian of your IRA. It will be up to you, however, to ensure that the custodian you select will permit the kinds of investments you want to make within your IRA. For example, if you want to invest in high-quality, well-known mutual funds, you probably won't want to keep your IRA at a bank. Although it's true that many banks now offer mutual funds and other securities products, your selection most likely will be limited to the bank's own proprietary investments. By the same token, if you aspire to do a lot of individual stock trading in your IRA, you will not want to set it up at one particular mutual fund company. In that scenario, you would probably want to pursue the possibility of having a brokerage house, particularly a discount brokerage house, serve as the custodian.

Actually, a discount brokerage might well be the best overall place to house your IRA (or any other retirement plan, for that matter). A discount brokerage affords you the opportunity to invest in almost all types of negotiable securities at commission prices that are much lower than those charged by the full-service retail outfits. Some of the more competitive discounters like Charles Schwab and Company will allow you to invest in many different high-quality, no-load (no commission) mutual funds for no transaction costs at all.

Here are a few more things you should be aware of regarding IRAs. For acting as the custodian of your plan, all custodians will charge an annual fee. This fee is used primarily to cover the costs associated with maintaining accurate records of account activity on behalf of yourself and the I.R.S. Custodial fees can vary greatly, depending on where you open your IRA and how much flexibility you wish to have in it. For most IRAs, though, an annual custodial fee of more than $50 would be considered excessive, and many will be as low as $25. Also, it's important to remember that if you withdraw money from your plan before you reach age 59, you will incur an I.R.S.-imposed penalty of 10% on the amount of the distribution. The latest you can wait to begin taking distributions is age 70. You'll find that these basic age requirements regarding distributions pertain to just about every type of retirement plan available.

SIMPLIFIED EMPLOYEE PENSION PLAN (SEP-IRA)

As the abbreviation above indicates, the Simplified Employee Pension plan is actually a special version of the good old IRA. The SEP was actually introduced to give small businesses an easy, cost-effective way to establish retirement plans for their employees, although they are used mainly by self-employed people to give themselves the opportunity to set aside more for retirement than is permitted in a regular IRA. While a regular IRA permits a maximum annual contribution of only $2,000 per person, the SEP-IRA contribution rules are much more liberal. Specifically, self-employed people may contribute up to 15% of their annual income, to a maximum of $30,000. Furthermore, because the SEP is really an IRA at heart, the simplicity and low cost of custodianship and administration are maintained. All of the other basic rules regarding regular IRAs apply as well to SEP-IRAs.

KEOGH

The Keogh plan, named after U.S. Representative Eugene Keogh, is actually two different kinds of plans, known as *defined contribution* and *defined benefit*. In fact, the term "Keogh" is used less frequently these days in favor of those more specific plan names. Like the SEP-IRA, the Keogh may also be used to cover employees of small businesses, but traditionally its major role is as the primary retirement plan of the self-employed.

Defined Contribution

As if it weren't enough that there exist two broad types of Keoghs, there are also two different versions of the defined contribution plan. The first one we'll look at is a *money purchase* plan, and it demands that you select a certain fixed percentage of your income as an annual contribution and contribute that same percentage year after year. The percentage chosen may be as small as 1%, and it can be as large as 20%, up to a maximum of $30,000. The problem with the money purchase plan is that you *must* contribute every year, regardless of how your business performs. If you don't, you will be penalized by the I.R.S.

It is for that reason that many people considering Keoghs opt for the *profit-sharing* plan. The profit-sharing Keogh is, for all intents and purposes, identical to the SEP-IRA. You may contribute up to 15% of your gross income, to a maximum of $30,000. That represents a change in the rules: up until recently, contributors to Keogh plans could contribute up to 25% of their income (to $30,000). As a result of the change, you should quickly see profit-sharing Keoghs fall by the wayside, as the increased cost and administration of the plan can no longer be justified by the greater contribution limit.

There *is* a third type of defined contribution Keogh available for your participation, but it is a hybrid that combines the money purchase and the profit-sharing versions, and its uniqueness makes it unqualified for inclusion here in our discussion. If you want to find out more about it, consult your tax adviser.

Defined Benefit

The defined benefit plan is the other broad type of Keogh available, and it's somewhat unique in the world of retirement plans. With the defined benefit Keogh, you decide at the outset how much money you want to have at retirement and fund the plan accordingly. As a result, it's very possible to have an annual contribution well in excess of the $30,000 cap imposed on most nonprivate, self-employed plans. Because of their design, defined benefit plans can be complicated and expensive to set up and maintain. However, these plans can be the saving graces of the highly successful self-employed who are fast approaching retirement and have done little to prepare for it. The defined benefit option allows these people to contribute huge sums to a plan in a very few years in order to reach a benefit level they have designated for retirement.

With the advent of the simpler, cheaper SEP-IRA, Keoghs have started to become somewhat obsolete. They still, however, have features that can make them the best choices for the self-employed. To find out for sure if the Keogh is for you, you'll probably want to consult your tax adviser. By the way, Keoghs, unlike IRAs and SEP-IRAs, must be opened by December 31st of the given tax year; you do *not* have until the following April 15th.

401(k), 403(b), AND 457 PLAN

The 401(k), 403(b), and 457 plans are each examples of *company-sponsored* retirement plans. The number and letter nomenclature of each is actually a reference to the section of the tax code where they are named and defined. These types of company-sponsored plans are known as *salary reduction* plans, because your company will reduce your weekly salary by a certain percentage (which you elect) and contribute that money into the plan. The three plans are essentially the same; the 401(k) is the precise plan that covers employees in the private sector, the 403(b) is the version that covers workers in tax-exempt organizations (schoolteachers, for example), and the 457 is reserved for government employees. For purposes of this discussion, we'll simply use the term 401(k) to refer to all of them.

The company that offers the 401(k) plan decides what sorts of investments it will make available in the plan, and the employees choose from those in constructing their own individual portfolios. This is an important point, because the quality of your 401(k) is dependent in no small way on the quality of vehicle selection you have to choose from. Some companies have excellent 401(k)s, offering a host of high-quality mutual funds that represent all types of stock, bond, and money market instruments. Others, however, are not so good. Some plans are downright pathetic, offering a small number of poor funds to their participants. Unfortunately, there are no mandates or guidelines that all companies must follow to ensure that all 401(k) participants everywhere are assured of having a quality, competitive 401(k) plan. Some plans allow you to make changes in your portfolio as often as you want; others limit you to twice a year. The government says that 401(k) plans may be borrowed against by participants, but only if the particular company allows it, and many do not. Furthermore, some companies offer generous matching contributions to their employees, while others offer nothing. These huge differences in plan quality mean that before you decide to participate in *your* company's 401(k), you need to get all the facts about it from the benefits administrator. There's no point in investing your money in a company-sponsored retirement plan if it's simply unsuited to your needs; better to open an IRA instead. As a rule of thumb, if your plan offers at least a few high-quality stock funds as well as some percentage of employer-matching contributions, you'll probably want to maximize it each year before placing money anywhere else.

ANNUITY

An annuity is an investment product that is designed to pay income to an investor once he or she retires. Annuities will pay that money in varying forms and durations, depending on which option the individual chooses. You can, for example, elect to receive the money that has accumulated over the years in one lump sum at retirement; or you can choose to have the money paid out at a rate designed to make the money last until both you and your spouse have died. Obviously, the longer the payout duration, the lower the monthly benefit will be.

It should be noted that annuities have been the sole province of insurance companies through the years, giving them a chance to compete in the arena of retirement investment planning. However, a recent Supreme Court decision has determined that annuities are more *investment* product than *insurance* product, and as a result, other institutions (like banks) will be able to offer them from now on.

Annuities come in two basic forms, *fixed* and *variable*. The distinctions are important, so let's spend some time looking at them now.

Fixed Annuity

A fixed annuity is basically a tax-deferred CD. The insurance company "guarantees" that your investment will grow at a stated rate of interest for a particular period of time. As with a CD, when a fixed annuity vehicle matures, you will then renew it at whatever the prevailing rate is at the time.

You'll notice that we put the word "guarantees" in quotation marks. The reason is that your investment and its return are guaranteed only by the *insurance company*; there is no such thing as F.D.I.C.-type insurance for fixed annuities, as there is for bank vehicles. Your fixed annuity investment becomes part of the assets of the life insurance company itself. If the insurance company goes out of business, there's a high probability that you'll lose some or all of your investment. This same problem doesn't exist with *variable* annuities, and you'll see why in a bit.

Because fixed annuities are very similar to CDs, they're not very good investments for growth-oriented investors. They do, however, provide a quality tax-deferred haven for those who are extremely conservative investors, or who have already accumulated a substantial amount of money and no longer feel comfortable having it exposed to market fluctuation.

Variable Annuity

The variable annuity gives the investor seeking long-term growth a much better opportunity to achieve that goal than the fixed version does. The reason? Variable annuities are generally made up of several stock, bond, and money market instruments (usually in the form of mutual funds), not unlike 401(k) plans.

This brings up a good point. Just as the specific investment vehicles available to you are selected by your company in a 401(k), the vehicles available to you in variable annuities have already been selected by the insurance company. Before purchasing a variable annuity, ensure that the one you're considering contains a wide selection of high-quality mutual funds from recognizable mutual fund companies. The variable annuity business has grown so much that there's plenty of competition for your dollars, so take advantage of the buyer's market.

Do you recall our statement earlier that variable annuity investors don't have to be concerned about losing their money through insurance company insolvency the way fixed annuity investors do? Well, the reason is that variable annuity money *must* be kept separate from the assets of the life insurance company. It is, after all, invested in actual mutual funds, and thus has no business being commingled with the insurance company's own assets.

A few more thoughts on annuities. Non-qualified annuities are like private retirement accounts, which means that while money grows for you on a tax-deferred basis as it does with all of the others, you don't have the opportunity to realize a current-year income tax benefit. Why? Because such annuities are purchased only with *after-tax* dollars. Therefore, you will want to maximize your other retirement plans before you place money in annuities. Also, annuities can assess some pretty stiff sales charges if you withdraw from them within the first few years of purchase. This is one of the reasons it's so important for you to select your annuity carefully; a good annuity with all sorts of quality investment options is one that you should never have to leave early. Finally, remember that the same age-59 rule applies to the withdrawal of money from annuities as from other retirement plans (although you need not begin taking distributions by age 70).

These, then, are the more common retirement plan umbrellas in a nutshell. We haven't told you every single thing there is to know about each one of them, but certainly we've told you enough to allow you to get a good idea as to which one(s) are probably best for you. Do remember that you're not limited to selecting just one type of retirement plan. Many people have two or three different plans, depending on what they qualify for, as well as how much money they have to set aside. Let's say, for example, that you and your spouse are both covered by retirement plans at work. Maybe you're both contributing all that you're allowed to, but you still have more that can be set aside. Why not open IRAs? While you may not necessarily be able to deduct your contributions, you'll have still another place to invest money that will grow tax-deferred for both of you. This brings up another important point we should address: *Do not decide whether or not to contribute to an IRA or any other type of plan based on the deductibility of the contribution.* Far too many people focus on their retirement plans (especially their IRAs) as a means to current-year tax relief while ignoring altogether the real benefit of the plan: the tax-deferred growth. To be honest, you can never put too much money into a retirement plan. That's especially true today, when continuous medical breakthroughs and a new emphasis on healthier lifestyles continue to lengthen human life expectancy. If you're 40 now and don't plan on retiring until age 65, how much longer after that will you live? To 80? To 90? Will you have enough money, or will it run out before you do? Don't take any chances; prioritize your retirement planning *now*.

One final thought. Many people agonize over whether they should place their investment monies in a retirement plan or a regular, fully taxable account. Some are scared off by the fact that if they need substantial money for one reason or another before they reach age 59, they'll be faced with having to pay a stiff penalty to the I.R.S. The answer to the problem lies in the word *prudence*. First of all, ensure that you're a full participant in at least one type of retirement plan. Once that goal has been met, you may then go through the process of analyzing how other monies should be allocated. It really isn't a bad idea to keep some invested monies available for easy access; just make sure that it's not a sum that is well beyond what you would likely need.

CHAPTER TWO
How to Select Your Retirement Investments

The greatest single factor in determining how successful a retirement you will enjoy is the performance of the specific investments you select for your plan. Granted, the judicious selection of an appropriate *type* of retirement plan is important, but remember, the plan is only the shell, the umbrella. It is the specific investments you choose to go *inside* the plan, as well as the method of *managing* those investments, that will have the greatest long-term influence on how large your account ultimately grows. Designing a plan is a careful process, and it starts with gaining an understanding of where you are at the outset. From there, you can begin to determine how to get where you want to go (isn't that how *everything* works?). In this chapter, we will introduce you to each of the factors you need to be familiar with in order to manage your retirement investing.

DEFINITION OF A SUCCESSFUL RETIREMENT

What *does* it mean to be retired, anyway? For some, a successful retirement means the ability to do whatever you want, whenever you want, without regard to what anything costs. For others, the definition may not be so grandiose. It may mean having enough money to start that business you always wanted to have. Perhaps it means having accumulated enough money to ensure that X number of dollars is generated for living expenses each year without dipping into principal. Or it may simply mean having $1,000,000 accumulated by the time you stop working. The fact is, the specifics of what makes a successful retirement will differ from individual to individual, but there *is* a common thread that runs through all these perceptions of retirement success: financial security.

Whether you aspire to have the freedom to buy whatever you want at any time, or simply want to have enough money to cover your basic necessities, you are looking for financial security. The amounts that are required to provide that security may differ from person to person, but we're talking about security nonetheless. Perhaps a minimal definition of a successful retirement that would apply to everyone is the ability to stop working entirely and still be assured of having enough money to live on until the point of death. Beyond that basic definition, everyone's personal wants and needs take over. *How* do you want to live, for example? Like a king? Or are you content to just get by? Whichever lifestyle you choose to maintain, you will need to do some hard planning to ensure that you're on the right road to reach your chosen destination.

WHERE ARE YOU NOW?

One of the most important factors in deciding how a plan should be formulated is, simply, your age. A 25-year-old who decides that he wants to begin planning for his retirement is going to have very different answers to the basic inquiries relating to retirement planning than will a 57-year-old who already has two retirement plans worth $1,000,000 apiece. For the sake of discussion, we have decided not to get too bogged down in accounting for every variable possibility that can exist for each individual. Rather, we want to introduce you to some broad guidelines that you can tailor to meet your own individual demands. The first order of business is to see into which phase of retirement planning you fit.

Accumulation Phase

The Accumulation Phase applies to those retirement planners who have at least ten years to go until the actual date of retirement. For these people, *capital accumulation* is of singular importance, while *capital preservation* is of little concern. Those who are in the Accumulation Phase will have the ability to select aggressive investments with a relatively high degree of security. Why? Principally because they have enough time to go until retirement to ride out whatever unfavorable fluctuation they may encounter while invested in their more aggressive selections. An Accumulator's sample investment choices might be growth and aggressive-growth mutual funds, growth stocks, high-yield (a.k.a. "junk") bonds and bond funds, as well as some funds that target the stocks of small, emerging countries. For obvious reasons, individuals who justifiably fit into the parameters of the Accumulation Phase are in the best position to realize a successful retirement.

Accumulation-Preservation Phase

This phase generally applies to those future retirees for whom retirement may not be tomorrow, but for whom it is no longer a distant eventuality, either. In real numbers, we're talking somewhere inside of ten years to retirement. The reason we've dubbed this time period the Accumulation-Preservation Phase is because those to whom it applies are in a situation in which they may still emphasize accumulation, or *growth*, overall in their portfolio structure, but they must also pay some attention to preserving what they've already worked so hard to produce. The reason we put the word "accumulation" before the word "preservation" is to emphasize that while accumulation concerns may still rank first in one's thinking during this phase, preservation concerns are now also present (but still secondary). Once someone reaches this phase, they should begin to reallocate their portfolio in such a way that their exposure to growth and aggressive-growth stocks and mutual funds is now somewhat diminished. Accumulation-Preservationists would begin to highlight growth and income mutual funds in their portfolios.

Preservation-Accumulation Phase

As you might expect, the Preservation-Accumulation Phase is one that reverses the order priority of capital accumulation and capital preservation. Those entering this phase are at a point where the desire to preserve what has been realized should take priority over the desire to make more. We're not saying that Preservation-Accumulationists must forsake their growth attempts altogether; just that they should be careful not to expose too much of what they've already earned to the precariousness of the stock market, particularly the NASDAQ (the stock market for small companies). In fact, it is our position that even the recently retired may want to consider maintaining somewhat of a growth posture throughout the early years of their retirement. Life expectancies are increasing all the time, and as a result a new dilemma has emerged: namely, how should the retiree invest if he or she may reasonably expect to live another twenty years past the date of retirement? It is really this person whom we had in mind when we developed this category. The time frame that corresponds to this phase is more difficult to define. In general, it can be anywhere from five years before retirement to five to ten years after retirement. Individual investors are going to have to decide for themselves, in this phase as in others, how they feel most comfortable constructing their portfolio.

Preservation Phase

Preservationists are those who are entering the later stages of their lives. They, by way of a personal inventory that includes evaluating several personal factors, are now at a point where they feel that they have nothing to gain and everything to lose by exposing their money to the elements of growth stocks and mutual funds. As with the Preservation-Accumulation Phase, the starting point of this phase is a little tough to define. Ideally, it's somewhere between five and ten years prior to the event of one's death, but obviously no one knows for sure when that's going to occur. All you can do is make an educated guess, keeping in mind that it's always better to err on the side of prudence; in other words, when in doubt, opt for the more conservative option. Preservationists would be wise to select their investments from balanced/income mutual funds, highly rated bonds and bond funds, Treasury instruments, and perhaps a *few* conservative equity funds and individual stocks.

ASSET ALLOCATION MODELS

The principle behind asset allocation is easy to understand. Asset allocation is the act of diversifying your portfolio in such a way that your investment objectives are reflected in the types of investments you select. For example, a 30-year-old man who plans on retiring at age 65 would want to set up his portfolio in such a way that growth investments are emphasized, perhaps to the complete exclusion of any other types of vehicles. By the same token, a 70-year-old retiree in uncertain health would probably want to have most of his money placed in very conservative stock funds, Treasury vehicles, municipal bonds, and even CDs and money markets. Any exposure to growth investments would have to be very limited.

Below you will find some broad asset allocation models that are designed to correspond to the four retirement phases we described above. Again, these are simply meant as guidelines, and the demands of your own particular situation should take precedence.

Accumulation Phase
70% to 100% growth and aggressive growth investments
0% to 30% growth and income investments

Accumulation-Preservation Phase
40% growth and income investments
30% growth and aggressive-growth investments
30% conservative investments

Preservation-Accumulation Phase
50% growth and income investments
30% conservative investments
20% growth and aggressive-growth investments

Preservation Phase
70% conservative investments
20% growth and income investments
10% growth investments

Here's what we mean by the terms we use above:

Growth and aggressive-growth investments: These are broad-based mutual funds that have as their primary investment objective capital accumulation, along with stocks that carry a corresponding objective. These investments also include sector, or specialty, mutual funds (those that target a particular industry), as well as high-yield ("junk") bonds and bond funds and international funds that concentrate in less-developed countries.

Growth and income investments: Chiefly, these are mutual funds that are so designated. The typical prospectus of a growth and income mutual fund will indicate that its investment objective is one that gives capital accumulation and capital preservation roughly equal consideration.

Conservative investments: Most of us probably have an idea of what qualifies as a conservative investment. For the authors, it could be any of the following: balanced/income mutual funds, municipal bonds and bond funds, Treasury securities, money markets, CDs, and anything else that greatly reduces the investor's exposure to market risk as well as interest rate risk. On the other hand, there will be investors reading this book who interpret "conservative" as "no possible risk to principal." Please understand that while we do not hold to that definition, we acknowledge those of you who do. If you are in that classification, you will need to limit your investment to CDs and short-term Treasury securities.

WHERE DO YOU WANT TO GO?

Some of you may think that the answer to this question is somewhat obvious; after all, the place *everyone* who is reading this chapter wants to go is "retirement-land," right? Well, yes, but you may recall that earlier we talked about the fact that retirement, in reality, means different things to different people. The plain fact is, the broad guidelines given above are just that, *broad*. How you *specifically* construct your portfolio will depend greatly on just how much money you want to have by the time you finally call it quits. Most people respond to this in one of two ways: either they simply put aside what they can, hoping it will be enough; or they take a more analytical approach and decide just how much money they want to have accumulated by retirement and design a relatively precise plan to get there.

Actually, the first method is not as haphazard as it sounds, as long as you commit to setting aside as much of your income as you can. In other words, the case can be made that it really doesn't matter how much you *want* at retirement—that you can only set aside what you *have*, no more. By doing that, and sticking to the asset allocation models that correspond to your particular phase, you're doing just about the best that you can.

The truth is, though, that you will *always* be better off by adopting a more scientific approach to this or any other kind of financial planning. The smart thing to do is to sit down and decide how much money you want to have saved by the time you retire. This will be a fairly personal determination, as you will have to account for all of your wants and needs and then estimate how they will have changed by the time you finally stop working. Perhaps you will decide that you want to have enough money by retirement so that if you invest it at 6%, it will yield $120,000 per year without requiring you to dip into principal. If that's what you want, great. The first question that must be answered, then, is just *how much* invested at 6% will throw off $120,000 a year. Some simple math tells us that the answer is $2,000,000. Great; now you know that you must have $2,000,000 accumulated by the time you retire. The next question is, how much money have you saved thus far and how many years do you have to go until retirement? Once you learn the answers to these questions, you'll have a better idea of how much money you need to set aside each month, and into which kinds of vehicles the dollars should be directed. It's at this point that you may want to consider purchasing a *financial calculator*.

The financial calculator looks just like any other type of calculator, save for the fact that it has a few extra keys. Although space limitations prevent us from giving a lesson in the financial calculator, suffice it to say that the financial calculator can make all the difference in helping you to realize *all* of your long-term financial goals. Specifically, the financial calculator has the ability to account for what is commonly known as the "time value of money," that almost-magical effect that occurs when money is invested for X number of years at X percent. Regular calculators can't help you with this stuff; only the *financial* calculator will do. We can't say it any more plainly: if you want to know *specifically* the answers to how much, how often, and how long, buy yourself a financial calculator. It will tell you where you're at and what you need to do to meet your goals. Buy one.

WHAT TO DO WHEN TIME IS RUNNING OUT

It's human nature to procrastinate. The maxim "Don't put off 'till tomorrow what you can do today" is, more than anything, wishful thinking on the part of the person who came up with it. The sad fact is, far too many Americans put off planning for retirement until there's little that can be done. In our roles as financial advisers, we too often come across individuals in their mid- to late fifties (and even early sixties) who decide that it's finally time to do some retirement planning. We said earlier that it's never too late to put money away for retirement, and in a general sense that's true. After all, even if planning gives you just another $10,000 dollars in a few years, are you not better off with the receipt of every additional dollar you can get your hands on? However, you must be realistic. It's not likely that a 57-year-old who makes $40,000 per year and has nothing set aside for retirement will be able to retire at 65 with a nest egg of $1,000,000. This person will have to do some *special* planning. First of all, he (or she) may want to continue working to age 70 or beyond in order to have enough time to let the money he's *now* putting away grow to a significant level. He may also have to sell his home and move to a much smaller residence, allowing him to live on a portion of the proceeds. He may even have to make arrangements to move in with his children once he retires. The average benefit paid by Social Security is quite small, and is nowhere near enough for a retiree who was reasonably prosperous in his or her working years to live on. In our opinion, your Social Security benefit should be excluded from your retirement planning altogether, and viewed simply as an added bonus.

OK. You're 60 years old and only now considering retirement; you've put nothing away on your own and are facing a retirement consisting of only a small Social Security stipend and the prospect of selling many of your worldly possessions in an effort to get by. You need help . . . fast!

Can anything be done to significantly improve your situation? Yes, but you have to be realistic. Retirement at 65, let alone 62, may be inadvisable. Shoot for an age-70 retirement, if you can. That will give you ten years to put money away in growth-oriented vehicles and allow the time value of money to work its magic. Now, at this point, you might be thinking "Hey, I thought that it was about this time that I become an Accumulation-Preservationist, *limiting* my exposure to pure growth vehicles." Under more reasonable circumstances, you'd be exactly right. However, in this case, you've accumulated nothing at all. You are now in the position of having to take a calculated risk and place your money in growth-oriented vehicles so that you may take advantage of the manic growth potential these securities offer. A good way for you to limit your risk in this case would be to stick to growth *mutual funds*, and stay away from individual stocks. If you place $2,000 per year into an IRA, and can scrape up another $3,000 per year to invest in a variable annuity, you'll be putting a total of $5,000 per year into mutual funds for the next ten years. Keeping the money in growth funds, you can assume that you'll earn an average of 12% a year. By the time you reach age 70, you'll have almost $88,000 saved. Not a king's ransom by any means, but still $88,000 more than you had ten years ago. Once you retire, you may have to continue to monitor your portfolio so that you can try to earn an annual rate of slightly higher than 6%, maybe 8%. A sum of $88,000 invested at 8% would give you a return of almost $600 per month without having to touch the principal. That figure, combined with your monthly Social Security benefit, might very well make the difference between an acceptable living standard and one that is quite unbearable. While the illustration we just gave is fictional, it is typical of the retirement scenarios of many. As you can see, getting a late start on your retirement planning can be most inconvenient and may limit the *quality* of your actual retirement somewhat, but it is by no means a financial death sentence. The later you wait to start, the more sacrifices you will have to make, but a successful retirement can still be had.

PASSIVE VERSUS ACTIVE INVESTING

The purpose of investing is to make money, plain and simple. In the historical course that investing has taken through the years, numerous philosophies and beliefs have emerged regarding the best way to do it. Many of these theories are still intact, primarily because they have enjoyed the good fortune of having at least a few practitioners use them with great success. Some people, for example, choose to make buys and sells on specific days of the week. Others trade on a seasonal basis, while still others use the stars to guide them. While these are certainly some of the more unscientific of the investment strategies, all of them can be divided into two broad categories: passive and active. We want to take a moment to briefly outline each of these investment methods, leaving you to do some additional investigation if you so desire. The truth is, entire books have been written on investment styles alone, and space limitations don't really allow us to include a comprehensive description. This chapter, however, would not be complete if we didn't give at least some attention to the subject.

Passive Investing

Passive investing is, essentially, investing without adherence to any sort of proactive money management style. Passive investors do not nimbly jump from security to security on the basis of any kind of system, signal, or data; in general, they are content to find some vehicles with a demonstrated long-term track record and stay with them for an extended period of time. This doesn't mean that they *never* trade their portfolios; just that they do it much less frequently than active investors, and generally only when their current holdings are showing clear signs of yielding unfavorable results for a long time to come. These investors are more commonly known as "buy and hold" investors. It's important, however, to make a distinction between "buy and hold" investors and "buy and forget" investors. Buy and hold investors *do* evaluate their portfolios from time to time and *do* make changes; they just do it less frequently and on the basis of data that is much less particular and scientific than that examined by active investors. Buy and forget investors are a different breed altogether, although we guess it could be said that they are passive investors as well . . . *very* passive.

Statistics will show that buy and hold investing is about as successful as anything out there. However, the key to doing it successfully is to do it with mutual funds; individual stocks are too uncertain to bank on for extended periods of time. Most people opt for buy and hold investing because it's the easiest (obviously). However, if you choose to buy and hold, remain mindful of the difference between buying and holding and buying and forgetting. Check your portfolio at least quarterly, and make changes as appropriate.

Active Investing

A number of different money management theories and philosophies fall under the category of "active investing," but the two most popular are technical analysis and fundamental analysis. Technical analysts concentrate on the historical price action of a security, watching its highs and lows and making buy/sell decisions based on the data. Technical analysts also evaluate the trading volume (when applying the strategy to individual stocks) as a means of determining when to trade particular securities. Pure technicians don't really care very much about what a company does, what its earnings record is, or any other data that is fundamental to the company or fund. They are solely concerned with its price action, along with the associated charts and graphs.

Fundamental investing is another type of active investing, but it is rather the *opposite* of technical analysis. Fundamental analysts are only concerned with what a company does, its book value, earnings per share, and other pieces of data that generate a very specific reflection of the company or fund at hand. Fundamental analysts care *everything* about the particulars of a company, whereas technicians care little or nothing at all.

Each of these two broad types of active investing has great numbers of adherents, and actually these subcategories can be broken down even further. The nature of technical analysis especially is such that it invites new, creative ways of examining and structuring charts and graphs based on different types of technical data. There is even a magazine available that is dedicated solely to the subject of technical analysis. In your travels, you'll probably run across people who will swear by this or that method of analyzing securities, but keep in mind that if any one method was clearly so much better than the rest, everyone would be using it. The bottom line is, each one of these types of investing has advantages as well as disadvantages. Developing a system that allows you to combine elements of *all* of them is probably your best bet.

CHAPTER THREE
Investing in Mutual Funds

Mutual funds have become the retirement investment of choice for many people, and it's easy to see why. Mutual fund investors are able to invest in stock markets, bond markets, and money markets without becoming burdened with the difficulties associated with buying individual securities. Take *stock* mutual funds, for example. An individual stock investor must have the wherewithal to identify, purchase, track, and sell his holdings in order to be successful. A stock *mutual fund* investor, however, effectively employs a professional money manager to accomplish these tasks *for* him. Additionally, while an individual stock investor is likely to maintain a portfolio of no more than several issues (at the most), the mutual fund investor may see his money diversified over the fortunes of *100-plus* companies, thereby preserving a strong measure of relative safety. In short, mutual funds represent a far superior option to long-term investors for a number of reasons—but to better understand their advantages, we should look at just what a mutual fund is.

WHAT IS A MUTUAL FUND?

A mutual fund is actually an *investment company*. An investment company is a company like any other, except that it seeks

to make money by investing in securities, as opposed to manufacturing automobiles, hamburgers, or anything else. From
where does an investment company get the money to invest in
these securities? From investors. These investors purchase
shares of this investment company (mutual fund) and thus
become shareholders. The mutual fund manager takes this
money and uses it to buy securities; as the value of the underlying securities changes, so does the value (specifically, the *net
asset value*) of the mutual fund. If the overall value of the
underlying securities increases, the value of the mutual fund's
shares will increase; if the securities decrease in value, the
fund shares will move accordingly. That is, admittedly, an
oversimplification of how it works, but it is essentially an
accurate description nonetheless.

MUTUAL FUND ADVANTAGES

There are several advantages to investing in mutual funds rather
than selecting individual stocks, bonds, and/or money markets
on your own, but the two most often cited are those of professional management and diversification. We've alluded to each
of these already, but let's discuss them further so that the benefits of these features are clear to you. First, almost all of us
could use professional help (of one kind or another), couldn't
we? Mutual fund managers are highly trained investment
experts—professionals who generally have years of securities
analysis and financial education under their belts. Furthermore,
these portfolio managers have a staff of analysts of their own to
help them make decisions on behalf of the fund, along with the
latest in high-tech tools to accomplish the job quickly and accu-
rately. How many of us have all of these resources to rely on
when trading individual securities? Few, if any.

Safety is an important issue for most investors in general,
and for retirement investors in particular. Mutual funds, by
their very structure, offer a measure of safety that is difficult to

achieve through investment in individual securities. The reason for this is *diversification*. If you choose to invest in a few individual stocks, you have elected to entrust your money with the fortunes of these few companies. Beyond that, your money is also exposed to risks associated with being invested in particular industries, and of course to the inherent broad-market risk that affects *all* equity investors. Mutual fund investors, however, have a leg up on this type of volatility. Investors in broad-based growth funds, for example, will likely have *their* money riding on the fortunes of one hundred or so companies representing a great number of different industries. Can you see the benefit of such a structure from a safety standpoint? If one or two companies in the fund portfolio has a particularly bad day, the performance of the other ninety or so stocks can limit the negative impact to the point where it's completely unnoticeable. Additionally, broad-based funds derive their stock selections from a large number of industries, which is also very helpful if and when certain industries run into trouble. Now, as far as broad-market risk is concerned, that's tough to dodge as long as you choose to invest in equity-based investments at all, but remember that safety is relative; stock mutual funds are, by and large, safer than individual stocks and bond mutual funds are safer than individual bonds. However, we don't think anyone would make the case that stock mutual funds are safer than bank CDs. The point is, investing in equities markets involves choosing to accept a measure of risk. Through mutual funds, however, you have the chance to limit that risk to a great extent.

There are other advantages to utilizing mutual funds as opposed to individual securities, including the fact that you are not burdened with paying commissions every time you buy or sell an individual stock or bond. This leads us to an important question, however: What *does* it cost to invest in a mutual fund?

MUTUAL FUND COSTS

Mutual funds are one of the most cost-effective ways to invest in equities markets, but they're not free. First of all, all mutual funds charge an annual expense fee of roughly 1% to 1.5%. The purpose of this fee is to compensate the manager and his team, as well as to defray the administrative expenses associated with operating the fund. You are not billed for the fee in any traditional sort of way; rather, it is precalculated in the fund's share price so that you don't really notice it (although you *are* paying it). Some funds, however, will charge a *commission* on top of this management fee simply for the privilege of investing in them. Funds that charge sales commissions are known as *load* funds—the opposite of funds that charge no sales commission of any kind and are referred to as *no-loads*. Let's take a peek at the differences between the two.

The predominant compensation structure within the securities industry is commission-based. Most financial salespeople earn their money through the commissions generated from the sales of products. In that spirit, load funds were born. Load funds are sold by brokers, and the cost of the load is generally 4% to 8% of the money invested in the fund. This load fee goes solely to compensating the broker for the sale of the fund; it does not pay the fund manager, nor does it go to defraying any other expenses related to the fund itself. It should be mentioned that some load fees are incurred only if and when you sell your shares; called *back-end* loads, these funds were introduced to be more competitive with no-loads by not demanding a commission up-front. Watch out for them, though, because you *will* pay a commission when you sell. Some brokers who pitch back-end load funds will try to do so in a way that makes the fund sound like a no-load. Just remember, if a broker is taking the time to sell you a fund, there's undoubtedly a commission in there somewhere.

No-loads are, simply, mutual funds that charge no commission whatsoever. They are not sold by brokers, but rather are marketed directly to the public by way of generally accepted media outlets. If you want to purchase a no-load fund, you need only contact the fund company (known as a "family") at the telephone number that almost always accompanies its ads. Many no-load funds are now available through discount brokers as well, which gives more active investors the advantage of being able to move interfamily without maintaining several different accounts with several different fund families (be advised, though, that you may incur a small transaction charge if you purchase your no-load through a discount broker).

For reasons that should be obvious, we are proponents of the use of no-load funds whenever possible. The paying of a load does nothing to enhance the performance of a fund, although there are actually some people who just "feel better" about paying extra for something, perhaps thinking that they'll get "something extra" for their money. Just about every type of fund that is sold with a load can be found *without* a load, so there's really no advantage to paying the commission as far as the fund itself is concerned. However, we would be remiss in not pointing out that one solid advantage (in theory) of paying a commission to a financial professional is that the fee entitles you to access the broker for advice on your investment path. Representatives of no-load funds will dispense no such advice. It is our position that it is worth the relatively small amount of work necessary to learn about mutual funds and basic investing in general to avoid paying a commission that doesn't do anything for the fund's performance, anyway. Furthermore, speaking as "insiders" in the securities industry, we know that most commission-based brokers dislike spending time conversing with a client unless the client is a constant source of revenue generation; in other words, don't expect that the load fee you paid will entitle you to a lot of time with your broker unless you're paying a lot of load fees.

HOW WE PICKED THE FUNDS FOR THIS BOOK

In the following pages you will find sixty-five funds featured as the "best." Right off the bat, we want to stress that there is really no such thing as a standardized test through which the "best" mutual funds may be determined. Mutual funds possess many inherent variables and characteristics, and some of these variables and characteristics carry more significance with certain individuals, while those same characteristics may be less important to other investors. However, it *is* fair to assume that performance is usually of paramount importance to prospective investors, and thus it is performance that we use as the screen for determining our list of finalists. You will notice that we also rate how a fund ranks within its peer group, as well as its level of safety, but these categories were not used to actually screen out competitors; we simply rate them once the final list of funds has been determined on the basis of performance.

You will notice that there doesn't even exist a standardized test for evaluating fund performance. Why? Simply because opinions differ among investors over what kind of performance is important, as well as what lengths of time (one year, three years, five years, ten years, fifteen years, twenty years) should be regarded as significant for determining the value of a fund's performance ability. The basic performance screen that *we* decided was important was a fund's *ten-year* average annualized return. This figure is generated by averaging a fund's twelve-month performance for the last ten years. We selected ten years because it is a time frame that fairly qualifies as being representative of long-term performance, but is not so long as to be unrepresentative of near-term financial and economic activity. If we could also reasonably screen out funds on the basis of *short-term* performance as well, we did so; even if we didn't actually screen out a fund on that basis, we evaluated it nonetheless. You will notice that some fund categories we look at here have their long-term performance rated on the basis of a *five-year* average annualized return.

This screen was adopted if we found that we could not come up with an adequate list of funds on the basis of a ten-year return. However, when you see "short-term performance," that always refers to a three-year average annualized return. When we rate a fund's long- and short-term performances, we're gauging it against the returns of all other available mutual funds, regardless of investment objective.

We've decided to adopt a star rating system with which to rate these funds, and the four individual categories to which we ascribe stars are as follows: Long-Term Performance, Short-Term Performance, Performance Against Peer Group, and Safety. We've already talked about the Long- and Short-Term Performance categories. Performance Against Peer Group involves the comparison of a fund's long-term performance against those of all other funds in the given fund type category (Growth, Growth and Income, and so on). Safety is intended to be an evaluation of a fund's risk/volatility level in comparison with all other funds in its respective instrument category. By *instrument category* we mean stock or bond. For example, when we rate the safety of the municipal bond funds featured here, we are doing so by comparing them with other bond funds—not with stock funds. As you might expect, each rated category can receive anywhere from one to five stars, with five indicating the highest or most favorable score.

For most of the fund-type categories here, we have included some type of commentary along with the raw data and star ratings. For the fund types we deemed to be the most relevant to investors at large (Growth and Income, International, Growth, Balanced, and Bond), we comment on the following characteristics: Performance, Management, Risk/Reward Analysis, and Expenses. We also include a section called Final Thoughts, which is intended to be a very brief summation about the fund and its appropriateness to one's portfolio. You will also notice that we've chosen to include three additional fund types for you to peruse: sector/specialty, index, and municipal bond, which are more specialized and will be of interest to fewer investors overall.

So, without further delay, let's look at the best growth and income, international, growth, balanced, and bond funds available today. Be advised that the funds in this book are not presented in any sort of order beyond their broad fund type categorization. So that everyone's on the same sheet of music, let's quickly look at definitions of the fund types included here, as well as any other pertinent features.

Growth and Income

A growth and income mutual fund has as its objective the realization of both capital appreciation and income. Growth and income funds are considered in general to be medium-risk funds, because they are not made up solely of the small companies that are terrific candidates for growth but possess no real dividend-paying abilities, nor are they made up predominantly of the larger, better-established companies that typically pay quality dividends and are attractive to more conservative investors. Growth and income funds, accordingly, will not increase in value as sharply as more pure growth-oriented funds when the market rises, nor will they typically fall as quickly when the market *drops* in value. These funds potentially have a place in every investor's portfolio, understanding that the more conservative an investor is, the smaller the allocation would likely be.

International

International funds are comprised primarily of common stocks that represent companies located in many different countries. Normally, a true international stock fund will invest at least 80 or 90% of its portfolio overseas, although the prospectuses of these funds will usually allow the managers the flexibility to invest as much as 25 or 30% of the portfolio domestically if they see fit. Furthermore, international funds are designed for long-term capital appreciation and are not usually good havens for those seeking income. The Long-Term Performance screen we used in evaluating the funds in this category was five-year, not ten-year average annualized performance.

Note: It is our intention to introduce you to what we have determined to be the very best funds in the fund type categories most heavily relied on by retirement investors seeking competitive total returns. Accordingly, while the vast majority of mutual funds featured here may be accessed by the average investor without any fanfare, we have decided to include funds that may be burdened with certain sales restrictions (for instance, the fund may be purchased only within a retirement plan, or may be purchased only by an institutional investor on your behalf), if they indeed made the final cut. Again, because so many of the funds found here are free of these encumbrances, we did not feel it inappropriate to include the few that aren't, in the spirit of presenting you with the "best." If you are interested in a particular fund that appears to carry a sales restriction of some sort, you may want to telephone the fund company to see how you may qualify to own shares. To give you a head start, we have included, when appropriate, a brief description of the relevant restriction.

One more thing. To ensure that you have as much information as possible at your disposal about the numerous funds contained herein, we've included some various, standard statistical measurements of volatility to help profile each of the funds. You will notice measurements for alpha, beta, R-2 (R-Squared), and standard deviation. Following are the nontechnical definitions for each as they apply to the investments features in this book:

Alpha
Alpha is a coefficient that measures the amount of return expected from a fund on the basis of its inherent, fundamental

characteristics rather than from its volatility. To generalize, the higher a fund's alpha, the better. Better still is a fund with a relatively high alpha and a relatively low beta (the most basic measurement of a fund's volatility), because such a disparity suggests that the fund will do well without putting the shareholder through a rollercoaster ride.

Beta

Beta, which we mentioned very briefly in the alpha definition, is a coefficient that measures a fund's volatility level in comparison to a stated index (stock funds featured here are measured against the Standard & Poor's 500 Index, while bond funds are measured against the Lehman Brothers Aggregate Index). The index for comparison is typically ascribed a beta of "1"; therefore, any fund that sports a beta of less than 1 is deemed to be less volatile than its respective, overall market, while any fund with a beta higher than 1 is considered more volatile than the overall market.

R-2, or R-Squared

R-2 is a coefficient that measures the similarity of a fund's portfolio to the index against which it is being compared. The stock funds featured here are all measured statistically against the S&P 500, and the R-2 figures are presented on a scale from 0% up to 100%. A fund that has an R-2 measurement of 90, for example, would be very similar in portfolio makeup to the S&P 500, while a fund with an R-2 of 15 would be very dissimilar to the S&P 500. You will notice that the S&P 500 index funds featured here all have R-2s of 100%, while some of the more aggressive stock offerings have R-2s well below 50%.

Standard Deviation

Standard deviation is a commonly used measurement that shows the degree to which a particular, given value of something varies from its mean, or average value. Here we offer for comparison the funds' three-year standard deviation measurement: The higher the standard deviation, the less predictable the fund's return; the lower the standard deviation, the greater the predictability. When examining the standard deviations of the funds that follow, you will want to compare and contrast them against other funds in the *same category*.

Growth

A growth mutual fund has as its objective long-term capital appreciation, with little or no regard for income. The companies that typically make up a growth fund portfolio are smaller and newer, and thus carry more risk for investors. Growth mutual funds, then, are also going to maintain a higher level of risk than many other types of funds. It is for that reason that more conservative investors will want to limit their exposure to growth funds, while more aggressive investors and those who have quite a while until retirement may want to weight their portfolios more heavily with this kind of vehicle.

Balanced

Balanced mutual funds are so named because they seek to "balance" their portfolios with fairly even apportionments of stocks and bonds, with perhaps some favoritism toward stocks. The classic balanced fund allocation, in fact, is considered to be 60% in stocks and 40% in bonds. Balanced funds are really an outgrowth of the dated notion that investors should keep their portfolios weighted evenly at all times among the basic investment vehicles of stocks, bonds, and perhaps money market instruments. This strategy may have some validity from a risk-reduction standpoint, but investors soon came to realize that overall investment performance suffered by maintaining a portfolio that contained even distributions of securities that at any given time were likely to work against one another. Nevertheless, balanced funds have remained popular options with more conservative investors who wish to take advantage of equities markets, and some balanced funds have been able to preserve a high degree of performance in addition to the high degree of safety. The best of that group are featured here. It should be mentioned that the Long-Term Performance screen utilized in evaluating this fund type was a *five*-year average annualized return.

Bond

"Bond fund" by itself is a very broad category, because there are all sorts of bond funds out there to choose from. We have elected to cull our list of finalists from the categories of intermediate-term bond funds that are made up primarily of U.S. government and corporate issues. None of the funds we considered are high-yield, or "junk" bond funds; the vast majority of bonds that make up these offerings are investment-grade or better and have average portfolio maturities no higher than fifteen years. It should be mentioned that bond funds with longer average portfolio maturities may have greater total returns overall than those featured here, but we felt it necessary to choose a maturity length that would be less impacted by interest rate risk while still maintaining the capability of realizing a worthwhile return.

CHAPTER FOUR
The 65 Best Mutual Funds for Retirement

GROWTH AND INCOME FUNDS

DODGE & COX STOCK FUND
Growth and Income

FUND FAMILY:	Dodge & Cox Group
TICKER SYMBOL:	DODGX
PORTFOLIO MANAGER:	Management Team
ADDRESS:	One Sansome St.
	35th Floor
	San Francisco, CA 94104
LONG-TERM PERFORMANCE:	★ ★ ★ ★ ★
SHORT-TERM PERFORMANCE:	★ ★ ★ ★
PERFORMANCE AGAINST PEER GROUP:	★ ★ ★ ★ ★
SAFETY:	★ ★ ★
TELEPHONE EXCHANGES:	N/A
BROKERAGE AVAILABILITY:	Yes
MANAGER TENURE:	21 Years
MINIMUM INITIAL PURCHASE:	$2,500/$1,000 for IRAs
ASSETS UNDER MANAGEMENT ($M):	675.10
PHONE NUMBER:	800-621-3979
TOTAL RETURNS, YEAR BY YEAR FOR THE PAST TEN:	1985—37.86% 1986—18.31% 1987—11.95% 1988—13.76% 1989—26.94% 1990— -5.09% 1991—21.48% 1992—10.81% 1993—18.37% 1994—5.17%

BETA (3-yr):	1.02
ALPHA (3-yr):	3.43
R2 (3-yr):	86
STANDARD DEVIATION (3-yr):	8.78
GROWTH OF $10,000 FROM JAN. 85 TO DEC. 94:	$41,937.36
PORTFOLIO TURNOVER:	7%
EXPENSE RATIO:	.61%

SUMMARY

Performance

Consistency in performance is the hallmark of Dodge & Cox Stock Fund. This investment's three-, five-, and ten-year performance records are solid, with each respective figure embedded solidly in the double-digit range. When the fund's performance is examined on a year-by-year basis, it becomes clear that management's desire for a defensive posture jettisons the fund's performance in rocky years. In dreadful 1990, only the Neuberger and Berman Guardian Fund posted a better performance record (of the funds featured here). Additionally, the Dodge & Cox Stock Fund finished ahead of the majority of our select group in 1994, a year that saw domestic-based funds post an average return of -2.0%. It is clear, then, that not only will investors be happy with this fund's long-term achievement, they will also enjoy its yearly steadiness.

Management

Dodge & Cox Stock Fund is guided by a management *team*, not by any one headliner in particular. This type of management is becoming favored with increasing frequency, as it prevents both fund company and customers from having to pin their collective hopes on one person. The team behind Dodge & Cox Stock Fund is both disciplined and deliberate. Team members avoid jumping in and out of sectors with great frequency, and ultimately earn their results with time-honored principles of investment analysis. Dodge & Cox management likes to keep the fund fully invested, with the clear majority of its holdings in common stock vehicles.

Risk/Reward Analysis

Interestingly, Dodge & Cox Stock Fund's volatility measurement is slightly worse than average when compared with the other funds in our group, but only marginally so. Its heavy reliance on cyclical stocks, combined with management's aversion to short-term trading, is probably what accounts for this. Nonetheless, our examination of the fund's *annual* performance records shows it to be quite stable in poor market years.

Expenses

Dodge & Cox Stock Fund's expenses are some of the lowest of our group offerings. The reason for this is clear: the fund's exceedingly low turnover rate. Management's conservative approach to trading gives this fund the lowest turnover rate of the bunch, and one of the lower expense ratios to be found here.

The Dodge & Cox Family

There are two other funds in the Dodge & Cox family besides Dodge & Cox Stock Fund: Dodge & Cox Balanced Fund, and Dodge & Cox Income Fund.

Final Thoughts

Dodge & Cox Stock Fund is unquestionably an excellent choice for anyone's portfolio. Both Accumulation–Preservationists *and* Preservation–Accumulators will find this fund to be tailor-made to their needs, and even pure Accumulators will benefit from the growth-oriented balance this fund will offer their portfolios.

MAS VALUE
Growth and Income

FUND FAMILY:	MAS Funds
TICKER SYMBOL:	MPVLX
PORTFOLIO MANAGER:	A. Morris Williams/Robert J. Marcin
ADDRESS:	One Tower Bridge #1150
	P.O. Box 868
	West Conshohocken, PA 19428-0868
LONG-TERM PERFORMANCE:	★ ★ ★ ★ ★
SHORT-TERM PERFORMANCE:	★ ★ ★ ★ ★
PERFORMANCE AGAINST PEER GROUP:	★ ★ ★ ★ ★
SAFETY:	★ ★ ★ ★
TELEPHONE EXCHANGES:	No
BROKERAGE AVAILABILITY:	Yes
MANAGER TENURE:	11 Years
MINIMUM INITIAL PURCHASE:	$1,000,000 (institutional investors only; may be purchased through discount broker for lower minimum)
ASSETS UNDER MANAGEMENT ($M):	954
PHONE NUMBER:	800-354-8185
TOTAL RETURNS, YEAR BY YEAR, FOR THE PAST TEN:	1985— 29.56% 1986— 24.05% 1987— -5.22% 1988— 22.16% 1989— 20.73% 1990— -6.16% 1991— 37.65% 1992— 14.61% 1993— 14.34% 1994— 3.48%
BETA (3-yr):	94
ALPHA (3-yr):	4.64
R2 (3-yr):	88
STANDARD DEVIATION (3-yr):	.04
GROWTH OF $10,000 FROM JAN. 85 TO DEC. 94:	$39,352.29
PORTFOLIO TURNOVER:	54%
EXPENSE RATIO:	.61%

SUMMARY

Performance

MAS Value represents another entry in the growth-and-income category, with both short- and long-term performance records standing in a most impressive posture. Its three- and ten-year annualized returns are in the upper half of the funds examined here, while its *five*-year return is tops, sitting at almost 17%. A per-year review of performance, however, shows that this fund does have a tendency toward inconsistency. In 1991, for example, MAS Value was the number-one performer of our group, posting a 37.65% return, phenomenal for any growth-and-income fund. Its performance the very next year, though, placed this fund in the bottom half of our group. Furthermore, in 1993, it was the absolute *worst* finisher overall. Bottom line: MAS Value multiyear performance records are some of the best, but you'd better be prepared to ride a bit of a roller coaster in order to earn them.

Management

The fund has the word "value" in its name, and a review of management indicates that they are not easily swayed from that particular focus. Managers A. Morris Williams and Robert J. Marcin are value purists, concentrating on medium- to large-capitalization stocks with extremely low price-to-earnings ratios.

Risk/Reward Analysis

Although the fund's three-year beta coefficient is certainly respectable, it may be important for prospective investors to again examine the per-year returns to see if this fund meets their risk tolerance levels. As we saw in our discussion on performance, this fund has a tendency to jump around the page each year. This is likely due to the fact that the fund keeps about 95% of its holdings in common stocks, a rather elevated figure for a growth-and-income fund. Furthermore, although it does invest primarily in large companies, the skittishness may also be attributed to management's fondness for technology companies, unpredictable in *any* size.

Expenses

MAS Value is pretty cheap as growth-and-income funds go, a fact to which its .61% annual expense ratio attests. Only Dodge & Cox Stock Fund carries an expense ratio as low, although its portfolio turnover is much higher. It's likely that the selection of so many income-producing stocks is the reason that costs are minimized throughout the portfolio.

The MAS Family

There are six other funds in the MAS family besides MAS Value: MAS Equity Portfolio, MAS High-Yield Securities Portfolio, MAS Limited Duration Fixed Income Portfolio, MAS Small Capitalization Value Portfolio, MAS Fixed Income Portfolio, and MAS International Equity Portfolio.

Final Thoughts

MAS Value is clearly a performance giant among growth-and-income funds, but very conservative investors need to be wary. Accumulators and Accumulation–Preservationists will like this fund just fine, but Preservation–Accumulators may want to limit their exposure. As long as you're not concerned with very short-term performance, you should get along very well with MAS Value.

MUTUAL BEACON
Growth and Income

FUND FAMILY:	Mutual Series
TICKER SYMBOL:	BEGRX
PORTFOLIO MANAGER:	Michael F. Price
ADDRESS:	51 John F. Kennedy Parkway
	Short Hills, NJ 07078
LONG-TERM PERFORMANCE:	★ ★ ★ ★ ★
SHORT-TERM PERFORMANCE:	★ ★ ★ ★ ★
PERFORMANCE AGAINST PEER GROUP:	★ ★ ★ ★ ★
SAFETY:	★ ★ ★ ★ ★
TELEPHONE EXCHANGES:	No
BROKERAGE AVAILABILITY:	Yes
MANAGER TENURE:	10 Years
MINIMUM INITIAL PURCHASE:	$5,000/$2,000 for IRAs
ASSETS UNDER MANAGEMENT ($M):	2,582
PHONE NUMBER:	800-553-3014
TOTAL RETURNS, YEAR BY YEAR, FOR THE PAST TEN:	1985— 23.31% 1986— 15.47% 1987— 12.73% 1988— 28.92% 1989— 17.46% 1990— -8.17% 1991— 17.60% 1992— 22.92% 1993— 22.93% 1994— 5.61%

BETA (3-yr):	.64
ALPHA (3-yr):	8.82
R2 (3-yr):	62
STANDARD DEVIATION (3-yr):	6.49
GROWTH OF $10,000 FROM JAN. 85 to DEC. 94:	$41,888.48
PORTFOLIO TURNOVER:	70%
EXPENSE RATIO:	.75%

SUMMARY

Performance

With Mutual Beacon, we find another fund that seems to have both short- and long-term performance consistency as its hallmark. The three-, five-, and ten-year track records of Mutual Beacon are, for the most part, excellent. Its average annual performance over the last three years beats those of all but one of our group members, while its average annual return for the last *ten* years is second to none. Curiously, its five-year annualized performance return is not quite as impressive, but is respectable nonetheless at over 14%. The best explanation for the fund's slightly substandard (relatively speaking) five-year record is that its holdings, which will be discussed shortly, are generally sensitive to recessionary economies. Except for years 1985 and 1991, the fund's per-year performance is *very* consistent, and even in those years investors would probably not likely have been disappointed.

Management

Mutual Beacon has been captained by Michael F. Price since 1985. Shareholders of Mutual Beacon should be very glad that he is as skilled as he is, because some of the securities selections he makes appear, at least on the surface, to be almost dangerous. To say that Price furiously searches for value is something of an understatement; Price has been known to invest portions of the fund's assets in companies involved in mergers, consolidations, reorganizations, and other similar types of circumstances that usually chase investors *away.*

Risk/Reward Analysis

Interestingly, although some of Mutual Beacon's holdings can look rather bizarre, the fund does not register very high on the risk scale. The primary reason for this is that Michael Price will spend a great deal of time in cash with much of his portfolio. A near-20% allocation in cash equivalents is huge, but it provides a nice balance to the rest of the holdings. The proof's in the pudding here: the fund's three-year beta coefficient is the lowest of any in our group.

Expenses

Although Mutual Beacon's turnover rate is rather high compared with other funds in our group, its annual expense ratio is an easy-to-take .75%. In the case of *this* fund, the mild expense ratio can be attributed to the fact that so much of the portfolio rests in cash at any given time, as well as the fact that the troubled securities Price thinks so highly of are, of course, dirt cheap.

The Mutual Series Family

There are three other funds in the Mutual Series family besides Mutual Beacon: Mutual Discovery Fund, Inc., Mutual Qualified Fund, Inc., and Mutual Shares Fund.

Final Thoughts

Mutual Beacon is clearly a fund for long-term investors. Although its per-year returns have been, overall, pretty consistent, the fund clearly has its moments. As long as you look to Mutual Beacon as a core addition to your portfolio, you should be quite pleased.

MUTUAL QUALIFIED
Growth and Income

FUND FAMILY:	Mutual Series
TICKER SYMBOL:	MQIFX
PORTFOLIO MANAGER:	Michael F. Price
ADDRESS:	51 John F. Kennedy Parkway
	Short Hills, NJ 07078
LONG-TERM PERFORMANCE:	★ ★ ★ ★ ★
SHORT-TERM PERFORMANCE:	★ ★ ★ ★ ★
PERFORMANCE AGAINST PEER GROUP:	★ ★ ★ ★ ★
SAFETY:	★ ★ ★ ★ ★
TELEPHONE EXCHANGES:	No
BROKERAGE AVAILABILITY:	Yes
MANAGER TENURE:	15 Years
MINIMUM INITIAL PURCHASE:	$1,000
ASSETS UNDER MANAGEMENT ($M):	2,096
PHONE NUMBER:	800-553-3014
TOTAL RETURNS, YEAR BY YEAR FOR THE PAST TEN:	1985— 25.62% 1986— 16.97% 1987— 7.66% 1988— 30.35% 1989— 14.44% 1990— -10.12% 1991— 21.13% 1992— 22.70% 1993— 22.71% 1994— 5.73%
BETA (3-yr):	.71
ALPHA (3-yr):	8.50
R2 (3-yr):	67
STANDARD DEVIATION (3-yr):	6.96
GROWTH OF $10,000 FROM JAN. 85 TO DEC. 94:	$40,899.13
PORTFOLIO TURNOVER:	67%
EXPENSE RATIO:	.73%

SUMMARY

Performance

Mutual Qualified is a sister fund to Mutual Beacon, and if you're not careful you might mistake it for a twin. The three-, five-, and ten-year average annual performance records of Mutual Qualified are very similar to those of Mutual Beacon; each figure is separated by less than a percentage point. A look at Qualified's per-year performance scores show it to be very solid indeed, much like its counterpart. To be honest, its similarity to Mutual Beacon is so great, there's not a whole lot that can be said that wasn't already said about Beacon.

Management

Michael Price manages Mutual Qualified along with Mutual Beacon, and his management philosophy is virtually identical with respect to both funds. As with Beacon, Price likes to concentrate in securities that are greatly undervalued, including those that may be involved in mergers, liquidations, and similar modes of discontent.

Risk/Reward Analysis

As with Beacon, Qualified's level of cash holdings is very high, reducing the risk associated with the many downtrodden securities Price likes to hold in the portfolio. Similarly, the fund's beta coefficient is quite low, second only to Beacon's. As with Beacon, Qualified is not shy about holding foreign securities in the portfolio. Although a high percentage of foreign securities may seem out of place in a growth-and-income fund, a conscientious manager like Price can reduce the inherent risks associated with those holdings.

Expenses

The tune doesn't change much here, either. Portfolio turnover is very similar to Beacon's, but the high concentration in cash as well as the low cost of questionable securities keep this fund's annual expense ratio fairly competitive.

The Mutual Series Family

There are three other funds in the Mutual Series family besides Mutual Qualified: Mutual Beacon Fund, Inc., Mutual Discovery Fund, Inc., and Mutual Shares Fund.

Final Thoughts

Mutual Qualified is ideal for longer-term investors, but not as good a choice for those who regard income and capital preservation as being very important. If you're looking for a fund that will provide you with nice returns but not a lot of homework, Mutual Qualified could be for you.

MUTUAL SHARES
Growth and Income

FUND FAMILY:	Mutual Series
TICKER SYMBOL:	MUTHX
PORTFOLIO MANAGER:	Michael F. Price
ADDRESS:	51 John F. Kennedy Parkway
	Short Hills, NJ 07078
LONG-TERM PERFORMANCE:	★ ★ ★ ★ ★
SHORT-TERM PERFORMANCE:	★ ★ ★ ★ ★
PERFORMANCE AGAINST PEER GROUP:	★ ★ ★ ★ ★
SAFETY:	★ ★ ★ ★ ★
TELEPHONE EXCHANGES:	No
BROKERAGE AVAILABILITY:	Yes
MANAGER TENURE:	20 Years
MINIMUM INITIAL PURCHASE:	$5,000/$2,000 for IRAs
ASSETS UNDER MANAGEMENT ($M):	4,144.60
PHONE NUMBER:	800-553-3014
TOTAL RETURNS, YEAR BY YEAR, FOR THE PAST TEN:	1985— 26.66% 1986— 16.98% 1987— 6.22% 1988— 30.92% 1989— 14.93% 1990— -9.82% 1991— 20.99% 1992— 21.33% 1993— 21.00% 1994— 4.53%
BETA (3-yr):	.75
ALPHA (3-yr):	7.46
R2 (3-yr):	69
STANDARD DEVIATION (3-yr):	7.23
GROWTH OF $10,000 FROM JAN. 85 TO DEC. 94:	$39,650.72
PORTFOLIO TURNOVER:	66%
EXPENSE RATIO:	.72%

SUMMARY

Performance

Mutual Shares is another relative of Mutual Beacon and Mutual Qualified. The three- and ten-year average annual performance records of Mutual Shares are solid—almost on a par with those of Beacon and Qualified, but not quite. Its five-year record of 14.52% beats Beacon but doesn't quite match Qualified. Regardless, whenever each of the three-, five-, and ten-year average annual performance scores are firmly ensconced in and around 15%, you know that's a winner of a growth-and-income fund. The performance data of Mutual

Shares does *not* disappoint. As you might expect, its per-year performance results show it to be virtually identical to Beacon and Qualified in that department. Its only "down" year in the past ten years was 1990, when *none* of the funds featured in this group finished on the "plus" side.

Management

Michael Price manages Mutual Shares, as well as Beacon and Qualified. The virtually identical performance data of all three funds should demonstrate that not only does he apply the same philosophies and strategies to all three, but he even buys many of the exact same securities for each of the funds. Price says that the funds are reflections of one another to about 90% of their portfolios. Of course, Price's pursuits are reserved for the most undervalued securities, including those with the most uncertain futures.

Risk/Reward Analysis

Given that Mutual Shares portfolio is structured so similarly to those of Beacon and Qualified, it should come as no surprise that the fund's beta coefficient is about as low. In fact, Mutual Beacon, Qualified, *and* Shares retain the three lowest three-year beta scores of all the funds in our group, as well as the three highest alphas.

Expenses

The annual expense ratio of Mutual Shares is .72%, which puts it in the upper half of the funds rated in this group. As with Beacon and Qualified, it is Price's addiction to cash and poor-quality securities that seems to keep the costs down, as the turnover percentage *is* fairly high relative to the other funds in our group.

The Mutual Series Family

There are three other funds in the Mutual Series family besides Mutual Shares: Mutual Beacon Fund, Inc., Mutual Discovery Fund, Inc., and Mutual Qualified Fund, Inc.

Final Thoughts

Mutual Shares, like Mutual Beacon and Mutual Qualified, is a top-notch choice for investors who like to emphasize the *growth* in their growth-and-income funds. As such, it makes for a less-than-stellar choice for superconservative investors who might be looking for a way to spice up their portfolios. However, for everyone else, *any* of these Mutual funds should be considered seriously.

NEUBERGER AND BERMAN GUARDIAN
Growth and Income

FUND FAMILY:	Neuberger and Berman Group
TICKER SYMBOL:	NGUAX
PORTFOLIO MANAGER:	Kent Simons/Lawrence Marx III
ADDRESS:	605 Third Ave.
	New York, NY 10158
LONG-TERM PERFORMANCE:	★ ★ ★ ★
SHORT-TERM PERFORMANCE:	★ ★ ★ ★
PERFORMANCE AGAINST PEER GROUP:	★ ★ ★ ★ ★
SAFETY:	★ ★ ★
TELEPHONE EXCHANGES:	Yes
BROKERAGE AVAILABILITY:	Yes
MANAGER TENURE:	14 Years
MINIMUM INITIAL PURCHASE:	$1,000/$250 for IRAs
ASSETS UNDER MANAGEMENT ($M):	2,833.10
PHONE NUMBER:	800-877-9700
TOTAL RETURNS, YEAR BY YEAR, FOR THE PAST TEN:	1985— 25.05% 1986— 11.91% 1987— -1.01% 1988— 28.08% 1989— 21.52% 1990— -4.71% 1991— 34.35% 1992— 18.99% 1993— 14.47% 1994— .60%
BETA (3-yr):	1.04
ALPHA (3-yr):	2.98
R2 (3-yr):	85
STANDARD DEVIATION (3-yr):	8.99
GROWTH OF $10,000 FROM JAN. 85 TO DEC. 94:	$37,823.19
PORTFOLIO TURNOVER RATE:	24%
EXPENSE RATIO:	.80%

SUMMARY

Performance

The Neuberger and Berman Guardian Fund is another solid-performance entry in our evaluation of the best growth-and-income funds for your retirement account. The average annualized three-year return is a respectable 13.99%, while the ten-year average annualized return is also impressive at 14.64%. Although these numbers rank this fund number eight and nine, respectively, of our group representatives, remember that we are dealing with the ten *best* growth-and-income funds out there. Furthermore, it is appropriate to point out that in the category of *five*-year average annual return, one to which we do not assign star ratings in this book, the Neuberger and Berman Guardian Fund placed second out of ten with a mark of 16.27%. There's not really much to mention when examining the fund's per-year performance results, although it might be worthwhile to mention that the Guardian Fund suffered the least amount of damage out of all the funds in our elite group of ten in the dismal year that was 1990.

Management

The Neuberger and Berman Guardian Fund enjoys the services of co-managers Kent Simons and Lawrence Marx III. The duo likes to pinpoint value stocks, the centerpieces of so many growth-and-income funds. However, Simons and Marx aren't reluctant to grab growth stocks either, and they have demonstrated an obvious inclination to try to benefit from in-favor sectors by weighting the portfolio accordingly.

Risk/Reward Analysis

Although this fund's beta coefficient ranks it ninth out of the ten funds featured here, the figure is only 1.04, just slightly above that of the entire S&P 500. The per-year returns of this fund have been, for the most part, quite steady. Although there have been several years in the past ten when this fund's annual performances were bested by the S&P 500, there was not one year when the distance was very great. This suggests that an investor who is content with earning what the S&P 500 earns will probably be happy here.

Expenses

The fund's annual expense ratio is quite reasonable at .80%, although with that figure it does rank eighth of the ten funds here. This is likely due to the fact that the Guardian Fund keeps a higher percentage of assets in stocks than any other fund featured here.

The Neuberger and Berman Family

There are fifteen other funds in the Neuberger and Berman family besides Neuberger and Berman Guardian Fund: Neuberger and Berman Cash Reserves, Neuberger and Berman Genesis Fund, Inc., Neuberger and Berman Government Income Fund, Inc., Neuberger and Berman Government Money Fund, Inc., Neuberger and Berman Limited Maturity Bond Fund, Inc., Neuberger and Berman Manhattan Fund, Inc., Neuberger and Berman Municipal Money Fund, Inc., Neuberger and Berman Municipal Securities Trust, Inc., Neuberger and Berman New York Insured Intermediate Fund, Inc., Neuberger and Berman Partners Fund, Inc., Neuberger and Berman Professional Investors Growth Fund, Inc., Neuberger and Berman Professional Investors Money Fund, Inc., Neuberger and Berman Selected Sectors, Inc., Neuberger and Berman Socially Responsive Fund, Inc., and Neuberger and Berman Ultra Short Bond Fund.

Final Thoughts

Neuberger and Berman Guardian Fund is another good growth-and-income selection for those who like a little more risk with their income. Unfortunately, the fund's three- and ten-year track records don't seem to justify the chances taken by the fund managers with their growth selections.

Nonetheless, performance being the overriding consideration, the portfolio mix is sufficient to rank this entry on our list of the ten best, and it is certainly worth a look by any prospective longer-term growth-and-income investor.

SAFECO EQUITY
Growth and Income

FUND FAMILY:	SAFECO Mutual Funds
TICKER SYMBOL:	SAFQX
PORTFOLIO MANAGER:	Richard Meagley
ADDRESS:	P.O. Box 34890
	Seattle, WA 98124-1890
LONG-TERM PERFORMANCE:	★ ★ ★ ★ ★
SHORT-TERM PERFORMANCE:	★ ★ ★ ★ ★
PERFORMANCE AGAINST PEER GROUP:	★ ★ ★ ★ ★
SAFETY:	★ ★ ★
TELEPHONE EXCHANGES:	Yes
BROKERAGE AVAILABILITY:	Yes
MANAGER TENURE:	Less than 1 year
MINIMUM INITIAL PURCHASE:	$1,000/$250 for IRAs
ASSETS UNDER MANAGEMENT ($M):	536.90
PHONE NUMBER:	800-426-6730
TOTAL RETURNS, YEAR BY YEAR, FOR THE PAST TEN:	1985— 33.27% 1986— 12.71% 1987— -4.80% 1988— 25.30% 1989— 35.79% 1990— -8.57% 1991— 27.91% 1992— 9.26% 1993— 30.91% 1994— 9.94%
BETA (3-yr):	1.14
ALPHA (3-yr):	5.76
R2 (3-yr):	60
STANDARD DEVIATION (3-yr):	11.69
GROWTH OF $10,000 FROM JAN. 85 TO DEC. 94:	$44,743.88
PORTFOLIO TURNOVER:	33%
EXPENSE RATIO:	.85%

SUMMARY

Performance

The SAFECO Equity Fund's performance numbers are indeed strong up and down the line. Of the ten funds we've selected here, SAFECO Equity finished ahead of seven of them in the three- and five-year annualized return categories, and ahead of *eight* of them in the ten-year annualized return screen. These returns rank SAFECO Equity as the growth-and-income fund with the best overall performance records of any in our evaluation. Peeking at how the fund's per-year results stacked up, we see that SAFECO Equity blew away the rest of the competition in years 1989, 1993, and 1994, and placed a solid second in 1985. In 1990, the year that saw *all* of our contestants finish in the red, SAFECO was absolutely average, ranking fifth. The truth is that based on historical performance, SAFECO Equity is tough to match in the category of growth-and-income.

Management

There has been a recent management change at SAFECO Equity. Former head man Doug Johnson left in 1994, and was replaced by Richard Meagley in January of 1995. Meagley is a vice-president with SAFECO Asset Management, and has been with them since 1983, except for a short break from '92 to '94. Early returns from '95 suggest that Meagley doesn't like to involve the fund in some of the more daring kinds of stocks of which his predecessor was most fond. Does this mean that the great returns in SAFECO Equity's past will never be repeated? Not at all; any time a new manager takes over, a fund may experience some turbulence as its portfolio is adjusted to more closely reflect the new captain's ideas. If anything, it appears that SAFECO Equity will begin to resemble *more* the structure of a true growth-and-income mutual fund.

Risk/Reward Analysis

The three-year beta coefficient of SAFECO Equity is 1.14, making it the fund with the highest beta in our group. This is undoubtedly due to former manager Johnson's love affair with small, growth-oriented companies that often represented the technology sector. Meagley's more conservative approach to the management of the fund will likely see this beta figure drop in the coming years. Looking at the fund's per-year standings, we see that it *has* had a propensity to jump around: of our ten funds, it finished second in '85, ninth in '86, ninth in '87, first in '89, eighth in '92, and first in '93 and '94. Although its beta is rather high for a growth-and-income fund, remember that its performance is, overall, the best.

Expenses

The fund's annual expense ratio is .85%, which places it ninth out of our group of ten, but the figure is still well below the industry standard of 1.00%. The truth is, with returns like these, it's hard to get upset if the fund charges a bit more than some of the others.

The SAFECO Family

There are thirteen other funds in the SAFECO family besides SAFECO Equity Fund: SAFECO California Tax-Free Income Fund, Inc., SAFECO GNMA Fund, Inc., SAFECO Growth Fund, Inc., SAFECO High-Yield Bond Fund, Inc., SAFECO Income Fund, Inc., SAFECO Insured Municipal Bond Fund, Inc., SAFECO Intermediate-Term Municipal Bond Fund, Inc., SAFECO Intermediate-Term U.S. Treasury Fund, Inc., SAFECO Money Market Mutual Fund, Inc., SAFECO Municipal Bond Fund, Inc., SAFECO Northwest Fund, Inc., SAFECO Tax-Free Money Market Fund, Inc., and SAFECO Washington State Municipal Bond Fund, Inc.

Final Thoughts

The returns of SAFECO Equity speak loud and clear. Investors in the past were probably content to endure the fund's slightly higher costs and increased volatility levels so that they might realize the reward of phenomenal returns. Although the new manager seems to be a bit more conservative in his ways, it's likely that SAFECO Equity will continue to represent a highly positive addition to the long-term growth-and-income investor's portfolio.

VANGUARD/WINDSOR
Growth and Income

FUND FAMILY:	Vanguard Group
TICKER SYMBOL:	VWNDX
PORTFOLIO MANAGER:	John B. Neff
ADDRESS:	P.O. Box 2600
	Valley Forge, PA 19482
LONG-TERM PERFORMANCE:	★ ★ ★ ★
SHORT-TERM PERFORMANCE:	★ ★ ★ ★
PERFORMANCE AGAINST PEER GROUP:	★ ★ ★ ★ ★
SAFETY:	★ ★ ★ ★
TELEPHONE EXCHANGES:	Yes
BROKERAGE AVAILABILITY:	Yes
MANAGER TENURE:	31 Years
MINIMUM INITIAL PURCHASE:	Currently closed
ASSETS UNDER MANAGEMENT ($M):	11,287.50
PHONE NUMBER:	800-662-7447
TOTAL RETURNS, YEAR BY YEAR, FOR THE PAST TEN:	1985— 28.03% 1986— 20.27% 1987— 1.23% 1988— 28.70% 1989— 15.02% 1990— -15.50% 1991— 28.55% 1992— 16.50% 1993— 19.37% 1994— -.15%
BETA (3-yr):	.99
ALPHA (3-yr):	2.44
R2 (3-yr):	66
STANDARD DEVIATION (3-yr):	9.74
GROWTH OF $10,000 FROM JAN. 85 to DEC. 94:	$34,803.92
PORTFOLIO TURNOVER:	34%
EXPENSE RATIO:	.45%

SUMMARY

Performance

The Vanguard/Windsor Fund, known simply as the Windsor Fund before May of 1993, still represents one of the most reliable performers in the growth-and-income arena more than thirty years after its inception. Although the fund ranked ninth out of our ten funds in the three- and five-year annualized return categories and dead last in our ten-year annualized return category, the fact is that each of those respective returns

(13.00%, 12.85%, 13.65%) is quite respectable and all are very consistent with one another. Furthermore, if we wish to examine its average annualized return over the last *fifteen* years, we see that of our fund selections that have been around that long, it's the champion with a whopping 17.33% result. Analyzing the fund's returns on a year-by-year basis, we see even more clearly that it is an adherent to the maxim that "slow and steady wins the race." In no year during the last ten did the fund finish higher than third of those in our group, and in two of those years it finished last. However, its long-term numbers are solid, and it's clear Windsor is content to be the wily tortoise in a mutual fund pack of hares.

Management
John B. Neff is the manager of Vanguard/Windsor, and has been for about thirty years now. Neff is a strict value investor, which means that he looks not only for stocks that reflect very favorable price-to-earnings ratios; he also seeks companies with quality price-to-book value ratios so that he may enhance the fund's yield capabilities. His obsession with seeking out top-value stocks keeps him on a constant search from industry to industry, pinpointing those currently out of favor. As performance results indicate, Neff's style does not usually result in returns such as those more closely associated with growth equities, but his solid, reliable performance through the years is considered more important by the true growth-and-income players.

Risk/Reward Analysis
Although this fund, at first glance, would hardly be considered volatile, a closer look will indicate that it can have some pretty rough years. 1990's return of -15.50% is rather scary for a true growth-and-income fund, and in 1994 the fund finished with the worst record of the ten measured here. Windsor's three-year beta is .99, which is a shade high considering that the

fund hasn't had any slam-bang years in recent history. Again, when you remember that we're talking about growth-and-income funds, you realize that risk is relative and Windsor is just not all that risky overall. However, the surest way to be happy with this fund is to buy it for the long term.

Expenses

The Vanguard/Windsor currently has a modest turnover rate of 34%, and that, along with its disciplined pursuit of value securities, keeps its annual expense ratio at a group-leading .45%.

The Vanguard Family

Vanguard is a comprehensive mutual fund company with too many funds to list here. Following is a brief selection of funds from Vanguard that might be of interest to growth-and-income investors: Vanguard Convertible Securities Fund, Vanguard Equity Income Fund, and Vanguard Index Trust-500 Portfolio.

Final Thoughts

If you aren't concerned with earning the *best* return but are content with the prospect of realizing a solid, competitive growth rate without having to run the risks associated with small-capitalization stocks, Vanguard/Windsor may be for you. A careful review of this fund's performance records should tell you, however, that you should plan on being here for at least three years or so in order to ensure a competitive return.

FIDELITY
Growth and Income

FUND FAMILY:	Fidelity Group
TICKER SYMBOL:	FFIDX
PORTFOLIO MANAGER:	Beth F. Terrana
ADDRESS:	82 Devonshire St.
	Boston, MA 02109
LONG-TERM PERFORMANCE:	★ ★ ★ ★
SHORT-TERM PERFORMANCE:	★ ★ ★ ★
PERFORMANCE AGAINST PEER GROUP:	★ ★ ★ ★ ★
SAFETY:	★ ★ ★ ★
TELEPHONE EXCHANGES:	Yes
BROKERAGE AVAILABILITY:	Yes
MANAGER TENURE:	2 Years
MINIMUM INITIAL PURCHASE:	$2,500/$500 for IRAs
ASSETS UNDER MANAGEMENT ($M):	2,152.70
PHONE NUMBER:	800-544-8888
TOTAL RETURNS, YEAR BY YEAR, FOR THE PAST TEN:	1985— 27.66% 1986— 15.76% 1987— 3.28% 1988— 17.85% 1989— 28.80% 1990— -5.10% 1991— 24.15% 1992— 8.46% 1993— 18.36% 1994— 2.58%
BETA (3-yr):	.89
ALPHA (3-yr):	2.33
R2 (3-yr):	79
STANDARD DEVIATION (3-yr):	8.00
GROWTH OF $10,000 FROM JAN. 85 to DEC. 94:	$35,943.90
PORTFOLIO TURNOVER:	207%
EXPENSE RATIO:	.65%

SUMMARY

Performance

Fidelity Fund, the most simply named fund in the arsenal of mutual fund powerhouse Fidelity, remains one of its cornerstones well over a half-century after its birth. Fidelity Fund made our list of the top growth-and-income funds primarily through its posting of solid performance numbers for all measured categories. In the performance categories we grade with stars, the three- and ten-year annualized return groups, this fund generated figures of 12.27% and 14.04%, respectively. Although these returns place the fund dead last against the other nine finalists, the fact remains that the numbers are excellent for growth-and-income vehicles. In the unstarred five- and fifteen-year annualized return categories, Fidelity Fund again notches strong performance figures with respective showings of 12.12% and 15.47%. A per-year performance review of this fund shows it to be quite steady: despite the fact that the fund placed last of our contenders in *all four* of the annualized multiyear performance categories we checked (three, five, ten, and fifteen years), the fund finished last only one year in the last ten. The conclusion? For slow-and-go growth-and-income investors, Fidelity's clear lack of rock 'n roll movement should be most welcome.

Management

Fidelity Fund is managed by Beth F. Terrana, a Harvard M.B.A., as well as a former assistant vice-president of Putnam Management. Terrana is no newcomer to Fidelity funds; she posted a strong showing while in charge of Fidelity Growth and Income from 1985 to 1990, and also did a great job with Fidelity Equity-Income as well from 1990 to 1993. Terrana's favorite portfolio acquisitions seem to be out-of-favor stocks that demonstrate the potential for a strong recovery—classic value investing.

Risk/Reward Analysis

A risk/reward analysis of Fidelity Fund shows that it should have appeal for the risk-averse set. We've already told you how its per-year performance has been most even-handed, and it is also worthwhile to note that in awful 1990 the fund posted a strong showing relative to its nine counterparts, finishing third that year. That's good news for those investors prone to heart failure. The fund's beta is relatively mild at .89. In short, Fidelity Fund's risk/reward relationship is very reasonable.

Expenses

Although the portfolio turnover rate of Fidelity Fund has been absolutely manic through the years (207% at last count), the fund enjoys a relatively mild annual expense ratio of .65%. Such an inoffensive number can likely be attributed to manager Terrana's disciplined search for value as well as the relatively high cash position the fund likes to maintain.

The Fidelity Family

Fidelity is a comprehensive mutual fund company with too many funds to list here. Following is a brief selection of funds from Fidelity that might be of interest to growth-and-income investors: Fidelity Equity-Income II Fund, Fidelity Growth and Income Portfolio, Fidelity Puritan Fund.

Final Thoughts

Fidelity Fund may be, all in all, the best fund in our group for those who prize stability as much as growth. Certainly there is always *some* risk with any vehicle that is primarily market-based, but Fidelity Fund does a nice job of limiting the volatility. While investors of *all* aggressiveness levels might like this fund, Preservation–Accumulators might like it best for the long haul.

BABSON VALUE
Growth and Income

FUND FAMILY:	Babson
TICKER SYMBOL:	BVALX
PORTFOLIO MANAGER:	Nick Whitridge
ADDRESS:	Three Crown Center
	2440 Pershing Rd.
	Kansas City, MO 64108
LONG-TERM PERFORMANCE:	★ ★ ★ ★
SHORT-TERM PERFORMANCE:	★ ★ ★ ★
PERFORMANCE AGAINST PEER GROUP:	★ ★ ★ ★ ★
SAFETY:	★ ★ ★ ★
TELEPHONE EXCHANGES:	Yes
BROKERAGE AVAILABILITY:	Yes

MANAGER TENURE:	10 Years
MINIMUM INITIAL PURCHASE:	$1,000/$250 for IRAs
ASSETS UNDER MANAGEMENT ($M):	119
PHONE NUMBER:	800-333-1001
TOTAL RETURNS, YEAR BY YEAR, FOR THE PAST TEN:	1985— 26.48% 1986— 20.81% 1987— 3.11% 1988— 18.88% 1989— 18.21% 1990— -11.39% 1991— 28.93% 1992— 15.40% 1993— 22.89% 1994— 2.51%
BETA (3-yr):	.88
ALPHA (3-yr):	4.02
R2 (3-yr):	79
STANDARD DEVIATION (3-yr):	7.93
GROWTH OF $10,000 FROM JAN. 85 TO DEC. 94:	$36,771.71
PORTFOLIO TURNOVER:	14%
EXPENSE RATIO:	.99%

SUMMARY

Performance

Babson Value has only had three years out of the last ten in which it did not produce attractive returns. In these years ('87, '90, '93) the overall market was down. The fund's worst year was 1990, in which it posted an 11% loss. During the important three- and ten-year annualized return periods the fund motored along at better than 14%. With a standard deviation of only 7.93, Babson Value makes an attractive addition to almost any portfolio. Consistency and predictability of returns are the fund's two most apparent traits. Although Babson Value is currently invested 95% in stocks, it does on occasion (for defensive purposes) move to bonds and cash. Even during a 1987 that saw the worst single-day market crash in history, the fund earned its shareholders a better-than-3% total return.

Management

Nick Whitridge is described by much of the financial press as a contrarian. He has earned this reputation through his willingness to buy out-of-favor stocks and invest in industries that are trending in a downward direction. More than a contrarian, we would consider him to be a value-oriented portfolio manager.

Undervalued issues in out-of-favor sectors are often overlooked, but not by Whitridge. He has made many gutsy decisions over the past few years, including taking large positions in industrial cyclicals before they showed strong signs of recovery. The fund has a portfolio price to earnings (P/E) ratio of less than 20 and is primarily investing in larger capitalized companies with a value approach.

Risk/Reward Analysis
The fund has about an average volatility among growth-and-income funds. Its worst year in our ten year review was 1990, when it lost 11%; its best was 1985, when it notched a 26.5% return. The fund takes approximately 83% of the risk of the S&P 500.

Expenses
The fund's expenses have averaged about 1% a year for the past five years. This is above average for all mutual funds but is slightly *below* average for the category of growth-and-income funds. The fund controls its expenses by holding its securities and thus keeping turnover low. The average turnover of the fund's portfolio is 14%, low for *any* type of equity fund. For this reason the fund is an excellent choice for nonretirement accounts as well, as tax costs are well-minimized.

The Babson Family
There are thirteen other funds in the Babson family besides Babson Value: Babson Bond L, Babson Bond S, Babson Enterprise, Babson Enterprise II, Babson Growth, Babson Tax-Free Income L, Babson Tax-Free Income S, Babson-Stewart Ivory International, Shadow Stock, UMB Bond, UMB Heartland, UMB Stock, and UMB Worldwide.

Final Thoughts
We are very impressed with Babson Value. It earns high marks in the areas of tax minimization, performance against peer group, risk-adjusted returns, and predictability of performance.

This fund would be an excellent addition to the portfolios of both Accumulators and Accumulation–Preservationists.

INTERNATIONAL FUNDS

HARBOR INTERNATIONAL
International Stock

FUND FAMILY:	Harbor Funds
TICKER SYMBOL:	HAINX
PORTFOLIO MANAGER:	Hakan Castegren
ADDRESS:	One Sea Gate
	Toledo, OH 43666
LONG-TERM PERFORMANCE:	★ ★ ★ ★
SHORT-TERM PERFORMANCE:	★ ★ ★ ★
PERFORMANCE AGAINST PEER GROUP:	★ ★ ★ ★ ★
SAFETY:	★ ★ ★ ★
TELEPHONE EXCHANGES:	Yes
BROKERAGE AVAILABILITY:	Yes
MANAGER TENURE:	8 Years
MINIMUM INITIAL PURCHASE:	Closed
ASSETS UNDER MANAGEMENT ($M):	3,003.50
PHONE NUMBER:	800-422-1050
TOTAL RETURNS, YEAR BY YEAR, FOR THE PAST FIVE:	1990— -9.76% 1991— 21.46% 1992— -.20% 1993— 45.42% 1994— 5.43%
BETA (3-yr):	1.00
ALPHA (3-yr):	3.67
R2 (3-yr):	32
STANDARD DEVIATION:	14.10
GROWTH OF $10,000 FROM JAN. 90 to DEC. 94:	$16,770.70
PORTFOLIO TURNOVER:	28%
EXPENSE RATIO:	1.10%

SUMMARY
Performance
Harbor International comes in with the best overall multiyear performance records of our group offerings. Its five-year average annualized return was tops, measuring 12.56%, while its three-year annualized performance figure was a very solid

13.86%, placing the fund third in *that* category. Interestingly, a review of the fund's per-year returns shows that despite its overall superior showing, Harbor International did not manage to finish first in any single year out of the past five. In fact, the fund couldn't manage to finish any higher than fourth in three out of the last five years. It should be mentioned, however, that neither did the fund place last in any of the last five years, offering prospective investors at least *some* measure of consistency over the long haul. Investors in international funds will find, however, that consistency is a relative term, as *all* of these funds are inclined to a greater measure of inconsistency than most other categories of mutual funds.

Management

The portfolio manager of Harbor International since 1987 has been Hakan Castegren, a 1957 graduate of the Stockholm School of Economics and president of Northern Cross Investments, the fund's adviser. Castegren is a traditional value investor who manages to utilize his professional financial education to the fund's advantage. Much of its strength in 1991, for example, can be attributed to Castegren's accurate targeting of the potential offered by so many emerging-markets countries at that time. In 1994, Castegren's economic shrewdness paid off again, as his foresight in staying clear of Latin American markets helped the fund dodge much of the damage wrought by Mexico's financial debacle. Investors in Harbor International should clearly welcome the careful analysis and forethought practiced by its portfolio manager.

Risk/Reward Analysis

As we said to in the Performance section, *all* international funds have a tendency to be a bit more skittish than funds of other broad objective categories. That fact must always be kept in perspective by overseas-fund investors. Harbor International has the highest beta coefficient of any fund in our group, but at

1.00 it's certainly not unreasonable. A heavy weighting in the financial sector probably accounts for this "top" score, but all in all the fund's risk/reward measurement is tolerable.

Expenses

Harbor International's expense ratio is perfectly average among the funds examined here, posting a figure of 1.10%. Prospective investors in international funds should realize that these vehicles are a bit more expensive to operate than domestic funds, for obvious reasons. That being said, there's nothing unusual about Harbor's expenses, especially when you consider that its turnover rate is closely in line with its expense ratio.

The Harbor Family

There are seven other funds in the Harbor family besides Harbor International: Harbor Bond Fund, Harbor Capital Appreciation Fund, Harbor Growth Fund, Harbor International Growth Fund, Harbor Money Market Fund, Harbor Short Duration Fund, and Harbor Value Fund.

Final Thoughts

As international funds go, it's tough to beat the performance of Harbor International, although it's safe to say that this fund should be negotiated only by Accumulators and others with a tolerance for some volatility.

MORGAN STANLEY INSTITUTIONAL INTERNATIONAL EQUITY
International Stock

FUND FAMILY:	Morgan Stanley Institutional Funds
TICKER SYMBOL:	MSIQX
PORTFOLIO MANAGER:	Dominic Caldecott
ADDRESS:	P.O. Box 2798
	Boston, MA 02208-2798
LONG-TERM PERFORMANCE:	★ ★ ★
SHORT-TERM PERFORMANCE:	★ ★ ★ ★ ★
PERFORMANCE AGAINST PEER GROUP:	★ ★ ★ ★ ★
SAFETY:	★ ★ ★ ★ ★
TELEPHONE EXCHANGES:	Yes
BROKERAGE AVAILABILITY:	No
MANAGER TENURE:	6 Years
MINIMUM INITIAL PURCHASE:	Closed
ASSETS UNDER MANAGEMENT ($M):	1,373.80
PHONE NUMBER:	800-548-7786
TOTAL RETURNS, YEAR BY YEAR, FOR THE PAST FIVE:	1990— -5.73% 1991— 8.92% 1992— -2.92% 1993— 46.60% 1994— 12.31%
BETA (3-yr):	.56
ALPHA (3-yr):	9.14
R2 (3-yr):	12
STANDARD DEVIATION (3-yr):	13.11
GROWTH OF $10,000 FROM JAN. 90 TO DEC. 94:	$16,412.07
PORTFOLIO TURNOVER:	16%
EXPENSE RATIO:	1.00%

SUMMARY

Performance

The Morgan Stanley Institutional International Equity Fund posts performance data that is as distinguished as the fund's name. Morgan Stanley has long been one of the world giants in money management, with an especially strong track record in overseas markets. That strength is certainly evident here, as the fund comes in fourth in our long-term, multiyear annualized return category of five years. Additionally, this fund wins the top spot in the *three*-year annualized return category with a tremendous 16.53% showing. If we look at the fund's per-year performance results for the past five years, we see that in three of those the fund managed to place in the top three of our offerings here. Only 1991 saw a worse-than-average return, but that was due mostly to the fund's insistence on staying out of the more volatile (but more *profitable*, at least in '91) emerging markets.

Management

The captain of the Morgan Stanley Institutional Equity Fund is Dominic Caldecott, a graduate of Oxford University. Caldecott has been running the fund since 1989, and before joining Morgan Stanley he sharpened his foreign-investment teeth at another international mutual fund giant, G. T. Management Group. His philosophy is more conservative in a realm that can be rather aggressive at times. Most of the fund's weightings are in Europe and Japan, and portfolio holdings are selected primarily for their value and monitored by way of fundamental analysis.

Risk/Reward Analysis

Morgan Stanley Institutional International Equity's three-year beta coefficient is third-lowest in our group of ten, with a measurement of .56. The reason its volatility level is so palatable is because management goes out of its way to forsake more aggressive markets, such as the so-called emerging markets that will likely ride the "boom-bust" cycle on many occasions. Accordingly, this fund is a prime candidate for more conservative investors who might like to add a little international flavor to their portfolios.

Expenses

The fund's expense ratio is a perfectly average 1.00%, the standard for mutual funds. The fund has a very low current turnover rate of just 16%, which is attributable to Caldecott's deliberate style of management and stock selection. The tax minimization that is a natural by-product of low-turnover funds such as this one makes it a great choice for those who are cost-conscious.

The Morgan Stanley Family

Morgan Stanley, in its capacity as a large institutional investment house, specializes in funds that are both international and closed-end in structure. Following are two open-end Morgan Stanley funds *besides* Institutional Equity that are available to overseas-minded investors: Morgan Stanley Institutional Asia Equity and Morgan Stanley Institutional Emerging Markets.

Final Thoughts

Morgan Stanley Institutional International Equity is a solid choice for just about anyone seeking to tap into the potential offered by overseas markets. The highly aggressive may be happier in a fund that seeks stock positions from upstart economies, but for the rest of us this fund is a great way to "see the world."

ELFUN GLOBAL
International Stock

FUND FAMILY:	Elfun Mutual Funds
TICKER SYMBOL:	EGLBX
PORTFOLIO MANAGER:	Ralph R. Layman
ADDRESS:	P.O. Box 120074
	Stamford, CT 06912-0074
LONG-TERM PERFORMANCE:	★ ★ ★
SHORT-TERM PERFORMANCE:	★ ★ ★ ★
PERFORMANCE AGAINST PEER GROUP:	★ ★ ★ ★ ★
SAFETY:	★ ★ ★ ★ ★
SALES RESTRICTIONS:	Elfun funds are available only to members of the Elfun Society, an organization affiliated with General Electric Co. For more information, contact General Electric Investment Corp. at the phone number below.
TELEPHONE EXCHANGES:	Yes
BROKERAGE AVAILABILITY:	No
MANAGER TENURE:	4 Years
MINIMUM INITIAL PURCHASE:	$100
ASSETS UNDER MANAGEMENT ($M):	126.10

PHONE NUMBER:	800-242-0134
TOTAL RETURNS, YEAR BY YEAR, FOR THE PAST FIVE:	1990— -8.65% 1991— 14.81% 1992— 5.93% 1993— 31.88% 1994— -.63%
BETA (3-yr):	.71
ALPHA (3-yr):	4.40
R2 (3-yr):	27
STANDARD DEVIATION (3-yr):	10.79
GROWTH OF $10,000 FROM JAN. 90 to DEC. 94:	$14,559.33
PORTFOLIO TURNOVER:	30%
EXPENSE RATIO:	.38%

SUMMARY

Performance

Elfun Global, a member of the Elfun Mutual Funds family that has historical ties to General Electric, registers with very consistent average performances over our three- and five-year average annualized periods. Elfun Global ranks fifth out of our ten funds in the five-year category with a return of 10.87%, quite respectable. In the *three*-year performance analysis, the fund places fourth with an even-more-respectable 12.89% average return. In a stock fund category that is prone to lower performance results than its domestic counterparts, these numbers prove to be very solid. A five-year review of the fund's per-year results shows that Elfun's best years are those in which international funds as a whole did poorly, while its worst years ('91 and '93) were also those in which the category as a whole did well. These results suggest that Elfun's portfolio prefers a risk-averse posture, sacrificing manic gains for a strong dose of safety.

Management

Elfun Global has been managed by Ralph Layman for four years now, and his style seems to be just what the doctor ordered for more conservative investors. Layman likes to keep his fund's allocations to the jumpy financial, cyclical, and technology sectors to a minimum, and he strives to find the kinds of companies that keep the fund's income ratio (1.44%)

the highest in our group. Additionally, it should be noted that under Layman's watchful eye, Elfun has the highest five-year earnings growth of any fund in our group at 10.93%.

Risk/Reward Analysis

Elfun Global enjoys a beta of .71, very acceptable, as well as a three-year alpha score of 4.40, third-highest of the ten. These volatility measurements go hand in hand with the per-year results of the fund during the past five years, which we have already indicated were investor-friendly to those who don't like much excitement with their overseas ventures. Overall, a risk/reward analysis of Elfun tells us that it is a very moderately tempered fund, great for the more conservative.

Expenses

Elfun Global's expense ratio is an unbelievably low .38%, a figure that is due chiefly to the fact that the Elfun funds are accessible to so few investors in general, which in turn means that administration costs are relatively low. Furthermore, Elfun's portfolio turnover rate is a very reasonable 30%, something that also helps to keep costs in line. Finally, a search for value as well as for stocks that offer a terrific yield also helps to keep the overall price tag in line.

The Elfun Family

There are five other funds in the Elfun family besides Elfun Global: Elfun Diversified Fund, Elfun Income Fund, Elfun Money Market Fund, Elfun Tax-Exempt Income Fund, and Elfun Trusts.

Final Thoughts

If you can gain access to it, Elfun Global would be a nice addition to the international section of one's portfolio. Although Preservationists and Preservation–Accumulators should be wary of overseas funds in general, these investors may want to give Elfun Global serious consideration if they're thinking of testing the waters *across* the water.

LEXINGTON WORLDWIDE EMERGING MARKETS FUND
International Stock

FUND FAMILY:	Lexington Group
TICKER SYMBOL:	LEXGX
PORTFOLIO MANAGER:	Richard T. Saler, et al.
ADDRESS:	Park 80 West Plaza Two
	Saddle Brook, NJ 07662
LONG-TERM PERFORMANCE:	★ ★
SHORT-TERM PERFORMANCE:	★ ★
PERFORMANCE AGAINST PEER GROUP:	★ ★ ★ ★ ★
SAFETY:	★ ★ ★ ★
TELEPHONE EXCHANGES:	Yes
BROKERAGE AVAILABILITY:	Yes
MANAGER TENURE:	1 Year
MINIMUM INITIAL PURCHASE:	$1,000/$250 for IRAs
ASSETS UNDER MANAGEMENT ($M):	262.40
PHONE NUMBER:	800-526-0057
TOTAL RETURNS, YEAR BY YEAR, FOR THE PAST FIVE:	1990— -14.15% 1991— 24.19% 1992— 3.77% 1993— 63.37% 1994— -13.81%
BETA (3-yr):	.89
ALPHA (3-yr):	1.23
R2 (3-yr):	15
STANDARD DEVIATION (3-yr):	17.96
GROWTH OF $10,000 FROM JAN. 90 to DEC. 94:	$15,578.58
PORTFOLIO TURNOVER:	79%
EXPENSE RATIO:	1.65%

SUMMARY

Performance

A look at the performance records of Lexington Worldwide Emerging Markets shows us how a classic volatile overseas fund can take unsuspecting investors on quite a roller-coaster ride. As we start our examination, we notice that the three- and five-year annualized performance results look innocuous enough: 9.57% for the five-year run, and an almost-identical 9.68% for the three-year test. A prospective investor who looked no further might think that he had a nice even-tempered international fund on his hands. Wrong! A look at Lexington's per-year performance results show that it's usually feast or famine with this entry. In 1990, this fund was down 14.15%, the worst showing of our group that year. The very next year, though, it was number one. Lexington placed a moderate fourth in 1992, but jumped back on the shuttle to the moon in '93 and scored a whopping 63.37%, far outdistancing its closest challenger, Harbor International. In 1994, it was famine time again, as emerging markets were just not the place to be and the fund posted a dismal -13.81%.

Management

Lexington has been managed by Richard T. Saler since 1994, and the fund supervisor takes many factors into account when he makes decisions on behalf of the portfolio. One of the most important is the condition of a particular country that may contain a number of promising companies. Regardless of *how* good the stocks look, Saler will pass on them if the representative nation is suffering from questionable economic/political stability. Although many of the world's definitive emerging markets are located in Latin America, Saler is still smarting after getting burned in them during '94 and plans not to return for a while.

Risk/Reward Analysis

Well, what do you think? Is this fund the riskiest of our group offerings? In the shorter term, it seems to be. After all, depending on what year you're in, you could do a minus 14% or a positive 63%! Although this fund's longer-term record is pretty good, its year-to-year volatility is something that risk investors should be acutely aware of. This fund's beta coefficient is not the highest of our group, but that is somewhat deceiving; the securities in the portfolio are clearly the most volatile, but Saler frequently holds high cash positions that tend to keep the fund's overall risk measurements lower.

Expenses

Lexington's expense ratio is high at 1.65%. Although the portfolio regularly maintains a high cash position, its turnover rate is quite high, which is to be expected in a fund that specializes in constantly changing emerging markets. If you want to ride *this* roller coaster, expect to pay a premium as these funds go.

The Lexington Family

There are eleven other funds in the Lexington family besides Lexington Worldwide Emerging Markets: Lexington Convertible Securities Fund, Inc., Lexington Corporate Leaders Trust Fund, Lexington Global Fund, Inc., Lexington GNMA Income Fund, Inc., Lexington Goldfund, Inc., Lexington Growth and Income Fund, Inc., Lexington International Fund, Inc., Lexington Money Market Trust, Lexington Short-Intermediate Government Securities Fund, Inc., Lexington Tax Exempt Bond Trust, and Lexington Tax Free Money Fund, Inc.

Final Thoughts

Although this fund made our list of best performances for international stock funds, we could say justifiably that it belongs in a different category altogether from other emerging markets funds. Be that as it may, Lexington Emerging Markets *is* a solid fund that should be reserved for those investors who have both a strong heart and the inclination to keep a close eye on it.

SCUDDER GLOBAL
International Stock

FUND FAMILY:	Scudder Funds
TICKER SYMBOL:	SCOBX
PORTFOLIO MANAGER:	William E. Holzer, et al.
ADDRESS:	P.O. Box 2291
	Boston, MA 02107-2291
LONG-TERM PERFORMANCE:	★ ★
SHORT-TERM PERFORMANCE:	★ ★ ★
PERFORMANCE AGAINST PEER GROUP:	★ ★ ★ ★ ★
SAFETY:	★ ★ ★ ★ ★
TELEPHONE EXCHANGES:	Yes
BROKERAGE AVAILABILITY:	Yes
MANAGER TENURE:	9 Years
MINIMUM INITIAL PURCHASE:	$1,000/$500 for IRAs
ASSETS UNDER MANAGEMENT ($M):	1,094.70
PHONE NUMBER:	800-225-2470
TOTAL RETURNS, YEAR BY YEAR, FOR THE PAST FIVE:	1990— -6.40% 1991— 17.07% 1992— 4.55% 1993— 31.10% 1994— -4.20%
BETA (3-yr):	.70
ALPHA (3-yr):	2.92
R2 (3-yr):	38
STANDARD DEVIATION (3-yr):	9.03
GROWTH OF $10,000 FROM JAN. 90 TO DEC. 94:	$14,388.44
PORTFOLIO TURNOVER:	59%
EXPENSE RATIO:	1.45

SUMMARY

Performance

Scudder Global is another fund that doesn't really have any standout performance numbers but nevertheless demonstrates a consistent overall strength. Its five-year annualized return standing is seventh out of our group of ten, posting a figure of 9.50%. Its three-year measurement raises its standing only one place, but its actual return is much improved at 11.39%. A per-year review of this fund's performance will show that Scudder Global finished in the upper half of the funds in our group from '90 to '92, and finished last and next-to-last in '93 and '94. There really isn't much that you can conclude from that, as its '93 showing was still a 30-plus percentage return and its '94 results simply reflected its traditionally bond-heavy weighting. Scudder is famous for its successful bond funds, and it seems to try to incorporate that same success in its other funds using debt securities in their portfolios. Normally, the strategy is successful; last year it wasn't.

Management

The manager of Scudder Global is William E. Holzer. Holzer, who earned his M.B.A. from New York University, has been in charge of this fund since its inception in 1986. Furthermore, Holzer is the man in charge of all global-equity investment strategies at Scudder, so he's a good man to have batting for you if you're a shareholder of this fund. Scudder Global's management is one that keeps the fund's stake in emerging markets very small, and, as mentioned above, its allocation in bonds unusually high.

Risk/Reward Analysis

This fund's beta coefficient is a nice .70—not so high as to indicate that the fund has nervous tendencies, and not as low as that of a fund that takes a too-conservative stance in these markets. The returns of this fund seem to bear this summation out: moderate risk for a moderate reward.

Expenses

Although we've already established that international funds will be more expensive in general, it would have been nice to see the fund with the third-highest expense ratio in our group post better overall results. Additionally, this fund also had the third-highest turnover rate of our group, and again it would have been nice to see results that better justified this kind of activity.

The Scudder Family

There are too many funds offered by Scudder to list here. Some that may be of interest to international investors are:

Scudder Emerging Markets Income Fund, Inc., Scudder Global Small Company Fund, Inc., Scudder International Fund, Inc., and Scudder Latin America Fund, Inc.

Final Thoughts

Scudder Global is a solid fund that won't, in general, give investors too many surprises. Nevertheless, its year-by-year performance results prove once again that prospective investors in international mutual funds should be of mostly the Accumulator and Accumulation–Preservationist mold; slow-and-go investors should always approach overseas investing with great caution.

T. ROWE PRICE FOREIGN EQUITY
International Stock

FUND FAMILY:	Price T. Rowe Funds
TICKER SYMBOL:	PRFEX
PORTFOLIO MANAGER:	Martin G. Wade
ADDRESS:	100 E. Pratt Street
	Baltimore, MD 21202
LONG-TERM PERFORMANCE:	★ ★
SHORT-TERM PERFORMANCE:	★ ★ ★
PERFORMANCE AGAINST PEER GROUP:	★ ★ ★ ★ ★
SAFETY:	★ ★ ★ ★ ★
SALES RESTRICTIONS:	T. Rowe Price Foreign Equity maybe purchased only by institutional investors currently. Contact Price at the number below for more information.
TELEPHONE EXCHANGES:	Yes
BROKERAGE AVAILABILITY:	Yes
MANAGER TENURE:	6 Years
MINIMUM INITIAL PURCHASE:	$100,000
ASSETS UNDER MANAGEMENT ($M):	1,046.20
PHONE NUMBER:	800-638-5660
TOTAL RETURNS, YEAR BY YEAR, FOR THE PAST FIVE:	1990— -8.21% 1991— 15.44% 1992— -3.74% 1993— 40.76% 1994— -.88%
BETA (3-yr):	.70
ALPHA (3-yr):	3.27
R2 (3-yr):	17

STANDARD DEVIATION (3-yr):	13.44
GROWTH OF $10,000 FROM JAN. 90 TO DEC. 94:	$14,231.09
PORTFOLIO TURNOVER:	23%
EXPENSE RATIO:	.84%

SUMMARY

Performance

Of the two T. Rowe Price funds we review here, Foreign Equity seems to be the superior performer of the two, at least in the recent several years. The five-year annualized return figure of this one is 9.18%, which is fair for international funds but not all that great for stock funds overall. The fund's three-year annualized performance is 11.28%, which isn't bad, but we wish the fund didn't have three down years in the last five. Unfortunately, this dubious distinction belongs to its sister as well, Price's International Stock Fund, making these two offerings from Price the *only* two of our group to be in the red three of the last five years. The fund's 1993 performance *was* strong, ranking it fifth of our ten, and despite its several down years recently, Foreign Equity did not come in last of our group in any of them.

Management

T. Rowe Price Foreign Equity is headed by Martin G. Wade, a Cambridge University graduate who manages several other foreign-based funds at Price. Wade's style of portfolio management here is very similar to the one he uses to manage International Stock: Wade preallocates percentages of the fund's portfolio to different regions of the world, and *then* begins his search for appropriate securities within the respective areas. Additionally, management likes to hold stocks for long periods of time, indicating that it is not easily swayed by the "flavor of the month" style of money management.

Risk/Reward Analysis

Foreign Equity runs with a beta of .70, which should be considered more than acceptable by investors. In fact, this mark ties it with Scudder Global at fourth-best in the beta rankings of the funds in this group. However, investors should pay close attention to the fact that while this fund suffers like the rest when international funds aren't doing well as a category, its positive years have not been the top-of-the-line standouts that help investors to *forget* those poor years.

Expenses

Although this fund generally maintains a 100% stock position, its expense ratio is kept moderate primarily through a low turnover rate of 23%. However, investors should closely examine this fund's performance against the cost. Will you only end up getting what you paid for?

The T. Rowe Price Family

There are too many funds offered by T. Rowe Price to list them all here. Some that may be of interest to international investors are: T. Rowe Price European Stock Fund, Inc., T. Rowe Price International Discovery Fund, Inc., T. Rowe Price International Stock Fund, Inc., T. Rowe Price Latin America Fund, Inc., and T. Rowe Price New Asia Fund, Inc.

Final Thoughts

As international funds go, T. Rowe Price Foreign Equity is one of the best. As equity mutual funds *in general* go, the returns are less than glorious. Although it is clear that favorable returns can be had in this fund during years that are good to international investing overall, investors should think twice before adopting a long-term buy-and-hold strategy with Foreign Equity.

T. ROWE PRICE INTERNATIONAL STOCK
International Stock

FUND FAMILY:	Price T. Rowe Funds
TICKER SYMBOL:	PRITX
PORTFOLIO MANAGER:	Martin G. Wade, et al.
ADDRESS:	100 E. Pratt St.
	Baltimore, MD 21202
LONG-TERM PERFORMANCE:	★ ★
SHORT-TERM PERFORMANCE:	★ ★ ★
PERFORMANCE AGAINST PEER GROUP:	★ ★ ★ ★ ★
SAFETY:	★ ★ ★ ★ ★
TELEPHONE EXCHANGES:	Yes
BROKERAGE AVAILABILITY:	Yes
MANAGER TENURE:	15 Years
MINIMUM INITIAL PURCHASE:	$2,500/$1,000 for IRAs
ASSETS UNDER MANAGEMENT ($M):	5,806.60
PHONE NUMBER:	800-638-5660
TOTAL RETURNS, YEAR BY YEAR, FOR THE PAST FIVE:	1990— -8.89% 1991— 15.87% 1992— -3.47% 1993— 40.11% 1994— -.76%
BETA (3-yr):	.72
ALPHA (3-yr):	3.05
R2 (3-yr):	19
STANDARD DEVIATION (3-yr):	13.25
GROWTH OF $10,000 FROM JAN. 90 TO DEC. 94:	$14,169.52
PORTFOLIO TURNOVER:	22%
EXPENSE RATIO:	.96%

SUMMARY

Performance

The T. Rowe Price International Stock Fund represents one of two funds in our group that notched an average annual return in the past five years of less than 9%. That's certainly not terrible, but it's important to note that once a stock fund of *any* kind generates a five-year track record of less than 9%, investors should sit up and take notice. Why? Well, remember that the reason you venture into the sometimes-rocky world of equities to begin with is so that you may realize a return that

justifies being there in the first place. With a five-year annual
return of 8.99%, this fund does so, but just barely. Its three-
year average annual record is certainly stronger at 11.18%, but
that five-year mark should be kept clearly in mind by any buyers-and-holders out there. Although its *ten*-year record is
admittedly excellent at 17.80%, the mark of a truly great fund
is that it will *always* post results that are at least good, regardless of the span measured (excluding time frames of two years
and less). Furthermore, it would be wise to keep that ten-year
record in perspective; in years '85 to '89, the fund's average
annual return was a terrific 31.25% with nary a down year in
the bunch, but its average annual return from '90 to '94 was
the previously mentioned 8.99%, with *three* down years in that
time span. Nevertheless, this fund did make our cut of best
international stock funds, and its three- and ten-year records
are good. All we're saying is that performance-hungry
investors should keep a close eye on this one.

Management

The ship at T. Rowe Price International Stock Fund is steered
by Martin G. Wade. Wade and his staff select securities by first
deciding how much of the portfolio should be allocated to different regions in the world, and *then* pick what they feel are
the most suitable securities from those areas. This method of
portfolio selection is a bit different from those used by other
fund managers, who generally don't lock themselves into specific parts of the world at the outset.

Risk/Reward Analysis

T. Rowe Price International enjoys a perfectly acceptable beta
coefficient of .72, but we would redirect your focus back to the
per-year performance of the fund, as well as to the dichotomy
in the fund's first- and second-half ten-year average annual
performance run.

Expenses

The expense ratio of this fund is .96%, certainly inoffensive. Additionally, the turnover rate is low at 22%, so tax minimization is achieved nicely here. Also, this fund's relatively low expense ratio is all the more impressive considering that the fund size is monstrous with roughly $6 billion in assets.

The T. Rowe Price Family

There are too many funds offered by T. Rowe Price to list them all here. Some that may be of interest to international investors are: T. Rowe Price European Stock Fund, Inc., T. Rowe Price International Discovery Fund, Inc., T. Rowe Price Latin America Fund, Inc., and T. Rowe Price New Asia Fund, Inc.

Final Thoughts

Some of you may be wondering why we included this fund in the book, considering that we don't spend a lot of time raving about it. Well, the truth is, performance records *do* establish this fund as one of the best in the entire stable of international stock funds; remember, if you made it into this book, you're among the best of the whole bunch. What's more, mutual fund champion performers that rule the roost with such seemingly average returns must have quite a challenge in their day-to-day existences. We must remain aware, however, of the fact that this fund is the only one from our group that did not have a top-five performance placing in any of the last five years.

BABSON-STEWART IVORY INTERNATIONAL
International Stock

FUND FAMILY:	Babson Fund Group
TICKER SYMBOL:	BAINX
PORTFOLIO MANAGER:	John G. L. Wright
ADDRESS:	Three Crown Center
	2440 Pershing Road
	Kansas City, MO 64108
LONG-TERM PERFORMANCE:	★ ★
SHORT-TERM PERFORMANCE:	★ ★ ★
PERFORMANCE AGAINST PEER GROUP:	★ ★ ★ ★ ★
SAFETY:	★ ★ ★ ★ ★
TELEPHONE EXCHANGES:	Yes
BROKERAGE AVAILABILITY:	Yes
MANAGER TENURE:	7 Years
MINIMUM INITIAL PURCHASE:	$2,500/$250 for IRAs
ASSETS UNDER MANAGEMENT ($M):	65.30
PHONE NUMBER:	800-422-2766
TOTAL RETURNS, YEAR BY YEAR,	
FOR THE PAST FIVE:	1990— -9.37% 1991— 15.08% 1992—
	-1.71% 1993— 33.47% 1994— 1.33%
BETA (3-yr):	.48
ALPHA (3-yr):	4.09
R2 (3-yr):	9
STANDARD DEVIATION (3-yr):	12.62
GROWTH OF $10,000	
FROM JAN. 90 TO DEC. 94:	$13,864.46
PORTFOLIO TURNOVER:	60%
EXPENSE RATIO:	1.32%

SUMMARY

Performance

Like T. Rowe Price International, Babson-Stewart Ivory International just barely breaks into our top ten in the international funds category. Its three-year average annualized return was 10.65%, which is decent, but its five-year annualized return was 8.93%, the worst of all of our offerings. Suffice it to say that international fund managers don't have it easy, wrestling as they must with currency challenges *as well as* the usual challenges associated with tracking down winning equity positions. However, whether their job is tough or not is not your concern; what *is* your concern is whether you should put your money with them. A per-year examination of Babson-Stewart shows us that it seems relatively comfortable in the bottom half of our list, although its performance in '94 earned it fourth place in our group of ten. The question you must answer for yourself is whether you could be happy in a fund that, over time, is likely to return no better than about 10% in any given year, and could likely return much less.

Management

Babson-Stewart Ivory International is managed by John G. L. Wright, and Mr. Wright has been running the show since 1988. Wright forsakes the oft-used strategy of currency hedging, as he believes it's virtually impossible to anticipate the movements of currency around the world.

Risk/Reward Analysis

The fund carries a low beta coefficient, which is due largely to its relatively light weightings in both the financial and industrial cyclical sectors. However, management's policy of refusing to currency-hedge the portfolio has the potential to come back and bite it (and, in turn, investors) from time to time. Although the fund's beta seems quite reasonable, we would have liked to see some better performance numbers posted. Bottom line: although the risk involved in being here is not great (relative to international stock funds in general), the reward is also nothing to get too excited about.

Expenses

Babson-Stewart's expense ratio is not unreasonable for international funds, but at 1.32 it would be nice to see better performance. Furthermore, the portfolio turnover rate is rather high at 60%. Again, with that kind of activity, we would have hoped for better results at the finish line.

The Babson Family

There are thirteen other funds in the Babson family besides Babson-Stewart Ivory International: Babson Bond L, Babson Bond S, Babson Enterprise, Babson Enterprise II, Babson Growth, Babson Tax-Free Income L, Babson Tax-Free Income S, Babson Value, Shadow Stock, UMB Bond, UMB Heartland, UMB Stock, and UMB Worldwide.

Final Thoughts

Babson-Stewart Ivory International is typical of many international mutual funds, in that when it's good it's pretty good, but when it's bad it's *really* bad. Many international funds go through years of mediocre-to-poor performance, and then have one really sensational year that boosts the overall numbers. Trouble is, you had better be in for that one great year; beyond that, if you're in for all the others, you're just spinning your wheels while other investors are making money. Babson-Stewart is a great illustration of the point that while good money can be made internationally on occasion, these funds are just not great for buyers-and-holders.

WARBURG PINCUS INTERNATIONAL EQUITY FUND–COMMON SHARES
International Stock

FUND FAMILY:	Warburg Pincus Funds
TICKER SYMBOL:	CUIEX
PORTFOLIO MANAGER:	Richard H. King/Harold W. Ehrlich
ADDRESS:	466 Lexington Ave.
	New York, NY 10017-3147
LONG-TERM PERFORMANCE:	★ ★ ★
SHORT-TERM PERFORMANCE:	★ ★ ★ ★
PERFORMANCE AGAINST PEER GROUP:	★ ★ ★ ★ ★
SAFETY:	★ ★ ★ ★
TELEPHONE EXCHANGES:	Yes
BROKERAGE AVAILABILITY:	Yes
MANAGER TENURE:	6 Years
MINIMUM INITIAL PURCHASE:	$2,500/$500 for IRAs
ASSETS UNDER MANAGEMENT ($M):	1,655.70

PHONE NUMBER:	800-257-5614
TOTAL RETURNS, YEAR BY YEAR,	
FOR THE PAST FIVE:	1990— -4.57% 1991— 20.60% 1992—
	-4.34% 1993— 51.26% 1994— .15%
BETA (3-yr):	.81
ALPHA (3-yr):	4.12
R2 (3-yr):	16
STANDARD DEVIATION (3-yr):	16.02
GROWTH OF $10,000	
FROM JAN. 90 TO DEC. 94:	$16,683.00
PORTFOLIO TURNOVER:	17%
EXPENSE RATIO:	1.44%

SUMMARY

Performance

Warburg Pincus International Equity Fund–Common Shares comes on strong in both our three- and five-year annualized return screens. The fund's three-year annualized return is a none-too-shabby 12.58%, although that figure places the fund fifth out of the ten funds evaluated here. Its five-year return of 11.67%, however, puts it at number two, strengthening its overall performance standing significantly. Given that international funds, on a year-to-year basis, will typically have widely varying performance returns, it's important for them to post a super-strong showing in the years when the whole category does well. Here, Warburg Pincus does not disappoint. Granted, the fund has its years like '90 and '92 when it realizes numbers in the negative range, but in years when the whole category is a winner, Warburg Pincus storms to the front. In 1991, the fund posted a 20.60% gain, placing it third of our elite ten. In 1993, the fund soared with a 51.26% return, second-best of our group that year.

Management

Warburg Pincus International Equity is co-managed by Richard H. King and Harold W. Ehrlich. King has been the manager since 1989, and his strict, disciplined value-driven approach seems to be the reason the fund has been so strong for so long. The fundamentals of all companies King considers have to be rock-hard, and his moves have long been shrewd and winning.

Risk/Reward Analysis

Warburg's beta coefficient is .81, a figure considered more than acceptable for an international stock fund. Although international funds in general are prone to more volatility than the average equity investments, Warburg's mark is pretty reasonable, although it *is* high for this group. No matter; this fund maintains a significant cash position, which always helps to reduce the inherent risk of any fund.

Expenses

The expense ratio of this fund is a sizable 1.44%. Although investors should always gauge what they are paying in relation to what they're receiving in performance, that comparison is especially important when considering international funds, which are as naturally expensive as they are plagued by checkered performance. Warburg Pincus International Equity seems to pass this test successfully. Although it has its ups and downs like all international funds, its up years can be super, posting some of the best scores of the funds in our group.

The Warburg Pincus Family

There are nine other funds in the Warburg Pincus family besides Warburg Pincus International Equity: Warburg Pincus Capital Appreciation Fund, Warburg Pincus Cash Reserve Fund, Inc., Warburg Pincus Emerging Growth Fund, Inc., Warburg Pincus Fixed Income Fund, Inc., Warburg Pincus Global Fixed Income Fund, Inc., Warburg Pincus Growth and Income Fund, Warburg Pincus Intermediate Maturity Government Fund, Inc., Warburg Pincus New York Municipal Bond Fund, Inc., and Warburg Pincus New York Tax Exempt Fund, Inc.

Final Thoughts

Warburg Pincus International Equity is tough to beat in this category. Its multiyear returns rank in the upper half of all funds in our group, and its results in years when international investing overall is favorable are sensational.

MANAGERS INTERNATIONAL EQUITY
International Stock

FUND FAMILY:	Managers Funds
TICKER SYMBOL:	MGITX
PORTFOLIO MANAGER:	William E. Holzer/John R. Reinsberg
ADDRESS:	200 Connecticut Avenue
	Norwalk, CT 06854
LONG-TERM PERFORMANCE:	★ ★ ★
SHORT-TERM PERFORMANCE:	★ ★ ★ ★ ★
PERFORMANCE AGAINST PEER GROUP:	★ ★ ★ ★ ★
SAFETY:	★ ★ ★ ★ ★
SALES RESTRICTIONS:	Managers International Equity may be accessed only by institutional investors or by financial advisers purchasing the fund on behalf of clients.
TELEPHONE EXCHANGES:	Yes
BROKERAGE AVAILABILITY:	Yes
MANAGER TENURE:	6 Years
MINIMUM INITIAL PURCHASE:	$10,000
ASSETS UNDER MANAGEMENT ($M):	81.50
PHONE NUMBER:	800-835-3879
TOTAL RETURNS, YEAR BY YEAR, FOR THE PAST FIVE:	1990— -9.69% 1991— 18.15% 1992— 4.26% 1993— 38.23% 1994— 2.00%
BETA (3-yr):	.51
ALPHA (3-yr):	7.94
R2 (3-yr):	17
STANDARD DEVIATION (3-yr):	10.04
GROWTH OF $10,000 FROM JAN. 90 TO DEC. 94:	$15,685.19
PORTFOLIO TURNOVER:	21%
EXPENSE RATIO:	1.49%

SUMMARY
Performance

Although Managers International Equity did not finish first in either the three-year or five-year screen, it may justifiably be regarded by many as the best of our bunch. Why? Consistency, plain and simple. The fund ranked third in our group in the category of five-year annualized return, and second in the three-year annualized return category. More significantly, Managers International had only one year in the last five when it posted a negative return; it was the only fund in our group to accomplish such a feat. For longer-term investors in the fund, that may be rather important. Our experience tells us that while everyone likes to make money when they can, they feel even more strongly about losing it. It appears that keeping individual losing years to a minimum is one of the many challenges faced by international funds, and as far as that goes, Managers acquits itself very nicely.

Management

Managers International is captained by William E. Holzer and John R. Reinsberg. Holzer has been the manager since 1989, and Reinsberg joined the team this year when the advisory firm of Lazard Frères was added as a subadvisor to the fund. The two have differing approaches to international investing, and it is believed that this diversity of styles will help ensure the fund's strength-of-performance in the future. For the record, Holzer tracks global trends and looks for companies that seem to offer potential riches within these trends. Reinsberg, on the other hand, is a pure value investor, searching *first* for out-of-favor companies with strong fundamentals.

Risk/Reward Analysis

The beta coefficient of this fund is a tasty .51, which makes it even more intriguing. Additionally, this fund is the only one in our group that had just one down year in the past five. Throw in the fact that its multiyear performance numbers are some of the best we've seen here, and you've got a winner.

Expenses

With an expense ratio of 1.49%, Managers International is one of the pricier offerings here for investors, but its performance figures are generally strong through and through, an important fact that helps significantly to justify such cost. The overall cost of the fund is kept down additionally with the tax minimization features associated with a fund that sports a portfolio turnover rate as low as that of Managers.

The Managers Family

There are thirteen other funds in the Managers family besides Managers International: The Managers Balanced Fund, The Managers Bond Fund, The Managers Capital Appreciation Fund, The Managers Global Bond Fund, The Managers Global Opportunity Fund, The Managers Income Equity Fund, The Managers Intermediate Mortgage Securities Fund, The Managers Money Market Fund, The Managers Municipal Bond Fund, The Managers Short and Intermediate Bond Fund, The Managers Short Government Income Fund, The Managers Short Municipal Fund, and The Managers Special Equity Fund.

Final Thoughts

Although the fund is a bit pricey, that factor pales in comparison with performance, the factor that is *always* the bottom line when it comes to investing. Both its longer-term and shorter-term returns are excellent, and fund management accomplishes this with a minimum of market risk, relatively speaking. Managers International should be a seriously considered choice of investors seeking to venture into foreign lands with their money.

GROWTH FUNDS

CLIPPER
Growth

FUND FAMILY:	Clipper Fund
TICKER SYMBOL:	CFIMX
PORTFOLIO MANAGER:	James H. Gipson/Michael C. Sandler
ADDRESS:	9601 Wilshire Blvd.
	Ste. 828
	Beverly Hills, CA 90210
LONG-TERM PERFORMANCE:	★ ★ ★ ★
SHORT-TERM PERFORMANCE:	★ ★ ★ ★
PERFORMANCE AGAINST PEER GROUP:	★ ★ ★ ★ ★
SAFETY:	★ ★ ★
TELEPHONE EXCHANGES:	N/A
BROKERAGE AVAILABILITY:	Yes
MANAGER TENURE:	11 Years
MINIMUM INITIAL PURCHASE:	$5,000/$1,000 for IRAs
ASSETS UNDER MANAGEMENT ($M):	290
PHONE NUMBER:	800-776-5033
TOTAL RETURNS, YEAR BY YEAR,	
FOR THE PAST TEN:	1985— 26.42% 1986— 18.74% 1987—
	3.41% 1988— 19.67% 1989— 22.11%
	1990— -7.57% 1991— 32.57% 1992—
	15.90% 1993— 11.26% 1994— -2.51%
BETA (3-yr):	1.19
ALPHA (3-yr):	2.00
R2 (3-yr):	80
STANDARD DEVIATION (3-yr):	10.66
GROWTH OF $10,000	
FROM JAN. 85 TO DEC. 94:	$34,942.39
PORTFOLIO TURNOVER:	45%
EXPENSE RATIO:	1.11%

SUMMARY

Performance

The Clipper Fund registers solid numbers for all of the multi-year performance periods we examined on behalf of growth funds. Although the fund did not achieve a five-star rating for either of the performance periods to which we *do* ascribe stars (three- and ten-year annualized returns), prospective investors should not be put off for that reason. The fact is, the annualized returns for the three-, five-, and ten-year periods we examined are excellent. Many people become a little too obsessed with finding funds that notch championship numbers, when in truth there are many well-managed funds that offer consistent long-term returns. Clipper is clearly one of these funds. This fund's ten-year annualized return is an excellent 14.49%, one that just barely deprived it of a fifth star in the Long-Term Performance category. Furthermore, although the fund achieved "only" a 13.86% average return in the three-year annualized return category, that result ranks it fourth out of our ten in that particular screen. In the five-year category, Clipper achieved a 14.70% annualized return, further indicating that its longer-term numbers are strongest. Regardless, if you decide to keep Clipper for a while, it's unlikely you will be disappointed.

Management

The Clipper Fund is co-managed by Harvard M.B.A. James H. Gipson and Michael C. Sandler, himself an M.B.A. from the University of Iowa. The duo are strict value players, and interestingly, their value test leads them to the financial sector time and time again. Beyond the bargains, Gipson and Sandler like to find companies that derive a significant portion of their income from overseas ventures; it is their way of receiving the rewards (indirect as they may be) of international investing without having to do much of it themselves.

Risk/Reward Analysis

In the Performance section above, we talked about how good the fund's longer-term numbers are. It should be mentioned, however, that Clipper Fund can have a tendency toward some short-term volatility—nothing too serious, but something that prospective investors should be aware of. The fund has not achieved either a first- or tenth-place finish in our group offerings in any of the last ten years, though, indicating that the roller-coaster ride isn't *too* fearsome. The fund's three-year beta is 1.19, not really outrageous for growth funds, but highest in this group.

Expenses
The Clipper Fund has a turnover rate of 45%, which is high for some categories but low for this one. In fact, that rate ranks this fund fourth in this group of finalists. The fund's expense ratio is 1.11%, which puts it in the lower half of the expense ratios here, but it's really not at all unreasonable considering its longer-term returns.

Final Thoughts
All things considered, Clipper Fund could justifiably make the final cut of anyone's growth fund list. Its volatility and expense figures, while not superb, are very satisfactory when compared with the results this fund has achieved through the years.

COLUMBIA GROWTH
Growth

FUND FAMILY:	Columbia Funds
TICKER SYMBOL:	CLMBX
PORTFOLIO MANAGER:	Alexander S. Macmillan, III
ADDRESS:	P. O. Box 1350
	Portland, OR 97207-1350
LONG-TERM PERFORMANCE:	★ ★ ★ ★
SHORT-TERM PERFORMANCE:	★ ★ ★ ★
PERFORMANCE AGAINST PEER GROUP:	★ ★ ★ ★ ★
SAFETY:	★ ★ ★
TELEPHONE EXCHANGES:	Yes
BROKERAGE AVAILABILITY:	Yes
MANAGER TENURE:	3 Years
MINIMUM INITIAL PURCHASE:	$1,000
ASSETS UNDER MANAGEMENT ($M):	657.60
PHONE NUMBER:	800-547-1707
TOTAL RETURNS, YEAR BY YEAR, FOR THE PAST TEN:	1985— 32.07% 1986— 7.06% 1987— 14.81% 1988— 10.89% 1989— 29.46% 1990— -3.27% 1991— 34.43% 1992— 11.90% 1993— 13.09% 1994— -.63%

BETA (3-yr):	1.15
ALPHA (3-yr):	.82
R2 (3-yr):	79
STANDARD DEVIATION (3-yr):	10.31
GROWTH OF $10,000	
FROM JAN. 85 TO DEC. 94:	$38,107.12
PORTFOLIO TURNOVER:	79%
EXPENSE RATIO:	.81%

SUMMARY

Performance

Although each of Columbia Growth's three-, five-, and ten-year annualized returns ranked in the bottom half of these categories of the funds evaluated here, the numbers that the fund *did* post were really quite good. In the ten-year category, this fund achieved an average annualized return of 14.18%—not stellar, but certainly nothing to sneeze at. In the three-year annualized return category, Columbia did well at 12.28%. Some might consider this to be a bit low for a true growth fund, but when one remembers that the average domestic-based fund returned -2.0% in 1994, an average annual three-year return of over 12% really stands out, as well it should. In the five-year annualized return category, Columbia realized a 13.53% return; again, not superb, but certainly representative of quality. Additionally, it should be mentioned that even though this fund's overall multi-year numbers place it in the bottom half of each of those categories, the fund *did* finish in the *top* half of the funds featured here in six of the last ten years.

Management

Alexander S. Macmillan is the portfolio manager of Columbia Growth Fund, and initially joined Columbia Management Company in 1989. Management's strategy in guiding this fund is really a combination of macro- and micro-money management. The "macro" involves the seeking out of broad economic and financial trends and following those trends into the respective industries and sectors. Once there, Macmillan and staff will then apply typical value-based tests to the securities in order to extract the most promising.

Risk/Reward Analysis

Columbia Growth sports a beta coefficient of 1.15, which indicates that the fund is generally more volatile than the S&P 500 Stock Index but not so volatile as to be a source of discomfort for investors. From years '85 to '88, this fund *was* somewhat prone to jumping around the board, but its year-to-year returns since 1989 have been much more consistent: Columbia Growth stayed between fourth and seventh place of the funds in this group when per-year returns were analyzed.

Expenses

Columbia Growth has the third-lowest expense ratio of all the funds in our group at .81%. As with many other funds managed with a value-oriented mind-set, this fund enjoys the cost-effectiveness that comes with purchasing securities priced below what fundamentals say they're worth. On the other hand, the turnover rate of this fund's portfolio is a noticeable 79%—not bad as these funds go, but not conducive to significant tax minimization.

The Columbia Family

There are nine other funds in the Columbia family besides Columbia Growth Fund: Columbia Balanced Fund, Inc., Columbia Common Stock Fund, Inc., Columbia Daily Income Co., Columbia Fixed Income Securities Fund, Inc., Columbia High Yield Fund, Inc., Columbia International Stock Fund, Inc., Columbia Municipal Bond Fund, Inc., Columbia Special Fund, Inc., and Columbia U.S. Government Securities Fund, Inc.

Final Thoughts

Columbia Growth is a fund that has enjoyed a relatively catastrophe-free existence. In 1990, when the NASDAQ Composite was down -17.8% and the S&P 500 was down

-6.6%, Columbia Growth was down only -3.27%, a return that ranked it in the upper half of all funds in our group for that year. The point? This one fact helps to show that while Columbia's returns haven't been *the* standard against which all other growth funds are compared, its performances *have* been most satisfactory and agreeable to less-adventurous growth investors.

ELFUN TRUSTS
Growth

FUND FAMILY:	Elfun Mutual Funds
TICKER SYMBOL:	ELFNX
PORTFOLIO MANAGER:	David B. Carlson
ADDRESS:	P.O. Box 120074
	Stamford, CT 06912-0074
LONG-TERM PERFORMANCE:	★ ★ ★ ★
SHORT-TERM PERFORMANCE:	★ ★ ★
PERFORMANCE AGAINST PEER GROUP:	★ ★ ★ ★ ★
SAFETY:	★ ★ ★ ★
SALES RESTRICTIONS:	Elfun funds are available only to members of the Elfun Society, an organization affiliated with General Electric Co. For more information, contact General Electric Investment Corp. at the phone number below.
TELEPHONE EXCHANGES:	Yes
BROKERAGE AVAILABILITY:	No
MANAGER TENURE:	7 Years
MINIMUM INITIAL PURCHASE:	None
ASSETS UNDER MANAGEMENT ($M):	987.60
PHONE NUMBER:	800-242-0134
TOTAL RETURNS, YEAR-BY-YEAR, FOR THE PAST TEN:	1985— 35.31% 1986— 14.39% 1987— 3.38% 1988— 18.41% 1989— 35.82% 1990— -3.73% 1991— 28.17% 1992— 9.43% 1993— 8.98% 1994— .23%
BETA (3-yr):	.99
ALPHA (3-yr):	-.05
R2 (3-yr):	93
STANDARD DEVIATION (3-yr):	8.26
GROWTH OF $10,000 FROM JAN. 85 TO DEC. 94:	$37,954.64
PORTFOLIO TURNOVER:	19%
EXPENSE RATIO:	.17%

SUMMARY

Performance

Elfun Trusts is perhaps the poorest performer overall of the ten funds we closely examine here, but that would only make it the worst of the best, and its year-to-year numbers may provide some enticement to less-aggressive growth investors. Elfun Trusts achieved an annualized ten-year return of 14.43%, which, when standing alone, really looks pretty good. Unfortunately, that return only placed Elfun ninth of ten in that category. Its five-year average annualized number wasn't quite as good at 12.14%, but that still kept the fund in ninth place overall in that screen. We must say that the fund's three-year average annualized return is not that great for a growth fund—10.40%. Although it's true that 1994 went a long way to depressing the multiyear performance numbers of almost all funds in this category, it would have been nice to see a return above the 10% range for this fund's three-year annualized return. Still, these numbers are certainly decent as a whole, and it's a good sign that the fund only lost -3.73% in 1990.

Management

Elfun Trusts is managed by David B. Carlson. Carlson's style of management is very value-oriented, as evidenced by the fact that his portfolio sports a price-to-earnings ratio that ranks as the fourth-best of the funds under consideration here. Furthermore, it's clear that Carlson likes to find solid companies that he can feel comfortable holding for long periods of time. In fact, this portfolio's turnover rate is only 19% currently, very low for a competitive growth fund.

Risk/Reward Analysis

Elfun Trusts carries a beta coefficient of .99, which is reasonable considering the inherent volatility associated with growth funds in general. Not surprisingly, though, the fund's *alpha* figure is rather poor. We say "not surprisingly" out of deference to the fact that the fund's performance has *not* been stellar overall. The conclusion we would be expected to reach is that the fund's performance figures do not justify its level of volatility, and while that may be technically true, we don't consider its volatility to be too unnerving.

Expenses

The expense ratio of Elfun Trusts is .17%, which is about as low as a fund's expense ratio can get. There are a number of reasons why this fund costs so little to administer and manage, but chief among them is the fact that its access is somewhat limited. Additionally, the fund has an extremely low turnover rate and also bones up on income-paying stocks, which also helps to absorb overall costs.

The Elfun Family

There are five other funds in the Elfun family besides Elfun Trusts: Elfun Diversified Fund, Elfun Global Fund, Elfun Income Fund, Elfun Money Market Fund, and Elfun Tax-Exempt Income Fund.

Final Thoughts

Although many will undoubtedly be put off by the multiyear performance numbers posted by Elfun Trusts, the fund clearly holds its own with the big boys. Elfun finished in the top half of these funds in four of the past ten years, an achievement not to be overlooked. We would have to say that this fund is a good all-around growth offering, worthy of a look by anyone seeking to strengthen their long-term numbers.

FIDELITY ADVISOR INSTITUTIONAL EQUITY GROWTH
Growth

FUND FAMILY:	Fidelity Advisor Funds
TICKER SYMBOL:	EQPGX
PORTFOLIO MANAGER:	Robert E. Stansky
ADDRESS:	82 Devonshire St.
	Boston, MA 02109
LONG-TERM PERFORMANCE:	★ ★ ★ ★ ★
SHORT-TERM PERFORMANCE:	★ ★ ★ ★
PERFORMANCE AGAINST PEER GROUP:	★ ★ ★ ★ ★
SAFETY:	★ ★ ★
SALES RESTRICTIONS:	Fidelity Advisor funds may only be purchased by institutional investors currently. Contact Fidelity at the number below for more information.
TELEPHONE EXCHANGES:	N/A
BROKERAGE AVAILABILITY:	N/A
MANAGER TENURE:	8 Years
MINIMUM INITIAL PURCHASE:	$100,000
ASSETS UNDER MANAGEMENT ($M):	501.40
PHONE NUMBER:	800-522-7297
TOTAL RETURNS, YEAR BY YEAR, FOR THE PAST TEN:	1985— 41.53% 1986— 14.51% 1987— -.57% 1988— 15.57% 1989— 44.84% 1990— 6.93% 1991— 64.71% 1992— 10.06% 1993— 15.71% 1994— -.04
BETA (3-yr):	1.02
ALPHA (3-yr):	3.07
R2 (3-yr):	62
STANDARD DEVIATION (3-yr):	10.35
GROWTH OF $10,000 FROM JAN. 85 TO DEC. 94:	$60,476.85
PORTFOLIO TURNOVER:	137%
EXPENSE RATIO:	.84%

SUMMARY

Performance

Fidelity Advisors Institutional Equity Growth: the *name* of this fund is a sentence unto itself, and so are its long-term performance numbers. This fund's ten-year annualized return is tops in the growth fund category here—19.39%. The five-year figure is even more impressive at a whopping 20.63%. It's tough to overemphasize this kind of performance; we all hear about funds that notch these kinds of numbers in particular years, but to see a fund that *averages* these returns is awesome. Fidelity's *three*-year average annualized return, 13.81%, is not quite as admirable as the others it has recorded, but that figure still places the fund in the upper half of these funds in that category. Its per-year performance results are nothing short of awesome: the fund did not finish any worse than eighth in any of the last ten years, and it in fact finished *first* in four of them. Incredible.

Management

Fast-becoming-legendary, Fidelity growth-guru Robert E. Stansky is the pilot of the Fidelity Advisors Institutional Equity Growth Fund. Stansky diligently searches for the manic ones, a fact to which his fund's portfolio turnover rate attests. Interestingly, Stansky does a good job of managing the fund's volatility level, accomplishing this in part with a consistently high position in cash. Stansky *is* a bit more motivated by growth than value but, after all, this *is* a growth fund.

Risk/Reward Analysis

Fidelity Advisors offers investors a beta coefficient of 1.02, which is very reasonable given this fund's terrific performance figures. We would have expected this fund's alpha number (3.07) to be a bit higher considering its performance, but the figure is a *three-year* alpha, and, as stated, this fund has slowed a little recently. No matter. We would have to say that this fund offers investors a great deal in the risk/reward trade-off.

Expenses

This fund's expense ratio is .84%, which is very low for growth funds in general and especially low for a fund with this kind of turnover rate. A prime reason for this cost-effectiveness is its cost-*efficiency*, as Fidelity Advisors cannot be accessed by anyone other than institutional investors. This means that the fund is not burdened with the administration associated with monitoring the activities of individual investors, and thus does not incur the costs involved.

The Fidelity Family

There are just too many funds available at Fidelity to mention them all here. Following are some choices that may be of interest to growth investors: Fidelity Capital Appreciation Fund, Fidelity Contrafund, Fidelity Emerging Growth Fund, and Fidelity Growth Company Fund.

Final Thoughts

Well, what else is there to say? Fidelity Advisors Institutional Equity Growth has an unbeatable long-term track record, and its short-term record is no slouch, either. While aggressive compared with the average mutual fund available to investors, it really isn't too skittish overall, and that makes this fund a good option for moderate-risk investors as well.

FIDELITY RETIREMENT GROWTH
Growth

FUND FAMILY:	Fidelity Group
TICKER SYMBOL:	FDFFX
PORTFOLIO MANAGER:	Harris B. Leviton
ADDRESS:	82 Devonshire St. Boston, MA 02109
LONG-TERM PERFORMANCE:	★ ★ ★ ★ ★
SHORT-TERM PERFORMANCE:	★ ★ ★ ★
PERFORMANCE AGAINST PEER GROUP:	★ ★ ★ ★ ★
SAFETY:	★ ★ ★ ★
TELEPHONE EXCHANGES:	Yes
BROKERAGE AVAILABILITY:	Yes
MANAGER TENURE:	3 Years
MINIMUM INITIAL PURCHASE:	$500
ASSETS UNDER MANAGEMENT ($M):	3,427.40
PHONE NUMBER:	800-544-8888
TOTAL RETURNS, YEAR BY YEAR, FOR THE PAST TEN:	1985— 28.90% 1986— 14.14% 1987— 9.32% 1988— 15.52% 1989— 30.41% 1990— -10.15% 1991— 45.58% 1992— 10.60% 1993— 22.13% 1994— .06%

BETA (3-yr):	.92
ALPHA (3-yr):	3.32
R2 (3-yr):	64
STANDARD DEVIATION (3-yr):	9.11
GROWTH OF $10,000 FROM JAN. 85 TO DEC. 94:	$42,836.73
PORTFOLIO TURNOVER:	72%
EXPENSE RATIO:	1.07%

SUMMARY

Performance

Very often, "consistent" is a descriptive word that is used to be polite to funds that lack excellent performance numbers. In the case of Fidelity Retirement Growth Fund, however, that's just not the case. Fidelity's ten-year average annualized return is a strong 15.91%, and its five-year return is an almost equally strong 15.13%. The three-year average annualized return is off from those numbers a bit, but not by much at 13.46%. The fact is, a range of 13% to 16% is a respectable place for all of these multiyear performance figures to reside. Looking at the per-year results, we see that in five of the last ten years this fund finished in the top half of the funds discussed here. The fund finished worse than seventh in only one of the last ten years, and topped the list in 1993. It must be noted, though, that this fund did record a double-digit *negative* return in 1990, although this wasn't the worst showing by a fund in our group in 1990.

Management

Harris B. Leviton is a growth fund manager with a strong concern for risk management. He obviously searches for growth opportunities in the same spirit as anyone in a similar position does, but he is perhaps more concerned with ensuring that the stocks he selects offer solid value-based numbers. This fund's highest sector allocation is in technology, but prospective investors shouldn't be put off by that; Leviton came aboard Fidelity in 1986 as an analyst of semiconductor and electronics stocks.

Risk/Reward Analysis

As mentioned, manager Leviton is a risk-averse growth investor, and his fund's beta coefficient of .92 helps to make this case. Furthermore, it speaks highly of Leviton's abilities that this fund has a three-year alpha of 3.32, fourth best in our group. Although Leviton can have an active portfolio from time to time, the high cash position he maintains goes far in keeping the fund's volatility numbers at a quality level. We *would* have been happier to see this fund perform better in challenging 1990, but this was really the only truly poor year of the last ten.

Expenses

Fidelity Retirement Growth's expense ratio ranks in the bottom half of the funds examined here, but the figure of 1.07% suggests that the fund is only slightly more volatile than the market as a whole. Although the portfolio turnover rate is a healthy 72%, the cash position of this fund is huge: 29.7%. Not only does this help to limit the fund's volatility, it also works to keep costs down as well.

The Fidelity Family

There are just too many funds available at Fidelity to mention here. Following are some choices that may be of interest to growth investors: Fidelity Capital Appreciation Fund, Fidelity Contrafund, Fidelity Emerging Growth Fund, and Fidelity Growth Company Fund.

Final Thoughts

Fidelity Retirement Growth is a high-quality growth mutual fund with perfectly reasonable numbers up and down the line. Accumulators should be most happy with this offering, but Accumulation–Preservationists and even some Preservation–Accumulators will probably find this fund's volatility level tolerable in relation to the return possibilities.

MAIRS AND POWER GROWTH
Growth

FUND FAMILY:	Mairs and Power Funds
TICKER SYMBOL:	N/A
PORTFOLIO MANAGER:	George A. Mairs, III
ADDRESS:	W-2062 First National Bank Bldg.
	St. Paul, MN 55101
LONG-TERM PERFORMANCE:	★ ★ ★ ★ ★
SHORT-TERM PERFORMANCE:	★ ★ ★ ★ ★
PERFORMANCE AGAINST PEER GROUP:	★ ★ ★ ★ ★
SAFETY:	★ ★ ★ ★
TELEPHONE EXCHANGES:	No
BROKERAGE AVAILABILITY:	No
MANAGER TENURE:	15 Years
MINIMUM INITIAL PURCHASE:	$1,000
ASSETS UNDER MANAGEMENT ($M):	47.50
PHONE NUMBER:	612-222-8478
TOTAL RETURNS, YEAR BY YEAR, FOR THE PAST TEN:	1985— 34.77% 1986— 11.54% 1987— -2.39% 1988— 9.97% 1989— 28.07% 1990— 3.55% 1991— 42.09% 1992— 7.84% 1993— 12.86% 1994— 5.63%
BETA (3-yr):	.96
ALPHA (3-yr):	4.81
R2 (3-yr):	73
STANDARD DEVIATION (3-yr):	9.06
GROWTH OF $10,000 FROM JAN. 85 TO DEC. 94:	$39,089.55
PORTFOLIO TURNOVER:	5%
EXPENSE RATIO:	.99%

SUMMARY

Performance

Mairs and Power Growth Fund is one of only three funds in our group that scored top-five multiyear returns in all of our rated categories. This fund's ten-year average annualized return is a wonderful 15.11%, a figure that should always make any investor sit up and take notice. In the three-year annualized return category, this fund posted a super-strong 15.42%, a remarkable return for a growth fund in light of the fact that 1994 was such a sorry year for this type of fund in general. In the unstarred five- and fifteen-year average annualized return screens, this fund also produced fine results. The five-year result was a powerful 17.69%, second only to Fidelity Advisor Institutional Equity Growth in that category. Over the past fifteen years, Mairs and Power Growth has averaged 15.43%, which is very remarkable over such a long period of time. Looking at the fund's per-year returns, it is noteworthy to mention that this fund was one of only two here that ended up on the "plus" side in 1990.

Management

George A. Mairs, III, is the portfolio manager of Mairs and Power Growth, and has been since 1980. Mairs apparently doesn't like to have to manage a vast portfolio, as the number of stocks contained in the portfolio usually numbers about thirty. His strategy of limiting portfolio size seems to be effective, as is his reliance on companies that are indigenous to the area in which the fund company is located. Clearly, it is management's policy to keep things simple. Anyone who doubts such simplistic logic need only glance at this fund's performance numbers.

Risk/Reward Analysis

Mairs and Power Growth offers investors a beta coefficient of .96 and a three-year alpha of 4.81, which are great volatility measurements for a growth fund with these performance numbers. The fund's standard deviation is only 9.06, low for growth funds overall. The fund has had only one "down" year in the past ten, and it posted a positive return in 1990, uncommon for growth funds that year. Mairs and Power Growth represents a favorable weighting for investors in the risk/reward balance.

Expenses

The expense ratio of this fund is .99%, a figure that is perfectly in line with the average mutual fund, and even consistent with the typical *growth* fund. More significant for the tax-conscious, the fund's turnover rate is about as low as we've ever heard of at 5%.

The Mairs and Power Family
There is one other fund in the Mairs and Power family besides Mairs and Power Growth: Mairs and Power Income Fund, Inc.

Final Thoughts
Mairs and Power isn't exactly the biggest fund family in the world with two funds, but with a growth fund like this one how many do you need? All of Mairs and Power's multiyear performance figures are at 15% and above, and if you compare those returns with the fund's relatively limited volatility, this fund emerges a winner for even the less-aggressive growth investor.

MANAGERS CAPITAL APPRECIATION
Growth

FUND FAMILY:	Managers Funds
TICKER SYMBOL:	MGCAX
PORTFOLIO MANAGERS:	Paul Dietche and Howard Shawn
ADDRESS:	40 Richards Ave.
	Norwalk, CT 06854
LONG-TERM PERFORMANCE:	★ ★ ★
SHORT-TERM PERFORMANCE:	★ ★ ★ ★
PERFORMANCE AGAINST PEER GROUP:	★ ★ ★ ★ ★
SAFETY:	★ ★ ★
SALES RESTRICTIONS:	Managers Capital Appreciation may be accessed only by institutional investors or by financial advisers purchasing the fund on behalf of clients.
TELEPHONE EXCHANGES:	Yes
BROKERAGE AVAILABILITY:	Yes
MANAGER TENURE:	9 Years
MINIMUM INITIAL PURCHASE:	$10,000
ASSETS UNDER MANAGEMENT ($M):	73.60
PHONE NUMBER:	800-835-3879
TOTAL RETURNS, YEAR BY YEAR, FOR THE PAST TEN:	1985— 27.67% 1986— 11.91% 1987— 8.02% 1988— 20.19% 1989— 22.03% 1990— -1.72% 1991— 32.94% 1992— 15.98% 1993— 16.68% 1994— -1.52%
BETA (3-yr):	1.07

ALPHA (3-yr):	1.44
R2 (3-yr):	69
STANDARD DEVIATION (3-yr):	10.26
GROWTH OF $10,000 FROM JAN. 85 TO DEC. 94:	$39,413.52
PORTFOLIO TURNOVER:	121%
EXPENSE RATIO:	1.29%

SUMMARY

Performance

Managers Capital Appreciation is another straightforward, no-nonsense offering in the fertile field of growth mutual funds. Although this fund does not earn a five-star rating for either long- or short-term performance, both of its numbers in those categories are impressive indeed. In the category of ten-year average annualized return, Managers returned a delightful 14.99%, effectively earning the much-sought-after benchmark mutual fund return of 15% per year. Although this fund's three-year average annualized return was a "mere" 12.42%, that return includes the unfortunate 1994; furthermore, there were three other funds in our group that finished below Managers in this particular screen. The fund's *five*-year annualized performance, a category to which we do not attribute star rankings here, was again very fine at 14.37%. When we take a peek at this fund's per-year performances, we see more cause for celebration; although this fund's multiyear returns rank it in the bottom half of the funds evaluated here, it *did* place in the *upper* half of our group in five of the last ten years.

Management

The portfolio of Managers Capital Appreciation is guided by Paul Dietche and Howard S. Shawn. Their style of management is unique for co-managers: rather than working closely together to evaluate the same types of securities in the same fashion, Dietche and Shawn effectively split the portfolio responsibilities down the middle—Dietche scours the markets for suitable small-cap offerings, while Shawn looks for winners among the grown-up contestants. This approach to portfolio management has helped this fund emerge looking like a champ from many different types of market battles.

Risk/Reward Analysis

Managers carries a beta coefficient of 1.07, which indicates that the fund is more volatile than the overall market, but not unbearably so. Readers will notice that the fund's three-year alpha is only 1.44, a fact that Managers' 1994 performance undoubtedly had something to do with. Nonetheless, the longer-term numbers are great, and even a 12.42% three-year run that includes a year like '94 is really pretty good.

Expenses

At 1.29%, Managers has one of the highest expense ratios of the funds in our group, and the portfolio turnover rate is a hefty 121%. Nonetheless, this fund's performance results seem worth the cost, especially if you commit to holding it for the long term.

The Managers Family

There are thirteen other funds in the Managers family besides Managers Capital Appreciation: The Managers Balanced Fund, The Managers Bond Fund, The Managers Global Bond Fund, The Managers Global Opportunity Fund, The Managers Income Equity Fund, The Managers Intermediate Mortgage Securities Fund, The Managers International Fund, The Managers Money Market Fund, The Managers Municipal Bond Fund, The Managers Short and Intermediate Bond Fund, The Managers Short Government Income Fund, The Managers Short Municipal Fund, and The Managers Special Equity Fund.

Final Thoughts

Managers Capital Appreciation is a growth fund that gives investors a fair shake at consistent capital appreciation over time, with an acceptable amount of risk for funds in this category. Managers should be considered an option for long-term Accumulators and others who prioritize growth in their portfolios.

OMNI INVESTMENT
Growth

FUND FAMILY:	Omni Investment Fund
TICKER SYMBOL:	OMNIX
PORTFOLIO MANAGER:	Robert Perkins
ADDRESS:	53 W. Jackson Blvd.
	Ste. 818
	Chicago, IL 60604
LONG-TERM PERFORMANCE:	★ ★ ★ ★
SHORT-TERM PERFORMANCE:	★ ★ ★ ★ ★
PERFORMANCE AGAINST PEER GROUP:	★ ★ ★ ★ ★
SAFETY:	★ ★ ★ ★
SALES RESTRICTIONS:	Not qualified to be sold in all states. Call at the number below for more information.
TELEPHONE EXCHANGES:	N/A
BROKERAGE AVAILABILITY:	No
MANAGER TENURE:	10 Years
MINIMUM INITIAL PURCHASE:	$3,000/$1,000 for IRAs
ASSETS UNDER MANAGEMENT ($M):	25.20
PHONE NUMBER:	800-223-9790
TOTAL RETURNS, YEAR-BY-YEAR, FOR THE PAST TEN:	1985— N/A 1986— 17.66% 1987— 8.45% 1988— 20.09% 1989— 26.44% 1990— -21.95% 1991— 24.86% 1992— 19.73% 1993— 16.07% 1994— 6.69%
BETA (3-yr):	.85
ALPHA (3-yr):	6.43
R2 (3-yr):	34
STANDARD DEVIATION (3-yr):	11.67
GROWTH OF $10,000 FROM JAN. 86 TO DEC. 94 (9 Years):	$27,995.79
PORTFOLIO TURNOVER:	125%
EXPENSE RATIO:	1.43%

SUMMARY

Performance

Omni Investment Fund has had a curious, but overall excellent, performance history. The fund's long-term numbers are solid: 14.65% in the ten-year average annualized return screen, which is very respectable even though that figure ranks the fund seventh out of the ten funds featured here. In the short-term category, the fund acquits itself even more auspiciously against its brethren, posting a three-year average annualized return of 16.03% and garnering a five-star rating. However, Omni came in last of this group in the five-year average annualized return category with a figure of 11.88%, which is way off the mark. The reason for this unfortunate performance can be found in years '90 and '91, when the fund finished dead last against its finalist competitors. In 1990, a miserable year for stock funds anyway, Omni posted a horrid -21.95% return. In 1991, when many growth funds bounced back and returned 30-plus percent, Omni could only generate 24.86%—a good return, to be sure, but in 1991 a mark that underperformed growth funds as a whole.

Management

Robert Perkins is the portfolio manager of Omni Investment Fund, and his style is an anomaly in the world of growth management. While most value-oriented managers concentrate on the bargains available among the larger, better-established companies, Perkins specializes in finding value among the little guys. As you might imagine, this can be a difficult chore, given the fact that small-cap company stocks are usually so young and relatively low-priced to begin with. Nonetheless, Perkins's approach seems to have worked for the *most* part, but did turn around on him badly in 1990.

Risk/Reward Analysis

Omni Investment Fund sports a beta coefficient of .85, which is number one in this group. It's not often that you find a growth fund with a beta that measures less than the overall market and manages to whip up the kinds of returns that this one does. As proof, simply gaze at the fund's alpha, which registers a sizable 6.43 (second-best of this group). In short, Omni investors are the clear winners in the ever-present battle of risk versus reward.

Expenses

Omni Investment Fund has the highest expense ratio of any fund in our group at 1.43%. At first glance, this figure would strike one as being somewhat high, but this fund *does* manage to come through for investors in the performance realm, where it counts. The 1994 result of 6.69% would undoubtedly be considered worth the price, considering what so many other investors had to endure that year. However, with a turnover rate of 125%, tax relief is not likely to be found here.

Final Thoughts

Notwithstanding this fund's terrible 1990 result, Omni has built a fine record in both the short and long term. One can only imagine what this fund's multiyear performance numbers would look like if it had not fallen so hard in '90, but the surrounding years indicate that investors should take a close look at this one.

STEINROE SPECIAL
Growth

FUND FAMILY:	Stein Roe Mutual Funds
TICKER SYMBOL:	SRSPX
PORTFOLIO MANAGER:	E. Bruce Dunn/Richard B. Peterson
ADDRESS:	P.O. Box 804058
	Chicago, IL 60680
LONG-TERM PERFORMANCE:	★ ★ ★ ★ ★
SHORT-TERM PERFORMANCE:	★ ★ ★
PERFORMANCE AGAINST PEER GROUP:	★ ★ ★ ★ ★
SAFETY:	★ ★ ★ ★
TELEPHONE EXCHANGES:	Yes
BROKERAGE AVAILABILITY:	Yes
MANAGER TENURE:	4 Years
MINIMUM INITIAL PURCHASE:	$2,500/$500 for IRAs
ASSETS UNDER MANAGEMENT ($M):	1,192.70
PHONE NUMBER:	800-662-7447
TOTAL RETURNS, YEAR BY YEAR, FOR THE PAST TEN:	1985— 29.42% 1986— 14.70% 1987— 4.27% 1988— 20.25% 1989— 37.84% 1990— -5.81% 1991— 34.04% 1992— 14.05% 1993— 20.42% 1994— -3.35%
BETA (3-yr):	.93

ALPHA (3-yr):	1.48
R2 (3-yr):	64
STANDARD DEVIATION (3-yr):	9.34
GROWTH OF $10,000	
FROM JAN. 85 TO DEC. 94:	$42,995.16
PORTFOLIO TURNOVER:	58%
EXPENSE RATIO:	.96%

SUMMARY

Performance

SteinRoe Special boasts some strong numbers, with an interesting accompanying trend. SteinRoe's ten-year average annualized return is marvelous, earning five stars with a figure of 15.28%. Its three-year number is not so good, however, but still satisfactory at 11.56%. What's interesting, though, is to watch the fund's average annualized returns decrease in an almost linear fashion through its fifteen-, ten-, five-, and three-year screens. The fifteen-year record *is* impressive at 17.78%, but the fund's annualized returns diminish noticeably as the time period gauged also decreases. A careless observer might believe that this trend was indicative of some sort of growing problem with SteinRoe, but that doesn't seem to be the case. In truth, the fund finished in the upper half of the funds featured here on the basis of per-year returns over the last five years. Unfortunately, the fund's 1994 performance was the worst of the bunch, which is undoubtedly the anchor that has brought down the fund's more recent multiyear performance numbers. However, at a return of -3.35%, it's no reason to discard the fund from consideration.

Management

SteinRoe Special enjoys the guidance of co-managers E. Bruce Dunn and Richard B. Peterson, who again represent portfolio managers who forsake tradition to some extent. While most portfolio managers are concerned with the fundamental numbers of the companies they consider, Dunn and Peterson put great weight on the abilities of the companies' *management*. In other words, Dunn and Peterson believe that if a company does right by its individual shareholders, it will necessarily do right by those who own it indirectly in a mutual fund as well. This approach seems to be working admirably, but it should be noted that the love affair these two pilots have with small, relatively untested stocks can cause the fund to trip over bumps in the road from time to time.

Risk/Reward Analysis

This fund's three-year beta measures .93, which is good news for risk-averse growth investors. Unfortunately, the fund's 1994 performance is probably a strong reason why the corresponding alpha is a mere 1.48, indicating that even at .93 this growth fund has been underperforming its volatility capacity somewhat in recent times. Regardless, this fund's long-term performance numbers are wonderful, and investors should not discount this entry on the basis of a dismal 1994.

Expenses

The expense ratio of SteinRoe Special is a perfectly acceptable .96%. The fund's longer-term returns make that figure even more palatable, although its shorter-term return could be better. Nevertheless, the cost of this fund to investors is very reasonable, as is the rate of portfolio turnover.

The Steinroe Family

There are fifteen other funds in the SteinRoe family besides SteinRoe Special: SteinRoe Capital Opportunities Fund, Inc., SteinRoe Cash Reserves, Inc., SteinRoe Government Income Fund, SteinRoe Government Reserves, Inc., SteinRoe High-Yield Municipals, Inc., SteinRoe Income Fund, SteinRoe Intermediate Bond Fund, Inc., SteinRoe Intermediate Municipals, Inc., SteinRoe International Fund, Inc., SteinRoe Limited Maturity Income Fund, SteinRoe Managed Municipals, Inc., SteinRoe Municipal Money Fund, Inc., SteinRoe Prime Equities, SteinRoe Stock Fund, Inc., and SteinRoe Total Return Fund, Inc.

Final Thoughts

SteinRoe Special is a growth fund that can certainly have its moments. Although it would have been nice to see a "best" growth fund weather the '94 storm a bit better than this one did, the longer-term numbers are nothing to scoff at. Serious growth investors would do well to give this fund a thorough evaluation before deciding against it.

VANGUARD/PRIMECAP
Growth

FUND FAMILY:	Vanguard Group
TICKER SYMBOL:	VPMCX
PORTFOLIO MANAGER:	Howard B. Schow, et al.
ADDRESS:	Vanguard Financial Ctr.
	P.O. Box 2600
	Valley Forge, PA 19482
LONG-TERM PERFORMANCE:	★ ★ ★ ★ ★
SHORT-TERM PERFORMANCE:	★ ★ ★ ★ ★
PERFORMANCE AGAINST PEER GROUP:	★ ★ ★ ★ ★
SAFETY:	★ ★ ★
TELEPHONE EXCHANGES:	Yes
BROKERAGE AVAILABILITY:	Yes
MANAGER TENURE:	11 Years
MINIMUM INITIAL PURCHASE:	Closed
ASSETS UNDER MANAGEMENT ($M):	2,184.70
PHONE NUMBER:	800-662-7447
TOTAL RETURNS, YEAR BY YEAR, FOR THE PAST TEN:	1985— 35.76% 1986— 23.51% 1987— -2.24% 1988— 14.68% 1989— 21.56% 1990— -2.79% 1991— 33.14% 1992— 8.99% 1993— 18.02% 1994— 11.41%
BETA (3-yr):	1.17
ALPHA (3-yr):	7.34
R2 (3-yr):	76
STANDARD DEVIATION (3-yr):	10.75
GROWTH OF $10,000 FROM JAN. 85 TO DEC. 94:	$42,383.76
PORTFOLIO TURNOVER:	8%
EXPENSE RATIO:	.64%

SUMMARY

Performance

Vanguard/Primecap Fund can certainly put up the numbers. Whether you look at its three-, five-, or ten-year average annualized returns, you won't find any under 16%. Specifically, the fund generated an average annual return of 16.45% for the last ten years, eye-catching no matter *how* successful you've been in the past with your holdings. This fund's five-year record, a category we do not grade with stars, notched a third-place ranking within our select group, posting a return of 16.76%— truly noteworthy. As if these numbers weren't enough, Vanguard/Primecap outdoes itself with an astonishing 19.64% average annual return for the last three years, crushing all of the competition here. Interestingly, despite the fund's five stars under both the long- and short-term performance screens, Vanguard/Primecap managed to finish in the bottom half of the funds listed here on the basis of per-year returns in five out of the last ten years. However, the strength of this fund's multi-year performance results pretty much relegate that fact to the Land of Unconcern.

Management

Any dedicated money movers who don't believe that buy-and-hold strategies are effective need look no further than this fund to be proven wrong. Howard B. Schow, a Harvard M.B.A. who has been at the investment game longer than many of us have been alive, loves to hang on to his purchases. The fund's turnover rate is unbelievably low for a top-performing growth fund: 8%. Several of this fund's portfolio stocks have been in there since the fund was started back in 1984. It is worth noting that Schow and company seem to have a love affair with the technology sector, allocating to it nearly 40% of the portfolio at last check. Such allegiance seems to bear out the notion that as volatile as that sector can be, it remains one of the strongest bastions of potential profitability available to investors.

Risk/Reward Analysis

If there were a risk/reward champ to be declared here, Vanguard/Primecap would easily be a finalist, if not the overall winner. While this fund has a three-year beta that is almost the highest of any in our group, its long- and short-term returns much more than offset that level of volatility. Accordingly, this fund's corresponding alpha measurement is a whopping 7.34, by far the highest of any in our group. Most impressively, in a year like '94 that saw many growth securities have their poorest years in quite a while, Vanguard/Primecap scored an almost-inconceivable 11.41%. If you can take a little volatility with your investing, Primecap's the one for you.

Expenses

As if the performance record of Vanguard/Primecap weren't enough to lure you, check out this fund's expense ratio: .64%. The reason it is so low undoubtedly has much to do with the fact that manager Schow and his crew don't like to move the portfolio around any more than they have to; but whatever the reason, this fund is a great deal all around.

The Vanguard Family

There are simply too many funds available at Vanguard to list them all here. Here are some that should be of interest to growth investors: Vanguard Explorer Fund, Vanguard/Morgan Growth Fund, Vanguard U.S. Growth Portfolio, and Vanguard Windsor Fund.

Final Thoughts

If it's not clear to you by now, it should be: true growth-oriented investors should make Vanguard/Primecap one of their first stops on the growth fund shopping trip. Although its volatility level might be a bit excessive for the tolerance levels of the more conservative investor, the performance to be had here is second to none.

BALANCED FUNDS

EVERGREEN FOUNDATION Y
Balanced

FUND FAMILY:	Evergreen Funds
TICKER SYMBOL:	EFONX
PORTFOLIO MANAGER:	Stephen A. Lieber
ADDRESS:	2500 Westchester Ave.
	Purchase, NY 10577
LONG-TERM PERFORMANCE:	★ ★ ★ ★ ★
SHORT-TERM PERFORMANCE:	★ ★ ★
PERFORMANCE AGAINST PEER GROUP:	★ ★ ★ ★ ★
SAFETY:	★ ★ ★ ★
TELEPHONE EXCHANGES:	Yes
BROKERAGE AVAILABILITY:	Yes
MANAGER TENURE:	5 Years
MINIMUM INITIAL PURCHASE:	$1,000
ASSETS UNDER MANAGEMENT ($M):	353.30
PHONE NUMBER:	800-807-2940
TOTAL RETURNS, YEAR-BY-YEAR,	
FOR THE PAST FIVE:	1990— 6.60% 1991— 37.38% 1992—
	19.97% 1993— 15.73% 1994— -1.12%
BETA (3-yr):	.82
ALPHA (3-yr):	2.35
R2 (3-yr):	81
STANDARD DEVIATION (3-yr):	7.27
GROWTH OF $10,000	
FROM JAN. 90 TO DEC. 94:	$20,105.17
PORTFOLIO TURNOVER:	33%
EXPENSE RATIO:	1.14%

SUMMARY

Performance

If you're not careful, you might mistake Evergreen Foundation Y for an honest-to-goodness growth fund. The fund's five-year average annualized return is a whopping 17.40%—amazing for a balanced mutual fund. Its three-year annualized return is no slouch either at 11.84%, and it makes you wonder why anyone would consider anything more aggressive when they can realize such fine returns in a fund category that is by nature quite conservative. A per-year look at this fund over the past five years shows us that it has finished no worse than fourth in our group in four of them. Even though the fund's 1994 return was -1.12%, that return beat the average return of domestic stock funds for that year and only placed as low as seventh out of the balanced offerings featured here.

Management

Stephen A. Lieber is the portfolio manager of Evergreen Foundation Y, and his style involves a mix of value investing with some contrarian twists. Although it's fair to say that value investors are by nature somewhat contrarian anyway, Lieber takes that a step further, as evidenced by his strong moves into the financial and health care sectors just *after* what were apparently their best surges in quite awhile. However, time proved the widom of his judgment, to which these phenomenal returns attest. Perhaps this fund's performance further shows that a shrewd stock-picker who has been at the game for over forty years can invariably be trusted.

Risk/Reward Analysis

Evergreen maintains a beta coefficient that is currently at .82. All good balanced funds should sport betas that are considerably below that of the overall market, and all of the funds in our group do just that. Although .82 is on the high end of the betas listed here, note that the fund also has one of the highest alphas, and that the fund's multiyear performance numbers are nothing short of excellent.

Expenses

Evergreen Foundation Y is really rather pricey for a balanced fund, with an annual expense ratio of 1.14%, but with performance numbers like the ones posted by this fund, it's tough to really care all that much. What a fund costs you should be constantly compared with what it *gives* you. The same principle applies with respect to a fund's volatility measurement. In this case, Evergreen is a fund that clearly favors investors in the battle of cost versus reward; cost may be a bit on the high side, but returns are very much on the high side as well.

The Evergreen Family

There are fifteen other funds in the Evergreen family besides Evergreen Foundation Y: The Evergreen American Retirement Trust, The Evergreen Fund, The Evergreen Global Real Estate Equity Fund, The Evergreen Insured National Tax-Free Fund, The Evergreen Limited Market Fund, The Evergreen Money Market Trust, The Evergreen Short-Intermediate Municipal Fund, The Evergreen Short-Intermediate Municipal Fund-California, The Evergreen Small Cap Equity Income Fund, The Evergreen Tax Exempt Money Market Fund, Evergreen Tax Strategic Foundation Fund, The Evergreen Total Return Fund, Inc., The Evergreen U.S. Government Securities Fund, The Evergreen U.S. Real Estate Equity Fund, and The Evergreen Value Timing Fund, Inc.

Final Thoughts

With a beta well below that of the overall market and a string of returns that resemble a quality growth fund more than a balanced fund, Evergreen Foundation Y is very tough to beat under any circumstances. This may not be a fund for the more conservative balanced investor, but it may be one of the best combinations of performance and safety that you'll find in a stock-based vehicle.

STATE FARM BALANCED
Balanced

FUND FAMILY:	State Farm Group
TICKER SYMBOL:	STFBX
PORTFOLIO MANAGER:	Kurt Moser
ADDRESS:	One State Farm Plaza
	Bloomington, IL 61710
LONG-TERM PERFORMANCE:	★ ★ ★ ★
SHORT-TERM PERFORMANCE:	★ ★

PERFORMANCE AGAINST PEER GROUP:	★ ★ ★ ★ ★
SAFETY:	★ ★ ★ ★ ★
SALES RESTRICTIONS:	State Farm mutual funds are available only to employees of State Farm Insurance Companies and to their family members.
TELEPHONE EXCHANGES:	Yes
BROKERAGE AVAILABILITY:	No
MANAGER TENURE:	4 Years
MINIMUM INITIAL PURCHASE:	$50
ASSETS UNDER MANAGEMENT ($M):	410.30
PHONE NUMBER:	309-766-2311
TOTAL RETURNS, YEAR BY YEAR, FOR THE PAST FIVE:	1990— 9.99% 1991— 39.22% 1992— 5.38% 1993— 3.32% 1994— 5.01%
BETA (3-yr):	.68
ALPHA (3-yr):	-.22
R2 (3-yr):	84
STANDARD DEVIATION (3-yr):	6.00
GROWTH OF $10,000 FROM JAN. 90 TO DEC. 94:	$17,507.66
PORTFOLIO TURNOVER:	4%
EXPENSE RATIO:	.17%

SUMMARY

Performance

State Farm Balanced is one of only two funds in our elite group of balanced offerings that did not realize a negative return in any of the past five calendar years. As nice as it is to have those years when returns rival those of more aggressive funds, we must not forget that balanced fund investors are here because they don't want to endure the volatility of more growth-oriented funds, and thus are happy earning less in exchange for their peace of mind. In that spirit we present State Farm Balanced, which has posted five- and three-year average annualized returns of 13.49% and 8.16%, respectively. Although the five-year number pales next to that of Evergreen's, don't kid yourself: that return is terrific for a balanced player. It's true that 8.16% is a bit low for an equity-based security over any multiyear time period, but it should be noted that the fund bested all of its competitors in 1994, a year that was about as bad as they get.

Management

Kurt Moser has been the portfolio manager of State Farm Balanced for four years now. Moser is the only manager in our group here who eschews the use of bonds to the extent he does. Rather, he likes to incorporate preferred stock where the bonds would probably be, and that strategy cost him in years when declining interest rates represented a boon to bond investors. Nevertheless, the stability his approach brings to the portfolio is admirable, and hard-core balanced fund investors will undoubtedly like his fund's above-ground returns in some of the most challenging years in recent market history.

Risk/Reward Analysis

State Farm Balanced has a three-year volatility measurement that is quite low at .68, and the fund's longer-term track record is even more welcome with that kind of number. However, the fund's three-year alpha, a measurement of how well the fund has done relative to its given level of volatility, is disappointing at -.22. The overriding reasons for this dismal number can be found in years '92 and '93, when the fund finished at the bottom of our group members. In '94, though, State Farm beat 'em all, demonstrating that the previous two years were not the beginning of the end.

Expenses

The expense ratio of State Farm Balanced is an incredibly low .17%. The nice thing about such a low expense ratio (from the standpoint of the fund) is that if the fund didn't do well, it would be tough for investors to gripe. However, this fund *does* do well, as evidenced by its five-year average annualized return of 13.49%. Administration cost seems to be limited by way of the very low turnover of portfolio securities, a rate of 4%. Such buy-and-hold strategies by fund managers will always save investors money.

The State Farm Family
There are three other funds in the State Farm family besides State Farm Balanced: State Farm Growth Fund, Inc., State Farm Interim Fund, Inc., and State Farm Municipal Bond Fund, Inc.

Final Thoughts
State Farm is a no-load family with which many are unfamiliar, but the performance record of State Farm Balanced makes you wonder why it's such a secret. This fund enjoys a nice low level of volatility that is complemented by strong results, and its cost to investors is very minimal; all the way around, State Farm Balanced is likely to be a strong competitor for your investment dollars.

CGM MUTUAL
Balanced

FUND FAMILY:	CGM Group
TICKER SYMBOL:	LOMMX
PORTFOLIO MANAGER:	G. Kenneth Heebner
ADDRESS:	222 Berkeley Street
	Ste. 1940
	Boston, MA 02116
LONG-TERM PERFORMANCE:	★ ★ ★ ★
SHORT-TERM PERFORMANCE:	★ ★
PERFORMANCE AGAINST PEER GROUP:	★ ★ ★ ★ ★
SAFETY:	★ ★ ★ ★
TELEPHONE EXCHANGES:	Yes
BROKERAGE AVAILABILITY:	Yes
MANAGER TENURE:	15 Years
MINIMUM INITIAL PURCHASE:	$2,500/$1,000 for IRAs
ASSETS UNDER MANAGEMENT ($M):	1,055.50
PHONE NUMBER:	800-345-4048
TOTAL RETURNS, YEAR BY YEAR, FOR THE PAST FIVE:	1990— 1.11% 1991— 40.88% 1992— 6.07% 1993— 21.83% 1994— -9.73%
BETA (3-yr):	.82
ALPHA (3-yr):	-.34
R2 (3-yr):	51
STANDARD DEVIATION (3-yr):	9.18
GROWTH OF $10,000 FROM JAN. 90 TO DEC. 94:	$16,616.28
PORTFOLIO TURNOVER:	173%
EXPENSE RATIO:	.92%

SUMMARY

Performance

CGM Mutual is another balanced fund that seems to be able to put up the numbers over time. The fund's five-year average annualized return is a strong 13.28%, very good for a fund that doesn't keep much more than 60% of its portfolio in stocks at any given time. When we review the fund's three-year return, we are again exposed to an equity-based fund that admittedly sports a return that is a bit disappointing. However, this fund has enjoyed some super years of late; notably 1991, when it scored a 40.88% return, which is sensational for any kind of fund but truly awe-inspiring for a balanced fund. Unfortunately, the fund can be prone to some volatility, as evidenced by the fact that it topped our list in 1993, but finished in the basement in 1994 with a -9.73% return. CGM Mutual *does* seem a bit hyper for a balanced fund, but long-term holders should be quite pleased.

Management

The manager of CGM Mutual is G. Kenneth Heebner, a Harvard M.B.A. with portfolio management experience at Loomis Sayles and Scudder. His stock picks are based on value principles, but Heebner is famous in the fund management community for moving in and out rather quickly, not unlike an aggressive growth manager. In fact, the current turnover rate of his portfolio is downright manic—173%. In short, investors in CGM Mutual are only as successful as the sometimes-curious stock selections of its manager, but it's clear that those who hang on for the whole ride will likely end up winners.

Risk/Reward Analysis

CGM Mutual has a beta that ties for the worst in our group at .82, but as stated previously, a beta of .82 is, by itself, very reasonable. Remember, the overall market is ascribed a beta of

1.00, so anything less is considered increasingly favorable. This fund's alpha, however, is a miserable -.34. How, then, can the fund have the third-best long-term track record in our group? Easy—while the beta is a more or less static figure, the alpha changes in direct relation to the fund's actual performances. The alpha here is a three-year measurement, and CGM performed very poorly in '94, returning -9.73%, the worst in our group by a mile.

Expenses

CGM Mutual's annual expense ratio is a tad high for a balanced fund at .92%, but when you see what the fund's portfolio turnover rate is, you'll be amazed that it's not a lot higher: 173%. For this fund, the key to keeping costs down lies in its insistence on maintaining high-yielding positions, income that always helps funds of this type to keep their bite on customers' pocketbooks minimal. Furthermore, gauging total return to investors, this fund's five-year average annualized number more than justifies its expense ratio.

The CGM Family

There are three other funds in the CGM family besides CGM Mutual: CGM American Tax Free Fund, CGM Capital Development Fund, and CGM Fixed Income Fund.

Final Thoughts

Although it would have been nice to see a better short-term track record in a balanced fund with a beta of .82, the longer-term numbers are quite good. Do not allow the beating the fund took in '94 to dissuade you from considering it for your portfolio; you could certainly do worse.

DODGE & COX BALANCED
Balanced

FUND FAMILY:	Dodge & Cox Group
TICKER SYMBOL:	DODBX
PORTFOLIO MANAGER:	Management Team
ADDRESS:	One Sansome St.
	35th Floor
	San Francisco, CA 94104
LONG-TERM PERFORMANCE:	★ ★ ★ ★
SHORT-TERM PERFORMANCE:	★ ★ ★
PERFORMANCE AGAINST PEER GROUP:	★ ★ ★ ★ ★
SAFETY:	★ ★ ★ ★ ★
TELEPHONE EXCHANGES:	No
BROKERAGE AVAILABILITY:	Yes
MANAGER TENURE:	21 Years
MINIMUM INITIAL PURCHASE:	$2,500/$1,000 for IRAs
ASSETS UNDER MANAGEMENT ($M):	966.50
PHONE NUMBER:	800-621-3979
TOTAL RETURNS, YEAR BY YEAR, FOR THE PAST FIVE:	1990— .94% 1991— 20.72% 1992— 10.59% 1993— 15.98% 1994— 2.05%
BETA (3-yr):	.73
ALPHA (3-yr):	2.97
R2 (3-yr):	84
STANDARD DEVIATION (3-yr):	6.35
GROWTH OF $10,000 FROM JAN. 90 TO DEC. 94:	$15,949.77
PORTFOLIO TURNOVER:	20%
EXPENSE RATIO:	.58%

SUMMARY

Performance

Dodge & Cox Balanced has put together some terrific performance numbers for the world to see. This fund's five-year average annualized return is a very respectable 12.69%, again a fine mark to be achieved by a fund that resides in a category deemed to be "home" by many risk-averse investors. While all of the funds in this group earned double-digit returns in the five-year average annualized return category, only half realized the same in the *three*-year screen; yes, Dodge & Cox was one of them. In fact, the 11.91% return in the three-year category places this fund at the head of the class for that screen. Although the fund finished with a 20.72% return in 1990, a year that seemed to be magical for just about everybody, the fund demonstrated its real value in 1994 when it posted a 2.05% return, making it one of only three funds in our group to finish in the black that year.

Management

Dodge & Cox Balanced is managed by a team of portfolio experts. Adhering to a belief that they will be successful if invested for the long term, the pilots strive for value in their selections. They don't care much for struggling to find those elusive growth complements that can so significantly boost any stock-based portfolio; rather, they like to locate the larger, better-known companies that, for one reason or another, are selling below their worth. Management has also been partial to ensuring that the bonds in the portfolio carry a fairly sizable yield. Here we get a good look at the benefits realized by having a fund managed by several people, professionals who are able to find the best securities to go in a fund made up of many different types.

Risk/Reward Analysis

Dodge & Cox Balanced registers a three-year beta coefficient of .73, again quite satisfactory for a conservative investor. The corresponding alpha figure is a terrific 2.97, which is best in our group. A look at this fund's three-year average annualized track record shows us why; at 11.91%, it's tops in our group of finalists. Because CGM's longer-term performance record is no slouch either, this fund would have to be considered a strong contender from a risk/reward standpoint.

Expenses

The annual expense ratio of Dodge & Cox Balanced is a comfortable .58%. When compared against the fund's multiyear performance numbers, we see that it's quite fair to investors.

There are a lot of funds in this world that will cost you more than .58% per year and won't deliver the dependable double-digit returns (over time) that this one does. The portfolio turnover rate of Dodge & Cox (20%) also helps quite a bit in keeping the cost to investors down.

The Dodge & Cox Family

There are two other funds in the Dodge & Cox family besides Dodge & Cox Balanced: Dodge & Cox Income Fund, and Dodge & Cox Stock Fund.

Final Thoughts

Dodge & Cox is a fine family of mutual funds, and Dodge & Cox Balanced certainly doesn't represent any exception. With strong multiyear performance returns in the three- and five-year average annualized categories, this fund is one of the most competitive balanced funds you'll find.

T. ROWE PRICE BALANCED
Balanced

FUND FAMILY:	Price T. Rowe Funds
TICKER SYMBOL:	RPBAX
PORTFOLIO MANAGER:	Richard T. Whitney/Edmund Notzon, III
ADDRESS:	100 E. Pratt St.
	Baltimore, MD 21202
LONG-TERM PERFORMANCE:	★ ★ ★
SHORT-TERM PERFORMANCE:	★ ★
PERFORMANCE AGAINST PEER GROUP:	★ ★ ★ ★ ★
SAFETY:	★ ★ ★ ★ ★
TELEPHONE EXCHANGES:	Yes
BROKERAGE AVAILABILITY:	Yes
MANAGER TENURE:	4 Years
MINIMUM INITIAL PURCHASE:	$2,500/$1,000 for IRAs
ASSETS UNDER MANAGEMENT ($M):	463.40
PHONE NUMBER:	800-638-5660
TOTAL RETURNS, YEAR BY YEAR, FOR THE PAST FIVE:	1990— 7.14% 1991— 21.99% 1992— 7.26% 1993— 13.35% 1994— -2.05%
BETA (3-yr):	.70
ALPHA (3-yr):	1.22

R2 (3-yr):	82
STANDARD DEVIATION (3-yr):	6.17
GROWTH OF $10,000 FROM JAN. 90 TO DEC. 94:	$15,564.66
PORTFOLIO TURNOVER:	33%
EXPENSE RATIO:	1.00%

SUMMARY

Performance

T. Rowe Price Balanced seems to realize returns that are a little more realistic for a true balanced fund; not that anyone should be dissuaded from purchasing a fund with returns way above the norm (after all, isn't that what this game is all about?), just that many conservative investors feel comforted by the sight of a balanced fund that seems to indeed act like one. A look at each of Price's multiyear performance numbers reads like a review of the quintessential balanced fund. Its fifteen-year average annualized return is a solid 13.14%, while its ten-year average mark is 12.61%. Both of these numbers are about where they should be for a good balanced fund—a little bit better than the overall market, but not as high as those realized by the high-quality growth counterparts. The fund's five-year annualized return is 11.73%, which makes it perfectly average in this small pack of the best. Finally, Price's three-year average return is 9.82%, which is again average (sixth out of ten) in this group of the best balanced. Overall, these numbers are very strong for investors so inclined to consider these funds in the first place.

Management

Richard T. Whitney and Edmund Notzon, III, are the co-managers of T. Rowe Price Balanced, and the style they use to guide this offering is indeed balanced in every sense of the word. Not only do these guys maintain the classic 60%/40% split between stocks and bonds, but they see fit to evenly distribute the stock allocations into each sector available. Furthermore, their bond portfolios are handled in the same fashion, with a spread from solid, investment-grade, mortgage-backed securities to corporate high-yield ventures. This fund's portfolio structure certainly runs the gamut, and more conservative equity investors should like that type of diversification just fine.

Risk/Reward Analysis

T. Rowe Price Balanced seems to be right where it belongs. It has the sixth-best beta, the fifth-best five-year track record, and the sixth-best three-year number. The fund's beta is .70, while its alpha is 1.22 (*seventh*-best in *that* category). Price Balanced seems to be a perfect fit for those struggling to find a fund that offers a great deal of evenhandedness all the way around.

Expenses

T. Rowe Price Balanced carries with it the industry-standard expense ratio of an even 1.00%. The turnover rate of the fund is a fairly mild 33%, which is pretty fair for a balanced fund. There *are* cheaper expense ratios out there for funds of this type, and you'll want to evaluate the track records of each of them in comparison with their costs, but it does seem that while you could do better than Price Balanced in this department, the ratio here could hardly be considered offensive.

The T. Rowe Price Family

There are too many funds in the Price family to list them here. Following are two selections that might be of interest to balanced investors: T. Rowe Price Dividend Growth Fund, Inc., and T. Rowe Price Equity Income Fund, Inc.

Final Thoughts

T. Rowe Price Balanced represents one more offering from the very fine family of Price funds. Price Balanced affords investors a moderate beta, a perfectly acceptable expense ratio, and very solid performance numbers. This fund obviously maintains the high standards of the terrific Price fund family, and should be a consideration for all balance-minded investors.

ECLIPSE FINANCIAL ASSET BALANCED
Balanced

FUND FAMILY:	Eclipse Financial Asset Group
TICKER SYMBOL:	EBALX
PORTFOLIO MANAGER:	Wesley G. McCain
ADDRESS:	P.O. Box 2196
	Peachtree City, GA 30269
LONG-TERM PERFORMANCE:	★ ★ ★
SHORT-TERM PERFORMANCE:	★ ★ ★
PERFORMANCE AGAINST PEER GROUP:	★ ★ ★ ★ ★
SAFETY:	★ ★ ★ ★ ★
TELEPHONE EXCHANGES:	Yes
BROKERAGE AVAILABILITY:	Yes
MANAGER TENURE:	6 Years
MINIMUM INITIAL PURCHASE:	$1,000
ASSETS UNDER MANAGEMENT ($M):	30.80
PHONE NUMBER:	800-872-2710
TOTAL RETURNS, YEAR BY YEAR, FOR THE PAST FIVE:	1990— 1.45% 1991— 20.84% 1992— 10.16% 1993— 17.08% 1994— -.06%
BETA (3-yr):	.62
ALPHA (3-yr):	2.43
R2 (3-yr):	68
STANDARD DEVIATION (3-yr):	6.00
GROWTH OF $10,000 FROM JAN. 90 TO DEC. 94:	$15,801.88
PORTFOLIO TURNOVER:	65%
EXPENSE RATIO:	.80%

SUMMARY

Performance

Eclipse Financial Asset Balanced is a fund that seems to be about as long on returns as it is in name. The fund's five-year average annualized return missed finishing in the upper half of these funds by just a whisker, with an 11.69% result. The fund's three-year annualized return was even stronger (in comparison with the competition) at 10.57%. These multiyear investment returns represent classic results for quality balanced entries, and were much helped by the fund's especially sturdy return in 1993—17.08%. Although this fund *did* suffer a losing year in '94 (like so many other funds), its loss was barely one at all, as Eclipse still finished in the fourth place among our offerings at -.06%. While it's always disconcerting to consider investing in a fund that has demonstrated a capacity for finishing in the red, it must be remembered that it can happen to many of the best, and longer-term conservative investors who review this fund's overall performance should not be put off much by occasional performance deficiencies.

Management

Eclipse Financial is helmed by Wesley G. McCain, and this pilot seems to like to keep his portfolio allocations along the lines of the classic balanced fund; currently, this fund is invested in the form of a rough 60%/40% stock and bond split, with a negligible portion of the portfolio in cash. It is worth noting that McCain has seen fit to forsake entirely the financial sector at this time and place a disproportionate number of the assets in the shaky industrial cyclical sector, a move that seems to want to anticipate a broad-based economic recovery. McCain moves a lot for a balanced fund manager, displaying a turnover rate of about 65%; while that might seem a bit excessive for a fund like this, the returns it garners are nothing to disregard.

Risk/Reward Analysis

Eclipse Financial shares with FBP Contrarian the record for having the lowest beta of our group offerings. Its beta of .62 is very low for a fund that is primarily stock-based, and its three-year alpha is thus even more impressive at 2.43. You might think that a fund with such a favorable risk/reward relationship would have a better longer-term track record; really, though, the fund's longer-term numbers aren't bad (consider the average annualized five-year run of 11.69%), and the alpha is more of a reflection of the fund's shorter-term numbers, which are solid.

Expenses

The expense ratio of Eclipse Financial is .80%, which puts this fund well below the cost level of many other mutual funds. Still, it's rather expensive in comparison with the other expense ratios outlined here in our group of ten. The performance numbers of this fund, though, put it in the "perfectly acceptable" category, as we see that the fund is capable of putting up double-digit returns in the short as well as the long term. The portfolio turnover rate of Eclipse is 65%, which helps to account for its expenses in the face of solid performance. Nonetheless, the fund could hardly be considered a rip-off, and it should not be dropped from consideration on the basis of cost.

The Eclipse Family

There is one other fund in the Eclipse family besides Eclipse Balanced: Eclipse Equity Fund.

Final Thoughts

With strong performance numbers in the short as well as the long term, Eclipse Financial should not go unnoticed by any astute balanced investor. Consistency is the word of the day here, and its performance in '94, while not scintillating on its own, is quite good in comparison with others out there.

AMERICAN AADVANTAGE BALANCED INSTITUTIONAL
Balanced

FUND FAMILY:	American AAdvantage Funds
TICKER SYMBOL:	AADBX
PORTFOLIO MANAGER:	Management Team
ADDRESS:	P.O. Box 4580
	Chicago, IL 60680
LONG-TERM PERFORMANCE:	★ ★ ★
SHORT-TERM PERFORMANCE:	★ ★ ★
PERFORMANCE AGAINST PEER GROUP:	★ ★ ★ ★ ★
SAFETY:	★ ★ ★ ★ ★
SALES RESTRICTIONS:	American AAdvantage Balanced Institutional may be purchased only by institutional investors currently. Contact American AAdvantage at the number below for more information.
TELEPHONE EXCHANGES:	N/A
BROKERAGE AVAILABILITY:	N/A
MANAGER TENURE:	8 Years
MINIMUM INITIAL PURCHASE:	None
ASSETS UNDER MANAGEMENT ($M):	224
PHONE NUMBER:	817-967-3509
TOTAL RETURNS, YEAR BY YEAR, FOR THE PAST FIVE:	1990— .59% 1991— 21.58% 1992— 9.30% 1993— 14.82% 1994— -1.66%
BETA (3-yr):	.68
ALPHA (3-yr):	1.59
R2 (3-yr):	79
STANDARD DEVIATION (3-yr):	6.15
GROWTH OF $10,000 FROM JAN. 90 TO DEC. 94:	$15,093.32
PORTFOLIO TURNOVER:	48%
EXPENSE RATIO:	.66%

SUMMARY

Performance

With American AAdvantage, we again see a balanced fund that posts very fair numbers for a quality fund in this category. American's five-year average annualized return is a very solid 11.67%. The three-year annualized return figure drops off just a bit, landing at 10.08%. Again, it must be remembered that these are *balanced* funds, funds that are designed to insulate investors from the inherent volatility found in each broad type of investment vehicle. Accordingly, the returns *will* reflect such adherence to safety concerns. Although this fund's 1994 was in the negative range, it was better than the average performance of domestic-based stock funds. All in all, the performance numbers posted by American AAdvantage are very good for this category, and this fund should be considered by those looking to limit the excitement in their investment experience.

Management

American AAdvantage is another in an increasingly long line of mutual funds that opt for team management as opposed to guidance by one particular manager. Value investing is the rule here, as evidenced by the fact that this fund sports the lowest price-to-earnings ratio of the funds in our group, as well as one of the lowest price-to-book value ratios. American's management likes to stock the portfolio with a lot of yield-producing securities, something dedicated balanced fund investors will likely appreciate. Although management seems to distribute assets fairly evenly among the available sectors, it *can* be prone to turning holdings over at a rate that is significant for a balanced fund (48%).

Risk/Reward Analysis

American AAdvantage offers investors a beta coefficient that ranks in the top half of those featured here, numbers which are already low to begin with. The added attraction of the low beta is the strong multiyear performance numbers that this fund has managed to notch over the last five years. For investors inclined to keep this fund over the long haul, the risk/reward ratio is very favorable.

Expenses

American AAdvantage carries with it an expense ratio that begins to get into the range of being truly competitive. At .66%, the annual expense figure paid by investors is very low, and the performance numbers needed to justify it don't have to be very high. In this case, they're excellent at 11.67% for the five-year average annualized return, and 10.08% for the three-year. On a cost-effectiveness basis, American AAdvantage is a good deal.

Final Thoughts

American AAdvantage is another balanced fund that has been able to garner double-digit returns in both the three- and five-year average annualized return screens—no easy feat in the topsy-turvy climate of the 1994. Fortunately, this fund maintains a relatively low volatility measurement as well, so investors have a lot to look at.

VANGUARD/WELLINGTON
Balanced

FUND FAMILY:	Vanguard Group
TICKER SYMBOL:	VWELX
PORTFOLIO MANAGER:	Vincent Bajakian
ADDRESS:	P.O. Box 2600
	Valley Forge, PA 19482
LONG-TERM PERFORMANCE:	★ ★ ★
SHORT-TERM PERFORMANCE:	★ ★ ★
PERFORMANCE AGAINST PEER GROUP:	★ ★ ★ ★ ★
SAFETY:	★ ★ ★ ★
TELEPHONE EXCHANGES:	Yes
BROKERAGE AVAILABILITY:	Yes
MANAGER TENURE:	23 Years
MINIMUM INITIAL PURCHASE:	$3,000/$500 for IRAs
ASSETS UNDER MANAGEMENT ($M):	9,586.90
PHONE NUMBER:	800-662-7447
TOTAL RETURNS, YEAR BY YEAR, FOR THE PAST FIVE:	1990— -2.81% 1991— 23.65% 1992— 7.93% 1993— 13.52% 1994— -.49%
BETA (3-yr):	.76
ALPHA (3-yr):	1.13
R2 (3-yr):	84
STANDARD DEVIATION (3-yr):	6.66
GROWTH OF $10,000 FROM JAN. 90 TO DEC. 94:	$14,652.00
PORTFOLIO TURNOVER:	32%
EXPENSE RATIO:	.35%

SUMMARY

Performance

Wellington is one of the benchmark offerings from the rock-solid Vanguard family. It is one of five funds in our group with a five-year average annualized return in the 11% range. As with all of the other 11-percenters featured here, Wellington's return is very much in line with what a good balanced fund *should* be expected to do. Additionally, Wellington's three-year average annualized return creeps over the 10% mark to come in precisely at 10.14%. It deserves mentioning, however, that the three-year finish of this fund *does* place it in the upper half of the funds evaluated here for that particular screen. Although this fund did not finish in the upper half of the funds in our group in any of the last five calendar year races, it should be noted that it didn't finish any worse than eighth, either. Conclusion? While Wellington may not be the fund to bet on to finish first in any annual race of balanced funds, neither should you bet *against* it in a contest of overall reliability and consistency.

Management

Vincent Bajakian, armed with an M.B.A. from New York University as well as twenty-three years of experience at the helm of Wellington, just may be the reigning "father" of balanced fund investing today. His current "children" include equity-team manager Bob Courtemanche and bond-team manager Paul Kaplan, both of whom have made shrewd decisions on behalf of the fund during difficult '94. Wellington management is clearly partial to stocks, and weights the portfolio heavily (for a balanced fund) in that area. Longer-term investors know that while bonds and money markets may serve strategic purposes at times for realizing quality growth results, it is stocks on which investors must hang their hats if they want to be sure to make some real money through the years. Overall, Bajakian likes to see his fund look for value in out-of-favor sectors, and success with these picks has helped to propel the fund very recently.

Risk/Reward Analysis

Although Wellington owns one of the highest betas of the funds in our elite group, a .76 measurement could hardly be considered dangerous. The fund's double-digit returns in our five- and three-year average annualized return categories complement this fund's volatility level very nicely, and although the corresponding alpha measurement is not one of the better of those featured in this group, the staying power of this fund is its strongest suit; *that* should be the characteristic on which prospective investors focus.

Expenses

Thanks primarily to a relatively low turnover rate (32%) and a relatively high yield/income rate, Vanguard/Wellington has an exceedingly low annual expense ratio of .35%. With a cost like that, how much performance should you really expect? Well, all we know is how much you actually *receive*, which is a lot here. Wellington's long- and short-term multiyear performance numbers are very solid, and this fund, on the basis of cost, should make every balanced fund investor's short list.

The Vanguard Family

There are too many funds in the Vanguard family to list them all here. Following are some examples of funds that may be of interest to balanced investors: Vanguard Equity Income Fund, Vanguard Wellesley Income Fund, and Vanguard STAR Fund.

Final Thoughts

If long-term dependability is your game, then Wellington may very well be your fund. The Vanguard family itself is one of the best in the business, and one that is a home to many conservative investors. The double-digit returns realized by this fund in both the short- and long-term screens are a big plus, as many funds faltered in the upheaval that was 1994.

VANGUARD STAR
Balanced

FUND FAMILY:	Vanguard Group
TICKER SYMBOL:	VGSTX
PORTFOILIO MANAGER:	Multiple Managers
ADDRESS:	P.O. Box 2600
	Valley Forge, PA 19482
LONG-TERM PERFORMANCE:	★ ★ ★
SHORT-TERM PERFORMANCE:	★ ★
PERFORMANCE AGAINST PEER GROUP:	★ ★ ★ ★ ★
SAFETY:	★ ★ ★ ★ ★
TELEPHONE EXCHANGES:	Yes
BROKERAGE AVAILABILITY:	Yes
MANAGER TENURE:	10 Years
MINIMUM INITIAL PURCHASE:	$500
ASSETS UNDER MANAGEMENT ($M):	4,008.40
PHONE NUMBER:	800-662-7447
TOTAL RETURNS, YEAR BY YEAR, FOR THE PAST FIVE:	1990— -3.63% 1991— 24.29% 1992— 10.42% 1993— 10.97% 1994— -.29%
BETA (3-yr):	.66
ALPHA (3-yr):	1.36
R2 (3-yr):	88
STANDARD DEVIATION (3-yr):	5.65
GROWTH OF $10,000 FROM JAN. 90 TO DEC. 94:	$14,634.24
PORTFOLIO TURNOVER:	9%
EXPENSE RATIO:	0.00

SUMMARY

Performance

Vanguard STAR is another charter member of the "11% Club." STAR recorded a five-year average annualized return of 11.17%, which is a perfectly fair return for a balanced fund that makes our "best" list. However, this fund also qualifies for membership in the "9% Club" out of deference to its three-year average annualized return. Although a three-year return of just under 10% (9.72%, to be precise) is really not bad at all for a balanced fund, such a figure *does* place this fund in the bottom half of the funds featured here in this category. A look at the per-year returns shows us that this fund has actually finished in the upper half of our finalists in three of the last five years, which should certainly give performance-sensitive balanced players some solace. Additionally, it should be mentioned that this fund *does* have a ten-year annualized return, and it is quite respectable at 11.47%. In reality, none of the performance numbers notched by this fund, either annual or multiyear, are really anything to be dismayed over, save for *maybe* STAR's 1990 return.

Management

Here again is another fund that forsakes the leadership of an individual manager in favor of the guidance of *several* managers. Vanguard STAR is actually a curious beast as mutual funds go, as its portfolio is made up entirely of shares from other Vanguard funds. STAR owns the shares of nine other Vanguard funds at this writing, and its precise asset base is structured accordingly. Management's clear desire is to weight the portfolio heavily in the stock realm; of the nine other Vanguard funds owned by STAR, seven are stock funds. The stocks themselves are primarily large-capitalization issues with a value bent (surprise, surprise), with an especially strong weighting in the financial sector at this time.

Risk/Reward Analysis

Vanguard STAR has the third-lowest beta of our group members, but it would have been nice to see a shade better performance in this fund's recent history. STAR's longer-term numbers, including its ten-year average annualized return, are quite good; here again, we are left with a fund that gives the risk/reward benefit to the safety-conscious if they are committed to this fund for the long term.

Expenses

It's tough to argue about the annual expense ratio charged by Vanguard STAR: 0.00%. That's right—nothing. This is possible, of course, because of the fact that STAR is actually a combination of other Vanguard offerings. However, pay close attention to the performance numbers here. Again, what ultimately matters is what the investment can return to you in real dollars. STAR's numbers are good, but they're not the best we've seen here. Consider the fund seriously, but don't allow yourself to be too enamored by the admittedly attractive cost structure.

The Vanguard Family

There are too many funds in the Vanguard family to list them all here. Following are examples of funds that may be of interest to balanced investors: Vanguard Equity Income Fund, Vanguard Wellesley Fund, and Vanguard Wellington Fund.

Final Thoughts

Based on cost alone, Vanguard STAR is a worthy competitor of any fund featured here. While you might opt for a fund that has performed better in the short term, the fund's numbers through the years are very strong, and it has not had a single year with truly poor returns.

FBP CONTRARIAN BALANCED
Balanced

FUND FAMILY:	Flippin, Bruce and Porter Funds
TICKER SYMBOL:	FBPBX
PORTFOLIO MANAGER:	John T. Bruce
ADDRESS:	P.O. Box 5354
	Cincinnati, OH 45201
LONG-TERM PERFORMANCE:	★ ★ ★
SHORT-TERM PERFORMANCE:	★ ★
PERFORMANCE AGAINST PEER GROUP:	★ ★ ★ ★ ★
SAFETY:	★ ★ ★ ★ ★
TELEPHONE EXCHANGES:	N/A
BROKERAGE AVAILABILITY:	N/A
MANAGER TENURE:	6 Years
MINIMUM INITIAL PURCHASE:	$25,000/$1,000 for IRAs
ASSETS UNDER MANAGEMENT ($M):	26.00
PHONE NUMBER:	800-543-0407
TOTAL RETURNS, YEAR BY YEAR, FOR THE PAST FIVE:	1990— -7.87% 1991— 27.30% 1992— 14.37% 1993— 9.96% 1994— 1.84%

BETA (3-yr):	.62
ALPHA (3-yr):	1.47
R2 (3-yr):	82
STANDARD DEVIATION (3-yr):	5.47
GROWTH OF $10,000 FROM JAN. 90 TO DEC. 94:	$15,020.86
PORTFOLIO TURNOVER:	27%
EXPENSE RATIO:	1.25%

SUMMARY

Performance

Of the two primary screens we used to evaluate the funds in this group, five-year average annualized return and three-year average annualized return, FBP Contrarian placed at or near the bottom in both of the performance categories featured here. However, things may not be what they seem, as we're about to show you. First, let's mention the five-year annualized return, which is our only one below 11% (FBP's is precisely 10.91%). Also, the fund's three-year annualized return result is 9.53%, which is really not so bad but nonetheless *does* put this fund in eighth place of our finalists. Curiously, though, this fund actually finished in the upper half of our group on the basis of annual returns in three of the last five years. The reason FBP's five-year return is so heavily weighted-down is due primarily to its '90 return, which was the clear loser here at -7.87%. Overall, though, this fund has substance, and if you take a closer look at each year's return individually, you will likely be more impressed than you are right now.

Management

FBP Contrarian Balanced is under the care of John T. Bruce. Bruce and his staff like to provide investors with a balanced fund that tries to avoid generating undue surprises. The volatility level is kept quite low, and its limited size is due chiefly to the fact that FBP likes to keep a relatively large position in cash. The portfolio's equity weightings are heaviest in financials and technology, sectors that show this team's management philosophy to be based fundamentally on value.

Furthermore, it is clear that the team in charge of FBP is of a buy-and-hold mentality overall, demonstrated clearly by the portfolio's current turnover rate of 27%. Although this fund's performances are not at the top of our elite group, it *is* made more attractive by its limited volatility, something as important to conservative investors as pure performance.

Risk/Reward Analysis

FBP Contrarian tied with Eclipse Financial for the lowest beta measurement of the funds in our group. Unfortunately, it did *not* tie Eclipse Financial for one of the higher alphas as well. Nonetheless, for the truly conservative who would like to keep a hand in the stock market, this isn't such a bad choice at all. Prospective investors might be scared off by the fund's 1990 performance, but shouldn't be; the fund has acquitted itself nicely in the years that have followed, and as long as you don't expect this fund to make you rich overnight, you should be quite content in the long run.

Expenses

At 1.25%, FBP Contrarian has the dubious distinction of owning the most expensive annual expense ratio of the funds featured here. If you consider that fact at the same time you look at this fund's performance numbers, you might want to be given more of a reason to invest. The fact remains, though, that this fund is one of the least volatile of the competitive balanced funds, so when you take all of these factors together, you *do* manage to emerge with a quality fund in hand.

Final Thoughts

FBP Contrarian Balanced is a little pricey for a balanced offering, but it does give conservative investors a quality home through which to realize some decent gains while sheltering themselves from the market's natural volatility. Although its '90 performance is tough to swallow, this fund *did* acquit itself nicely in a '94 that was about as challenging.

BOND FUNDS

BABSON BOND L
Bond

FUND FAMILY:	Babson Fund Group
TICKER SYMBOL:	BABIX
PORTFOLIO MANAGER:	Edward L. Martin
ADDRESS:	Three Crown Center
	2440 Pershing Rd.
	Kansas City, MO 64108
LONG-TERM PERFORMANCE:	★ ★
SHORT-TERM PERFORMANCE:	★
PERFORMANCE AGAINST PEER GROUP:	★ ★ ★ ★ ★
SAFETY:	★ ★ ★ ★
TELEPHONE EXCHANGES:	Yes
BROKERAGE AVAILABILITY:	Yes
MANAGER TENURE:	11 Years
MINIMUM INITIAL PURCHASE:	$500/$250 for IRAs
ASSETS UNDER MANAGEMENT ($M):	148.20
PHONE NUMBER:	800-422-2766
TOTAL RETURNS, YEAR BY YEAR, FOR THE PAST TEN:	1985— 20.65% 1986— 13.88% 1987— 1.93% 1988— 7.17% 1989— 13.12% 1990— 7.78% 1991— 14.99% 1992— 7.97% 1993— 11.15% 1994— -3.29%
BETA (3-yr):	.98
ALPHA (3-yr):	.13
R2 (3-yr):	88
STANDARD DEVIATION (3-yr):	4.26
GROWTH OF $10,000 FROM JAN. 85 TO DEC. 94:	$24,421.46
PORTFOLIO TURNOVER:	40%
EXPENSE RATIO:	.97%

SUMMARY

Performance

Babson Bond L has posted some fine longer-term performance numbers for an intermediate-term bond fund, but suffered through a poor '94 and thus realized considerably less auspicious numbers in the short term. Babson's fifteen-year track record for average annualized returns is very sound, posting a total return figure of 10.27%. The ten-year number is also decent at 9.39%. The fund's *five*-year annualized return, although lower (9%), is still representative of a vehicle that is found outside the safety of a bank. Unfortunately, the fund suffers in the recent term, due mostly to its '94 total return of -3.29%. Nonetheless, it should be noted that the fund's individual 1994 return *did* rank the fund in the upper half of the bond vehicles featured here. Overall, this fund's returns, while not the best in the bunch, are still very fine.

Management

Edward L. Martin is the portfolio manager of Babson Bond L. Interestingly, manager Martin is not really a yield-chaser, as he aspires to bolster total return numbers. What makes that interesting is that the fund has one of the better yields of the offerings here at 7.1% (accomplished chiefly through the maintenance of a hefty average weighted coupon). Martin has also been wise to stuff the portfolio in part with some bargain Canadian issues, which he can do successfully given his experience as an investment analyst with Sun Life of Canada.

Risk/Reward Analysis

Babson's risk level is basically average for this category, as evidenced in part by a beta of .98. The returns of this fund overall, however, are clearly *better* than average, if not among the best of the group of finalists. The fund also sports a positive three-year alpha, which is actually saying something considering that three funds in this group carry negative alphas, while one other is flat. Babson's per-year returns saw this fund finish in the top half of the funds featured here in four of the last ten calendar years, although this fund's average maturity is long for this category.

Expenses

Babson Bond L carries an expense ratio of .97%, which is on the high side for a fund of this type. The figure is also high with respect to the fund's performance numbers, but really anything under 1.00% is not going to be too objectionable; just make sure you don't pay too much for too little.

The Babson Family

There are thirteen other funds in the Babson family besides Babson Bond L: Babson Bond S, Babson Enterprise, Babson Enterprise II, Babson Growth, Babson Tax-Free Income L, Babson Tax-Free Income S, Babson Value, Babson-Stewart Ivory International, Shadow Stock, UMB Bond, UMB Heartland, UMB Stock, and UMB Worldwide.

Final Thoughts

Babson Bond L is a fund with a consistent record of multiyear returns that doesn't cost investors too much or ask too much of them as far as their blood pressure is concerned. Longer-term investors aren't likely to be disappointed.

BOND PORTFOLIO FOR ENDOWMENTS
Bond

FUND FAMILY:	Endowments Funds
TICKER SYMBOL:	BENDX
PORTFOLIO MANAGER:	Multiple Managers
ADDRESS:	P.O. Box 7650
	San Francisco, CA 94120
LONG-TERM PERFORMANCE:	★ ★ ★
SHORT-TERM PERFORMANCE:	★
PERFORMANCE AGAINST PEER GROUP:	★ ★ ★ ★ ★
SAFETY:	★ ★ ★
SALES RESTRICTIONS:	Endowments funds may be purchased only by institutional investors currently. Contact Endowments at the number below for more information.
TELEPHONE EXCHANGES:	N/A
BROKERAGE AVAILABILITY:	N/A
MANAGER TENURE:	20 Years
MINIMUM INITIAL PURCHASE:	$50,000
ASSETS UNDER MANAGEMENT ($M):	44.20
PHONE NUMBER:	415-421-9360

TOTAL RETURNS, YEAR BY YEAR, FOR THE PAST TEN:	1985— 23.14% 1986— 15.75% 1987— -1.69% 1988— 9.18% 1989— 12.56% 1990— 6.04% 1991— 20.32% 1992— 9.40% 1993— 12.23% 1994— -4.31%
BETA (3-yr):	1.15
ALPHA (3-yr):	0.00
R2 (3-yr):	91
STANDARD DEVIATION (3-yr):	4.88
GROWTH OF $10,000 FROM JAN. 85 TO DEC. 94:	$25,813.41
PORTFOLIO TURNOVER:	82%
EXPENSE RATIO:	.77%

SUMMARY

Performance

Although the returns of our top ten are wrapped pretty closely around a tight range, there *are* going to be those funds that post consistently better returns than others. Bond Portfolio for Endowments is one of them. Of the funds that have a fifteen-year average annualized return to report, Bond Portfolio's is best at 10.82%. The fund's ten-year average annualized return is solid as well at 10.02%. The fund's five-year annualized return ranks in the upper half of the funds featured here, as does its three-year return. The only identifiable "black marks" the fund has in the performance department are its return in '87, when it was one of only two group members to finish in the red that year (although not by a lot), and its return in '94, when it finished in the bottom half of our group in a year that was already bad to begin with. However, Bond Portfolio has managed to finish in the top three of our offerings in five of the last ten calendar years, something with which performance junkies should be very pleased.

Management

Bond Portfolio for Endowments is guided by multiple managers who seem to favor high-coupon issues, giving this fund its terrific yield. Management is also partial to clinging to its holdings a bit more tenaciously than many in this group, operating at a portfolio turnover rate of 82%, which puts it in the upper half of these funds in the "low turnover" contest. Management also likes to deal in short maturity issues, a fact to which its 5.3-year average maturity will attest.

Risk/Reward Analysis

This fund's overall returns are superior, placing it in the top four of our group in the three-, five-, and ten-year average annualized return screens. Not surprisingly, Endowment's risk level is a bit elevated, as we can see by its three-year beta coefficient of 1.15. What's more, the fund's three-year alpha is flat, indicating that as good as performance is, investors aren't really getting a bargain in the risk/reward trade-off. Nevertheless, these returns *are* better than most, and this fund should make any bond investor's list of finalists.

Expenses

Endowment's expense ratio is an easy-to-take .77%, a figure made even more palatable when viewed in the light of the fund's performance numbers, which are solid in the multiyear screens.

Final Thoughts

Bond Portfolio for Endowments offers a strange name but a welcome profile. Prospective investors will be enticed by returns, but should ensure that the accompanying volatility is acceptable; it *should* be, save perhaps for the more conservative of investors.

COLUMBIA FIXED-INCOME SECURITIES
Bond

FUND FAMILY:	Columbia Funds
TICKER SYMBOL:	CFISX
PORTFOLIO MANAGER:	Thomas L. Thomsen, et al.
ADDRESS:	P.O. Box 1350
	Portland, OR 97207
LONG-TERM PERFORMANCE:	★ ★
SHORT-TERM PERFORMANCE:	★

PERFORMANCE AGAINST PEER GROUP:	★ ★ ★ ★ ★
SAFETY:	★ ★ ★
TELEPHONE EXCHANGES:	Yes
BROKERAGE AVAILABILITY:	Yes
MANAGER TENURE:	12 Years
MINIMUM INITIAL PURCHASE:	$1,000
ASSETS UNDER MANAGEMENT ($M):	265.90
PHONE NUMBER:	800-547-1707
TOTAL RETURNS, YEAR BY YEAR, FOR THE PAST TEN:	1985— 20.19% 1986— 12.31% 1987— 1.36% 1988— 7.72% 1989— 14.35% 1990— 8.30% 1991— 16.85% 1992— 8.01% 1993— 10.48% 1994— -3.36%
BETA (3-yr):	1.11
ALPHA (3-yr):	-.07
R2 (3-yr):	98
STANDARD DEVIATION (3-yr):	4.58
GROWTH OF $10,000 FROM JAN. 85 TO DEC. 94:	$24,595.04
PORTFOLIO TURNOVER:	139%
EXPENSE RATIO:	.66%

SUMMARY

Performance

Columbia Fixed-Income maintains the apparent tradition of the intermediate-term funds in this group, which suggests that they agree to finish in the top half in annual performance about as frequently as they finish in the bottom half. The fund's ten-year average annualized return is 9.63%, which is quite good for this category but does not put the fund among the best in this group. On the strength of a good '90 and a competitive '92 and '94, Columbia was able to realize a five-year annualized return that was actually better than its ten-year number. The fund, like all bond funds for the most part, posts a shorter-term track record that is pretty disappointing for securities overall but reasonably good for bond funds in general.

Management

Thomas L. Thomsen, who gained part of his fixed income expertise as the senior investment officer for Oregon's Treasury, is the portfolio manager of Columbia Fixed-Income

Securities. While Thomsen is fond of employing sector-based investing within this portfolio, he is *not* one to gamble on interest rates and, accordingly, avoids becoming too focused on anything other than matters of total return. Thomsen also likes to keep his average portfolio maturity fairly short, which helps to keep volatility levels in line.

Risk/Reward Analysis

Columbia's three-year beta coefficient is 1.11, which is a bit high but not really offensive. However, the returns posted by this fund indicate that it may be underperforming its risk level a bit, an idea further supported by its three-year alpha, which is negative. Of the three-, five-, and ten-year screens used here, Columbia finished in the top half in only one of them (the five-year), but on a per-year basis the fund finished in the top half of our group in half of the last ten years.

Expenses

Columbia's annual expense ratio of .66% puts the fund in the top half (as in lowest cost) of our offerings for that category. Although Columbia's returns are quite reasonable, investors can be sure that they're not getting ripped off in order to achieve them.

The Columbia Family

There are nine other funds in the Columbia family besides Columbia Fixed-Income Securities: Columbia Balanced Fund, Inc., Columbia Common Stock Fund, Inc., Columbia Daily Income Co., Columbia Growth Fund, Columbia High-Yield Fund, Inc., Columbia International Stock Fund, Inc., Columbia Municipal Bond Fund, Inc., Columbia Special Fund, Inc., and Columbia U.S. Government Securities Fund, Inc.

Final Thoughts

Columbia is another one of the many entries here that post very consistent performance numbers up and down the line. The beta's a tad high, but the overall volatility level is nothing a longer-term investor should have to worry about.

DREYFUS A BONDS PLUS
Bond

FUND FAMILY:	Dreyfus Group
TICKER SYMBOL:	DRBDX
PORTFOLIO MANAGER:	Garitt Kono
ADDRESS:	EAB Plaza
	144 Glenn Curtis Blvd. Plaza Level
	Uniondale, NY 11556
LONG-TERM PERFORMANCE:	★ ★
SHORT-TERM PERFORMANCE:	★
PERFORMANCE AGAINST PEER GROUP:	★ ★ ★ ★ ★
SAFETY:	★ ★ ★
TELEPHONE EXCHANGES:	Yes
BROKERAGE AVAILABILITY:	Yes
MANAGER TENURE:	1 Year
MINIMUM INITIAL PURCHASE:	$2,500/$750 for IRAs
ASSETS UNDER MANAGEMENT ($M):	540.30
PHONE NUMBER:	800-645-6561
TOTAL RETURNS, YEAR BY YEAR, FOR THE PAST TEN:	1985— 23.31% 1986— 14.11% 1987— -.31% 1988— 9.02% 1989— 14.22% 1990— 4.80% 1991— 18.76% 1992— 8.21% 1993— 14.95% 1994— -6.16%
BETA (3-yr):	1.39
ALPHA (3-yr):	-.25
R2 (3-yr):	93
STANDARD DEVIATION (3-yr):	5.88
GROWTH OF $10,000 FROM JAN. 85 TO DEC. 94:	$25,375.69
PORTFOLIO TURNOVER:	93%
EXPENSE RATIO:	.90%

SUMMARY

Performance

Dreyfus A Bonds Plus is clearly one of the better overall performers of the offerings featured here in our elite group of ten. The fund has posted a fifteen-year average annualized return of 10.65%, which is an excellent total return figure. In the ten-year screen, the fund barely missed out on a three-star rating, while its *five*-year annualized return is a terrific 10.12%, second-best of the bond funds featured here. The fund's three-year annualized return, while not glowing by itself, was also second-best in our group at 7.91%; what makes this so amazing is that the fund suffered more than any other in our group during miserable 1994, but its '92 and '93 performances were clearly helpful. Looking at the fund's per-year returns, it's interesting to notice that while the fund finished dead last in two of the last ten calendar years of the funds in our group, the fund offset those returns with top-five finishes in seven of the last ten years.

Management
Garitt Kono runs the show at Dreyfus A Bonds Plus, which he took over from Barbara Kenworthy halfway through 1994. Kono is a more conservative debt securities investor than was Kenworthy, as evidenced by his insistence in removing some of the longer-term and overall riskier holdings from the portfolio (although the fund still sports a hefty, average-maturity length of nearly thirteen years). It is only natural to assume that Kono's conservative bent will continue to become more apparent in the fund, especially when you consider that he's also the manager of a couple of high-profile Ginnie Mae funds.

Risk/Reward Analysis
Dreyfus A Bonds Plus has the highest three-year beta of all the funds in our group, but much of that is probably due to the more aggressive posture the fund had taken in the past. Still, without accounting for circumstances, the fund has the highest beta and the lowest alpha here—nothing to be proud of. However, the fund's bottom line is not too shabby, as we saw in the Performance section. The conclusion? If you can stand some volatility with your bond investing, it's clear that Dreyfus A Bonds Plus will reward you nicely.

Expenses
Dreyfus A Bonds Plus carries with it an annual expense ratio of .90%, which is not pricey in comparison with the splendid results it has achieved through the years.

The Dreyfus Family

There are too many funds in the Dreyfus family to list all of them here. Following are some selections that may be of interest to bond investors: Dreyfus GNMA Fund, Inc., Dreyfus Investors GNMA Fund, L.P., and Dreyfus Short-Term Income Fund.

Final Thoughts

This fund offers a great performance record and some of the highest volatility in the bond fund game. Shorter-term investors might want to remain wary, but those in for the long haul are not as obligated to be too deferential to roller-coaster rides.

ELFUN INCOME
Bond

FUND FAMILY:	Elfun Mutual Funds
TICKER SYMBOL:	EINFX
PORTFOLIO MANAGER:	Robert A. MacDougall
ADDRESS:	P.O. Box 120074
	Stamford, CT 06912-0074
LONG-TERM PERFORMANCE:	★ ★ ★
SHORT-TERM PERFORMANCE:	★ ★
PERFORMANCE AGAINST PEER GROUP:	★ ★ ★ ★ ★
SAFETY:	★ ★ ★ ★
SALES RESTRICTIONS:	Elfun funds are available only to members of the Elfun Society, an organization affiliated with General Electric Co. For more information, contact General Electric Investment Corp. at the phone number below.
TELEPHONE EXCHANGES:	Yes
BROKERAGE AVAILABILITY:	No
MANAGER TENURE:	8 Years
MINIMUM INITIAL PURCHASE:	$100
ASSETS UNDER MANAGEMENT ($M):	193.80
PHONE NUMBER:	800-242-0134
TOTAL RETURNS, YEAR BY YEAR, FOR THE PAST TEN:	1985— 21.53% 1986— 16.46% 1987— .79% 1988— 7.52% 1989— 14.34% 1990— 8.61% 1991— 16.13% 1992— 6.62% 1993— 9.72% 1994— -2.33%
BETA (3-yr):	.96
ALPHA (3-yr):	.12
R2 (3-yr):	97

```
        STANDARD DEVIATION (3-yr):   3.97
               GROWTH OF $10,000
        FROM JAN. 85 TO DEC. 94:  $25,273.48
             PORTFOLIO TURNOVER:   215%
                  EXPENSE RATIO:   .30%
```

SUMMARY

Performance

Here is another offering from the very fine but quite unknown
Elfun mutual fund family, and it is no less admirable than any
of its other intrafamily counterparts. Elfun Income completes
its ten-year average annualized return screen with a figure of
10.05%, qualifying it to receive a three-star rating in this category. Unfortunately, the fund's five-year annualized return,
while still good overall, falls to 9.41% and a seventh-place
ranking of the funds featured here. The fund's short-term
(three-year) multiyear annualized performance falls off
noticeably from its loftier levels, lagging behind the group for
that screen at 6.95%. Given that, you might expect the fund's
'94 run to have been one of the worst here, but it wasn't; in
fact, it was third-best. Although 6.95% might be enough to
drive one back to banks, review the fund's per-year returns
and you'll see that, for the most part, the annual returns are
high-quality.

Management

Robert A. MacDougall is the portfolio manager of Elfun
Income and has been for eight years running. MacDougall's
approach clearly leans to the conservative side, as evidenced
(in part) by his desire to keep portfolio maturities on the low
side of intermediate (8.3 years). The fund's yield is not blister-
ing, but neither is its average weighted coupon at 7.8%. Total
return is the name of the game here, and MacDougall's unwill-
ingness to gamble is testament to that fact.

Risk/Reward Analysis

Elfun Income offers investors a three-year beta that is slightly less volatile than the standard bond index (Lehman Brothers Aggregate) applicable here, and a corresponding alpha that lands on the "plus" side. Although the fund's three-year annualized return is nothing to write home about, its ten-year return is excellent, second-best overall here. Longer-term investors will find they can be quite content with this fund's overall performance, and will not have to wrestle with the volatility concerns that other greater-maturity fund investors must deal with.

Expenses

Elfun Income enjoys (or, more correctly, its *investors* enjoy) the lowest expense ratio of the funds in our group. It has also had, however, some less-than-scintillating performance runs, although the fund's longer-term numbers have been pretty good. From a cost perspective, it's tough to find fault with Elfun.

The Elfun Family

There are five other funds in the Elfun family besides Elfun Income: Elfun Diversified Fund, Elfun Global Fund, Elfun Money Market Fund, Elfun Tax-Exempt Income Fund, and Elfun Trusts.

Final Thoughts

Bond investors looking for a solid intermediate-term haven could certainly do worse than Elfun Income; the fund manages to keep costs way down, volatility in line, and performance at a premium for the long-term investor.

FIDELITY ADVISOR INSTITUTIONAL LIMITED TERM BOND
Bond

FUND FAMILY:	Fidelity Advisor Funds
TICKER SYMBOL:	EFIPX
PORTFOLIO MANAGER:	Michael S. Gray
ADDRESS:	82 Devonshire St.
	Boston, MA 02109
LONG-TERM PERFORMANCE:	★ ★
SHORT-TERM PERFORMANCE:	★
PERFORMANCE AGAINST PEER GROUP:	★ ★ ★ ★ ★
SAFETY:	★ ★ ★ ★
SALES RESTRICTIONS:	Fidelity Advisor funds may be purchased only by institutional investors currently. Contact Fidelity at the number below for more information.
TELEPHONE EXCHANGES:	N/A
BROKERAGE AVAILABILITY:	N/A
MANAGER TENURE:	8 Years
MINIMUM INITIAL PURCHASE:	$100,000
ASSETS UNDER MANAGEMENT ($M):	173.70
PHONE NUMBER:	800-522-7297
TOTAL RETURNS, YEAR BY YEAR, FOR THE PAST TEN:	1985— 17.63% 1986— 13.56% 1987— 1.56% 1988— 7.84% 1989— 12.11% 1990— 7.91% 1991— 15.16% 1992— 6.90% 1993— 12.51% 1994— -2.13%
BETA (3-yr):	.83
ALPHA (3-yr):	.77
R2 (3-yr):	86
STANDARD DEVIATION (3-yr):	3.62
GROWTH OF $10,000 FROM JAN. 85 TO DEC. 94:	$23,992.32
PORTFOLIO TURNOVER:	68%
EXPENSE RATIO:	.61%

SUMMARY

Performance

Fidelity Advisor Institutional Limited Term Bond Fund is one of the less stunning entries here, but posts very satisfactory results nonetheless. The ten-year average annualized return is somewhat disappointing, as the figure is closer to 9% than it is to 10%. The fund *does* hold tough at the 9%-plus mark in the five-year annualized return screen, but joins the "7% Club" with its three-year average annualized return. However, readers wondering why they should consider this fund at all would do well to notice that Fidelity Advisor has slowly but surely ascended in the ranks of these funds from its ten-year to its three-year annualized return results: it finished ninth in its ten-year run, eighth in its five-year run, and sixth in its three-year run. Furthermore, it is pertinent to note that the fund was down only -2.13% in '94, ranking it second among our group offerings for that year.

Management

Michael S. Gray has become the portfolio manager of three Fidelity bond funds, including Fidelity Advisor, after joining the mutual fund giant as a lowly bond analyst in 1982. Gray employs a tried-and-true conservative approach to bond portfolio management, a fact attested to by his short average portfolio maturity, as well as his maintenance of a low average weighted coupon. In fact, the yield on this fund is the second-lowest of any here, indicating that Gray prefers not to tempt interest rate difficulties.

Risk/Reward Analysis

Fidelity Advisor maintains nice risk numbers, something the volatility-averse should be happy to see. This fund's three-year beta coefficient is a calm .83, which is the lowest in our group, while its alpha is the second-highest. That this fund has some of the lowest performance numbers here should not be surprising, but keep something in mind: when you consider that the spread between the lowest-ranking fund and the highest-ranking fund in each of our multiyear performance screens is less than 3%, a conservative-minded option like Fidelity Advisor really doesn't seem so bad.

Expenses

Fidelity Advisor assesses a modest .61% as an annual expense ratio, third-lowest of our group. In comparison with the fund's performance figures, the expenses borne by investors are not at all unreasonable.

The Fidelity Family

There are too many funds in the Fidelity family to list all of them here. Following are some selections that may be of interest to bond investors: Fidelity Ginnie Mae Portfolio, Fidelity Global Bond Fund, Fidelity Intermediate Bond Fund, and Fidelity Investment Grade Bond Fund.

Final Thoughts

This fund is a good choice for the more conservative bond investor, one who is not averse to forsaking some performance for a greater measure of safety; in broad terms, though, this fund is still one of the best in the bond fund category.

FIDELITY INTERMEDIATE BOND
Bond

FUND FAMILY:	Fidelity Group
TICKER SYMBOL:	FTHRX
PORTFOLIO MANAGER:	Michael S. Gray
ADDRESS:	82 Devonshire St.
	Boston, MA 02109
LONG-TERM PERFORMANCE:	★ ★
SHORT-TERM PERFORMANCE:	★
PERFORMANCE AGAINST PEER GROUP:	★ ★ ★ ★ ★
SAFETY:	★ ★ ★ ★
TELEPHONE EXCHANGES:	Yes
BROKERAGE AVAILABILITY:	Yes
MANAGER TENURE:	8 Years
MINIMUM INITIAL PURCHASE:	$2,500/$500 for IRAs
ASSETS UNDER MANAGEMENT ($M):	2,455.00
PHONE NUMBER:	800-544-8888
TOTAL RETURNS, YEAR BY YEAR, FOR THE PAST TEN:	1985— 20.78% 1986— 13.08% 1987— 2.00% 1988— 7.22% 1989— 11.82% 1990— 7.54% 1991— 14.50% 1992— 6.08% 1993— 11.96% 1994— -2.01%
BETA (3-yr):	.84
ALPHA (3-yr):	.48
R2 (3-yr):	87

STANDARD DEVIATION (3-yr):   3.64
GROWTH OF $10,000
FROM JAN. 85 TO DEC. 94: $23,934.81
PORTFOLIO TURNOVER: 81%
EXPENSE RATIO: .64%

SUMMARY

Performance

Fidelity Intermediate Bond Fund wins the award of Worst of the Best for the bond fund category here. This is with respect to performance only, and does not pertain to any of the fund's other features. However, a close look at this fund is warranted by any prospective investor. The fund's ten-year average annualized return is 9.12%, which we would consider to be barely acceptable as a long-term return. Fidelity's five-year annualized return is a modest 8.64%, and its *three*-year return is kind of tough to take at 6.96%. On a per-year basis, the fund finished in ninth or tenth place of the funds evaluated here in five of the last ten years. It should be noted, though, that this fund's performance results are made more palatable by the fund's modest volatility level, indicating that performance, while counting for a lot, isn't necessarily everything.

Management

Michael S. Gray, a Wharton M.B.A., is content to earn good (not great) performance results on behalf of his fund while limiting the volatility level, something so important to bond investors anyway. The fund's average portfolio maturity is a very short (for an intermediate-term fund) 6.5 years, and its average weighted coupon is fifth-lowest of our contestants.

Risk/Reward Analysis

Not surprisingly, Fidelity Intermediate Bond Fund offers volatility numbers that are very close to those found with Fidelity Advisor Institutional. The fund's beta coefficient is virtually identical, coming in at .84. The alpha is not quite as good, which makes sense considering that this fund is slightly worse in performance than Advisor and is, in fact, the poorest performer overall in this group. However, heed the words we used in this section when the subject was Fidelity Advisor; remember that the performance figures of these funds are very close together.

Expenses
Fidelity Intermediate Bond's expense ratio is .64%, which is low for this group. However, this fund's total returns are the worst (overall) of the entries here.

The Fidelity Family
There are too many funds in the Fidelity family to list all of them here. Following are some selections that may be of interest to bond investors: Fidelity Advisor Institutional Limited Term Bond Fund, Fidelity Ginnie Mae Portfolio, Fidelity Global Bond Fund, and Fidelity Investment Grade Bond Fund.

Final Thoughts
This fund is very similar to Fidelity Advisor in every way; accordingly, we would ask you to regard it similarly as a prospective choice. If you're content to give up a bit of return for a lessening of volatility, this just might be the bond fund for you.

FIDELITY INVESTMENT GRADE BOND
Bond

FUND FAMILY:	Fidelity Group
TICKER SYMBOL:	FBNDX
PORTFOLIO MANAGER:	Michael S. Gray
ADDRESS:	82 Devonshire St.
	Boston, MA 02109
LONG-TERM PERFORMANCE:	★ ★
SHORT-TERM PERFORMANCE:	★
PERFORMANCE AGAINST PEER GROUP:	★ ★ ★ ★ ★
SAFETY:	★ ★ ★
TELEPHONE EXCHANGES:	Yes
BROKERAGE AVAILABILITY:	Yes

MANAGER TENURE:	8 Years
MINIMUM INITIAL PURCHASE:	$2,500/$500 for IRAs
ASSETS UNDER MANAGEMENT ($M):	1,082.70
PHONE NUMBER:	800-544-8888
TOTAL RETURNS, YEAR BY YEAR, FOR THE PAST TEN:	1985— 21.10% 1986— 13.62% 1987— .11% 1988— 7.93% 1989— 13.00% 1990— 6.07% 1991— 18.92% 1992— 8.31% 1993— 16.23% 1994— -5.35%
BETA (3-yr):	1.10
ALPHA (3-yr):	.43
R2 (3-yr):	84
STANDARD DEVIATION (3-yr):	4.88
GROWTH OF $10,000 FROM JAN. 85 TO DEC. 94:	$25,249.45
PORTFOLIO TURNOVER:	61%
EXPENSE RATIO:	.74%

SUMMARY

Performance

Fidelity Investment Grade Bond Portfolio represents the third Fidelity offering in our group, and while none of them have registered earth-shattering performances, there is something to be said for the fact that Fidelity does have three funds in the top ten, and that all three are under the supervision of Michael S. Gray. Investment Grade's fifteen-year average annualized return is a satisfactory 10.17%, while its ten-year annualized return drags a bit at 9.73%. The fund does redeem itself in the five-year screen (9.89%), and its three-year annualized return is a top-three performer at 7.73%, thanks mostly to a '93 return that topped the competition. Investment Grade is a fund that never finished worse than eighth in any of the last ten years, but *did* finish in the top three in '91, '92, and '93.

Management

Michael S. Gray is the resident intermediate-term portfolio manager at Fidelity, a fact that is evident in his care of three of Fidelity's mid-term bond funds. Gray keeps the fund's average maturity at a longer duration than he does his others, maintaining it at about 9.5 years. The yield on this fund is not insignificant

(6.83%), and neither is the fund's average weighted coupon—8.0%. Gray clearly invites a bit more volatility in Investment Grade, but compared with the other Fidelity finalists, this fund is a superior performer.

Risk/Reward Analysis

The beta coefficient of Fidelity Investment Grade is a higher-than-standard 1.10, but the figure is not so great as to be off-putting. In fact, the fund also has a three-year alpha that is also pretty nice, relatively speaking. The fund's performance numbers are, as we've seen, quite good, and thus we may be looking at the fund that offers one of the best risk/reward trade-offs of any in our group.

Expenses

Fidelity Investment Grade's annual expense ratio is solidly under what is considered the standard for mutual funds (1.00%), and its returns are quite good overall. The relationship between cost and return with regard to this fund is pretty fair, we must say.

The Fidelity Family

There are too many funds in the Fidelity family to list all of them here. Following are some selections that may be of interest to bond investors: Fidelity Advisor Institutional Limited Term Bond Fund, Fidelity Ginnie Mae Portfolio, Fidelity Global Bond Fund, and Fidelity Intermediate Bond Fund.

Final Thoughts

Fidelity Investment Grade seems to be one of the more reliable performers here, and doesn't ask a lot from investors as far as risk tolerance is concerned. The verdict? Worth a look from any bond investor with a long-term horizon.

MAS FIXED-INCOME
Bond

FUND FAMILY:	MAS Funds
TICKER SYMBOL:	MPFIX
PORTFOLIO MANAGER:	Management Team
ADDRESS:	One Tower Bridge
	West Conshohocken, PA 19428
LONG-TERM PERFORMANCE:	★ ★ ★
SHORT-TERM PERFORMANCE:	★ ★
PERFORMANCE AGAINST PEER GROUP:	★ ★ ★ ★ ★
SAFETY:	★ ★ ★
TELEPHONE EXCHANGES:	No
BROKERAGE AVAILABILITY:	Yes
MANAGER TENURE:	11 Years
MINIMUM INITIAL PURCHASE:	$1,000,000 (institutional figure only; may be purchased through discount broker for lower minimum)
ASSETS UNDER MANAGEMENT ($M):	1,307.30
PHONE NUMBER:	800-354-8185
TOTAL RETURNS, YEAR BY YEAR, FOR THE PAST TEN:	1985— 24.86% 1986— 16.41% 1987— 3.42% 1988— 8.84% 1989— 11.19% 1990— 7.24% 1991— 21.49% 1992— 8.47% 1993— 13.81% 1994— -5.43%
BETA (3-yr):	1.13
ALPHA (3-yr):	.89
R2 (3-yr):	90
STANDARD DEVIATION (3-yr):	4.85
GROWTH OF $10,000 FROM JAN. 85 TO JAN. 94:	$27,670.26
PORTFOLIO TURNOVER:	100%
EXPENSE RATIO:	.49%

SUMMARY

Performance

Although it's true that the performance numbers realized by the bond funds in this group are fairly close together, there *is* still an undisputed king, at least as far as the three-, five-, and ten-year average annualized returns are concerned: MAS Fixed-Income. MAS is the only entry here that achieved an annualized return in the 11% range for the benchmark ten-year screen, which of course places it first among the group members. The fund did *almost* as well in the five-year annualized screen, posting a 10.98% return. MAS maintains its perfect record with a first-place rank in the three-year screen as well, leading the pack with an 8.33% return. An examination of the fund's per-year returns demonstrates that even though MAS swept all three multiyear performance categories evaluated here, the fund did manage to finish last in '89 and ninth in '94. The lesson? Just that overall champions are determined over the course of several years, not several months.

Management

MAS Fixed-Income is piloted by a management team, and the record these captains have compiled sure does make a strong argument for the team concept. Actually, this type of management *has* apparently made it easier for management to weight the portfolio in profitable sectors in a timely fashion. The desire to keep portfolio maturities on the long side cannot be ignored, and it speaks to the truth that a presence in longer-term bonds, if timed correctly, cannot be beaten. Accordingly, volatility is a bit elevated here for a mid-term bond fund, but as long as management continues to move from sector to sector with agility, who cares?

Risk/Reward Analysis

Observing MAS Fixed-Income's performance figures as you have, you will probably not be surprised to find that this fund has the highest three-year alpha of the funds evaluated here, even with a beta of 1.13. The truth is, this fund's numbers are terrific up and down the line, and it would take volatility numbers much shakier than those indicated here to warrant discarding this fund on the basis of risk.

Expenses

What *more* do you want? Not only does this fund rule the roost as far as performance is concerned, it offers investors the second-lowest annual expense ratio of those featured here at .49%.

The MAS Family

There are six other funds in the MAS family besides MAS Fixed-Income: MAS Equity Portfolio, MAS High-Yield Securities Portfolio, MAS International Equity Portfolio, MAS Limited Duration Fixed Income Portfolio, MAS Small Capitalization Value Portfolio, and MAS Value Portfolio.

Final Thoughts

MAS Fixed-Income is perhaps the single best offering here. If you can stand the heat, definitely take up residence in the kitchen.

SCUDDER INCOME
Bond

FUND FAMILY:	Scudder Funds
TICKER SYMBOL:	SCSBX
PORTFOLIO MANAGER:	William M. Hutchinson/Stephen Wohler
ADDRESS:	P.O. Box 2291
	Boston, MA 02107-2291
LONG-TERM PERFORMANCE:	★ ★
SHORT-TERM PERFORMANCE:	★
PERFORMANCE AGAINST PEER GROUP:	★ ★ ★ ★ ★
SAFETY:	★ ★ ★
TELEPHONE EXCHANGES:	Yes
BROKERAGE AVAILABILITY:	Yes
MANAGER TENURE:	9 Years
MINIMUM INITIAL PURCHASE:	$1,000/$500 for IRAs
ASSETS UNDER MANAGEMENT ($M):	489.80
PHONE NUMBER:	800-225-2470
TOTAL RETURNS, YEAR BY YEAR, FOR THE PAST TEN:	1985— 21.80% 1986— 14.75% 1987— .67% 1988— 8.99% 1989— 12.75% 1990— 8.32% 1991— 17.32% 1992— 6.74% 1993— 12.66% 1994— -4.50%
BETA (3-yr):	1.17
ALPHA (3-yr):	-.10
R2 (3-yr):	93
STANDARD DEVIATION (3-yr):	4.96
GROWTH OF $10,000 FROM JAN. 85 TO DEC. 94:	$25,233.89
PORTFOLIO TURNOVER:	60%
EXPENSE RATIO:	.97%

SUMMARY

Performance
Scudder Income has been around for a while, posting some great long-term numbers along with some competitive short-term figures. Scudder's fifteen-year average annualized return is squarely on the high side of the 10% range, coming in at 10.79%. The fund's *ten*-year annualized return, while not qualifying for anything higher than a two-star rating, did place the fund in the upper half of the funds in our group. The five-year annualized return just barely missed out on an upper-half placing (9.58%), while the three-year mark was in there at 7.40%. On a per-year basis, Scudder Income placed in the top half of our group in six of the last ten calendar years, indicating that it's at least one of the *better* of the best. Of note also is that in the last ten years the fund did not finish any worse than eighth out of our group offerings.

Management
Scudder Income enjoys the services of co-managers William M. Hutchinson and Stephen Wohler. The average portfolio maturity of the fund is currently at 11.1 years, which is clearly on the high end of this category. The duo are clearly total return-oriented, indicated in part by the maintenance of a low average coupon (and thus a low yield). However, anyone who's familiar with successful bond investing knows that yield is ultimately *not* the name of the game, and that Hutchinson and Wohler's nimble moves to keep the portfolio duration where it's supposed to be with respect to rate variations is what's really important.

Risk/Reward Analysis
Although this fund's beta is not too hard to swallow, the alpha measurement does seem to indicate that the fund is underperforming its volatility level a bit. The three-year beta sits at 1.17, which places it ninth out of the ten funds here. The alpha

is negative, which is never a good sign, but the performance numbers realized by this fund are, in actuality, pretty fair. Scudder Income does not seem to burden investors with an undue level of risk in relation to performance, but a prospective purchaser might want to avail himself of a closer look before taking the plunge.

Expenses

Scudder Income ties with Babson Bond L for the highest annual expense ratio of the bunch at .97%. However, we would remind you that as long as these expense ratios remain under 1.00%, they're really OK regardless of how the fund performs. There is some benefit, though, to getting the most bang for your buck in mutual fund investing through an analysis of expense ratios; with that in mind, we will tell you that Scudder's cost numbers are a bit high (on paper) for what you get, but that must be weighed with the fact that these are the best bond funds to be had.

The Scudder Family

There are too many funds in the Scudder family to list all of them here. Following are some selections that may be of interest to bond investors: Scudder GNMA Fund, Scudder International Bond Fund, Inc., and Scudder Short-Term Bond Fund.

Final Thoughts

The Scudder fund family is not exactly famous for unleashing "dogs" on the general public, and Scudder Income does nothing to begin a new trend. Longer-term investors will really find nothing disagreeable about this offering.

THE BEST OF THE REST

We have just completed a comprehensive review of five major categories of mutual fund: Growth and Income, International, Growth, Balanced, and Bond. These broad fund types are featured prominently here because they traditionally carry the most relevance for the typical long-term stock mutual fund investor, inside as well as outside of a retirement plan. There are, however, several other types of funds available to retirement investors that generally serve a more specialized purpose. Many of these could actually be considered subcategories of some of the broader versions of mutual fund, but they are regarded by the mutual fund community as entities unto themselves nonetheless. We would now like to profile the five best funds from three more categories that are rather specialized but are quite popular with many members of the fund-purchasing community.

Sector/Specialty Funds

These are stock mutual funds that target a specific industry. The majority (at a minimum) of the stocks that make up the portfolio of the particular specialty fund come from the industry that is pinpointed. For example, you'll find that a technology fund is made up almost entirely of stocks from the technology industry. Likewise, a health care fund will be made up of stocks that are based in the health care industry. Some specialty funds are even more specific in scope, focusing on industries *within* industries. One way to identify specialty funds as being just that is to look for the name of an industry in the title of the fund. Accordingly, Fidelity Select Retail, Invesco Strategic Technology, and Rushmore Precious Metals should all be recognizable to you as examples of specialty funds.

It should be mentioned that specialty funds are among the most aggressive of all mutual funds. The primary reason for this has to do with the fact that these funds are among the least diversified of *all* funds, focusing as they do on just one particular industry and not several. When a given industry is popular, a representative mutual fund may be wildly successful; by the same token, if that same industry falls out of favor, investors may experience some dramatic declines in the value of their fund, because there's no cushion provided through interindustry diversification. Remember, too, that many industries and specialty areas (such as biotechnology and precious metals) are prone to great volatility to *begin* with, so that investing in these kinds of areas exclusively will torque the risk level up a notch or two further. Retirement investors in specialty/sector funds need to have both a high tolerance for risk and a willingness to pay close attention to the funds' market behavior. It is a category that should not be delved into by more passive investors.

Following are the five best specialty mutual funds to be found, per our performance screens based on three- and five-year average annualized returns. Be advised that we were forced to include *low-load* mutual funds among our candidates, as to exclude them would have drastically reduced the pool of availables and would thus have left you with an unsatisfactory representation of "the best."

FIDELITY SELECT COMPUTERS
Specialty

FUND FAMILY:	Fidelity Group
TICKER SYMBOL:	FDCPX
PORTFOLIO MANAGER:	Harry Lange
ADDRESS:	82 Devonshire St.
	Boston, MA 02109
LONG-TERM PERFORMANCE:	★ ★ ★ ★ ★
SHORT-TERM PERFORMANCE:	★ ★ ★ ★ ★
PERFORMANCE AGAINST PEER GROUP:	★ ★ ★ ★ ★
SAFETY:	★ ★
LOAD:	3% (Front End)
TELEPHONE EXCHANGES:	Yes
BROKERAGE AVAILABILITY:	No
MANAGER TENURE:	3 Years
MINIMUM INITIAL PURCHASE:	$2,500/$500 for IRAs
ASSETS UNDER MANAGEMENT ($M):	273.50
PHONE NUMBER:	800-544-8888
TOTAL RETURNS, YEAR BY YEAR,	
FOR THE PAST FIVE:	1990— 18.41% 1991— 30.76% 1992—
	21.96% 1993— 28.87% 1994— 20.45%
BETA (3-Yr):	1.23
ALPHA (3-Yr):	17.23
R2 (3-Yr):	31
STANDARD DEVIATION (3-Yr):	17.83
GROWTH OF $10,000	
FROM JAN. 90 TO DEC. 94:	$29,311.59
PORTFOLIO TURNOVER:	145%
EXPENSE RATIO:	1.89%

FIDELITY SELECT ELECTRONICS
Specialty

FUND FAMILY:	Fidelity Group
TICKER SYMBOL:	FSELX
PORTFOLIO MANAGER:	Marc Kaufman
ADDRESS:	82 Devonshire St.
	Boston, MA 02109
LONG-TERM PERFORMANCE:	★ ★ ★ ★ ★
SHORT-TERM PERFORMANCE:	★ ★ ★ ★ ★
PERFORMANCE AGAINST PEER GROUP:	★ ★ ★ ★ ★
SAFETY:	★ ★
LOAD:	3% (Front End)
TELEPHONE EXCHANGES:	Yes
BROKERAGE AVAILABILITY:	No
MANAGER TENURE:	Less than 1 year
MINIMUM INITIAL PURCHASE:	$2,500/$500 for IRAs
ASSETS UNDER MANAGEMENT ($M):	411
PHONE NUMBER:	800-544-8888
TOTAL RETURNS, YEAR BY YEAR,	
FOR THE PAST FIVE:	1990— 5.81% 1991— 35.29% 1992— 27.44% 1993— 32.08% 1994— 17.17%
BETA (3-Yr):	1.25
ALPHA (3-Yr):	20.89
R2 (3-Yr):	40
STANDARD DEVIATION (3-Yr):	15.96
GROWTH OF $10,000	
FROM JAN. 90 TO DEC. 94:	$28,232.65
PORTFOLIO TURNOVER:	163%
EXPENSE RATIO:	1.67%

FIDELITY SELECT HOME FINANCE
Specialty

FUND FAMILY:	Fidelity Group
TICKER SYMBOL:	FSVLX
PORTFOLIO MANAGER:	David Ellison
ADDRESS:	82 Devonshire St.
	Boston, MA 02109
LONG-TERM PERFORMANCE:	★ ★ ★ ★ ★
SHORT-TERM PERFORMANCE:	★ ★ ★ ★ ★
PERFORMANCE AGAINST PEER GROUP:	★ ★ ★ ★ ★
SAFETY:	★ ★ ★ ★
LOAD:	3% (Front End)
TELEPHONE EXCHANGES:	Yes
BROKERAGE AVAILABILITY:	No
MANAGER TENURE:	10 Years
MINIMUM INITIAL PURCHASE:	$2,500/$500 for IRAs
ASSETS UNDER MANAGEMENT ($M):	200.80
PHONE NUMBER:	800-544-8888
TOTAL RETURNS, YEAR BY YEAR,	
FOR THE PAST FIVE:	1990— -15.08% 1991— 64.61% 1992—
	57.85% 1993— 27.30% 1994— 2.66%
BETA (3-Yr):	1.00
ALPHA (3-Yr):	16.28
R2 (3-Yr):	28
STANDARD DEVIATION (3-Yr):	15.05
GROWTH OF $10,000	
FROM JAN. 90 TO JAN. 94:	$28,836.36
PORTFOLIO TURNOVER:	95%
EXPENSE RATIO:	1.58%

FIDELITY SELECT SOFTWARE AND COMPUTERS
Specialty

FUND FAMILY:	Fidelity Group
TICKER SYMBOL:	FSCSX
PORTFOLIO MANAGER:	John Hurley
ADDRESS:	82 Devonshire St.
	Boston, MA 02109
LONG-TERM PERFORMANCE:	★ ★ ★ ★ ★
SHORT-TERM PERFORMANCE:	★ ★ ★ ★ ★
PERFORMANCE AGAINST PEER GROUP:	★ ★ ★ ★ ★
SAFETY:	★
LOAD:	3% (Front End)
TELEPHONE EXCHANGES:	Yes
BROKERAGE AVAILABILITY:	No
MANAGER TENURE:	1 Year
MINIMUM INITIAL PURCHASE:	$2,500/$500 for IRAs
ASSETS UNDER MANAGEMENT ($M):	257.70
PHONE NUMBER:	800-544-8888
TOTAL RETURNS, YEAR BY YEAR,	
FOR THE PAST FIVE:	1990— .86% 1991— 45.85% 1992—
	35.54% 1993— 32.73% 1994— .39%
BETA (3-Yr):	1.58
ALPHA (3-Yr):	9.44
R2 (3-Yr):	43
STANDARD DEVIATION (3-Yr):	19.28
GROWTH OF $10,000	
FROM JAN. 90 TO DEC. 94:	$26,567.61
PORTFOLIO TURNOVER:	376%
EXPENSE RATIO:	1.57%

T. ROWE PRICE SCIENCE AND TECHNOLOGY
Specialty

FUND FAMILY:	Price T. Rowe Funds
TICKER SYMBOL:	PRSCX
PORTFOLIO MANAGER:	Charles A. Morris
ADDRESS:	100 E. Pratt St.
	Baltimore, MD 21202
LONG-TERM PERFORMANCE:	★ ★ ★ ★ ★
SHORT-TERM PERFORMANCE:	★ ★ ★ ★ ★
PERFORMANCE AGAINST PEER GROUP:	★ ★ ★ ★ ★
SAFETY:	★ ★
TELEPHONE EXCHANGES:	Yes
BROKERAGE AVAILABILITY:	Yes
MANAGER TENURE:	4 Years
MINIMUM INITIAL PURCHASE:	$2,500/$1,000 for IRAs
ASSETS UNDER MANAGEMENT ($M):	1200.50
PHONE NUMBER:	800-638-5660
TOTAL RETURNS, YEAR BY YEAR, FOR THE PAST FIVE:	1990— -1.33% 1991— 60.17% 1992— 18.75% 1993— 24.25% 1994— 15.79%
BETA (3-Yr):	1.36
ALPHA (3-Yr):	12.73
R2 (3-Yr):	43
STANDARD DEVIATION (3-Yr):	16.50
GROWTH OF $10,000 FROM JAN. 90 TO DEC. 94:	$27,000.22
PORTFOLIO TURNOVER:	113%
EXPENSE RATIO:	1.11%

Index Funds

Index funds are mutual funds that are designed to be representative of a particular market index. The S&P 500 is an example of an index that is used frequently in this regard, but an index fund may be designed to mirror *any* particular index. It is imperative, therefore, that you look closely to see which index is being represented in a fund so named. You cannot presume that "XYZ Index Fund" is tracking the S&P 500, the Wilshire 5000, or any other market index; you must look beyond the name to ensure that the index being tracked is the one you're interested in tying your money to. Be advised also that index funds are generally considered to be long-term growth funds; the more representative the index is of small companies, the more aggressive its corresponding fund is.

Because the S&P 500 is the index considered by many to be most representative of the market at large, and is therefore the one to which most mutual fund managers compare their performances, that is the index we chose to select our "best" list from. Following you will find a list of the five best index funds that were culled from our performance screens of short-term (three-year) and long-term (five-year) average annualized performance. You will find that because mutual funds that track a particular index have portfolios that are all structured very similarly, there isn't much opportunity for these funds to distinguish themselves from one another. In fact, it is said that index funds are basically unmanaged, because they need only ensure that they're tracking the appropriate index in order to completely fulfill their objective. They are very popular options for less-active retirement investors nonetheless, because these investors may be reasonably assured of duplicating (or nearly duplicating) the performance of the benchmark S&P 500 in any given year.

VANGUARD INDEX 500
Index

FUND FAMILY:	Vanguard Group
TICKER SYMBOL:	VFINX
PORTFOLIO MANAGER:	George U. Sauter
ADDRESS:	P.O. Box 2600
	Valley Forge, PA 19482
LONG-TERM PERFORMANCE:	★ ★ ★ ★
SHORT-TERM PERFORMANCE:	★ ★ ★
PERFORMANCE AGAINST PEER GROUP:	★ ★ ★ ★ ★
SAFETY:	★ ★ ★ ★
TELEPHONE EXCHANGES:	Yes
BROKERAGE AVAILABILITY:	Yes
MANAGER TENURE:	8 Years
MINIMUM INITIAL PURCHASE:	$3,000/$500 for IRAs
ASSETS UNDER MANAGEMENT ($M):	10654.90
PHONE NUMBER:	800-662-7447
TOTAL RETURNS, YEAR BY YEAR, FOR THE PAST FIVE:	1990— -3.33% 1991— 30.22% 1992— 7.42% 1993— 9.89% 1994— 1.18%
BETA (3-Yr):	1.00
ALPHA (3-Yr):	-.14
R2 (3-Yr):	100
STANDARD DEVIATION (3-Yr):	8.05
GROWTH OF $10,000 FROM JAN. 90 TO DEC. 94:	$15,035.14
PORTFOLIO TURNOVER:	6%
EXPENSE RATIO:	.19%

FIDELITY MARKET INDEX
Index

FUND FAMILY:	Fidelity Group
TICKER SYMBOL:	FSMKX
PORTFOLIO MANAGER:	Jennifer Farrelly
ADDRESS:	82 Devonshire St.
	Boston, MA 02109
LONG-TERM PERFORMANCE:	★ ★ ★ ★
SHORT-TERM PERFORMANCE:	★ ★ ★
PERFORMANCE AGAINST PEER GROUP:	★ ★ ★ ★ ★
SAFETY:	★ ★ ★ ★
TELEPHONE EXCHANGES:	Yes
BROKERAGE AVAILABILITY:	No
MANAGER TENURE:	1 Year
MINIMUM INITIAL PURCHASE:	$2,500/$500 for IRAs
ASSETS UNDER MANAGEMENT ($M):	361.50
PHONE NUMBER:	800-544-8888
TOTAL RETURNS, YEAR BY YEAR, FOR THE PAST FOUR:	1991— 30.33% 1992— 7.31% 1993— 9.62% 1994— 1.02%
BETA (3-Yr):	1.00
ALPHA (3-Yr):	-.33
R2 (3-Yr):	100
STANDARD DEVIATION (3-Yr):	8.04
GROWTH OF $10,000 FROM JAN. 91 TO DEC. 94:	$15,487.52
PORTFOLIO TURNOVER:	3%
EXPENSE RATIO:	.45%

SEI S&P 500 INDEX
Index

FUND FAMILY:	SEI Funds
TICKER SYMBOL:	TRQIX
PORTFOLIO MANAGER:	
ADDRESS:	680 East Swedesford Rd.
	Wayne, PA 19087-1658
LONG-TERM PERFORMANCE:	★ ★ ★ ★
SHORT-TERM PERFORMANCE:	★ ★ ★
PERFORMANCE AGAINST PEER GROUP:	★ ★ ★ ★ ★
SAFETY:	★ ★ ★ ★
SALES RESTRICTIONS:	SEI S&P 500 Index may be accessed only by institutional investors or by financial advisors purchasing the fund on behalf of clients.
TELEPHONE EXCHANGES:	N/A
BROKERAGE AVAILABILITY:	Yes (through financial advisers)
MANAGER TENURE:	4 Years
MINIMUM INITIAL PURCHASE:	None
ASSETS UNDER MANAGEMENT ($M):	456.10
PHONE NUMBER:	800-342-5734
TOTAL RETURNS, YEAR BY YEAR, FOR THE PAST FIVE:	1990— -3.16% 1991— 29.94% 1992— 7.36% 1993— 9.83% 1994— .99%
BETA (3-Yr):	1.00
ALPHA (3-Yr):	-.22
R2 (3-Yr):	100
STANDARD DEVIATION (3-Yr):	8.05
GROWTH OF $10,000 FROM JAN. 90 TO DEC. 94:	$14,984.40
PORTFOLIO TURNOVER:	23%
EXPENSE RATIO:	.25%

DREYFUS PEOPLES INDEX FUND, INC.
Index

FUND FAMILY:	Dreyfus Group
TICKER SYMBOL:	PEOPX
PORTFOLIO MANAGER:	Management Team
ADDRESS:	EAB Plaza
	144 Glenn Curtis Blvd., Plaza Level
	Uniondale, NY 11556
LONG-TERM PERFORMANCE:	★ ★ ★ ★
SHORT-TERM PERFORMANCE:	★ ★ ★
PERFORMANCE AGAINST PEER GROUP:	★ ★ ★ ★ ★
SAFETY:	★ ★ ★ ★
TELEPHONE EXCHANGES:	Yes
BROKERAGE AVAILABILITY:	Yes
MANAGER TENURE:	5 Years
MINIMUM INITIAL PURCHASE:	$2,500/$750 for IRAs
ASSETS UNDER MANAGEMENT ($M):	262.30
PHONE NUMBER:	800-645-6561
TOTAL RETURNS, YEAR BY YEAR, FOR THE PAST FIVE:	1990— -4.97% 1991— 29.90% 1992— 7.70% 1993— 9.53% 1994— .66%
BETA (3-Yr):	1.00
ALPHA (3-Yr):	-.42
R2 (3-Yr):	100
STANDARD DEVIATION (3-Yr):	8.01
GROWTH OF $10,000 FROM JAN. 90 TO DEC. 94:	$14,658.03
PORTFOLIO TURNOVER:	18%
EXPENSE RATIO:	.61%

T. ROWE PRICE EQUITY INDEX
Index

FUND FAMILY:	Price T. Rowe Funds
TICKER SYMBOL:	PREIX
PORTFOLIO MANAGER:	Richard T. Whitney
ADDRESS:	100 E. Pratt St.
	Baltimore, MD 21202
LONG-TERM PERFORMANCE:	★ ★ ★ ★
SHORT-TERM PERFORMANCE:	★ ★ ★
PERFORMANCE AGAINST PEER GROUP:	★ ★ ★ ★ ★
SAFETY:	★ ★ ★ ★
SALES RESTRICTIONS:	T. Rowe Price Equity Index is available only through employer-sponsored retirement plans. Contact Price at the number below for more information.
TELEPHONE EXCHANGES:	Yes
BROKERAGE AVAILABILITY:	No
MANAGER TENURE:	5 Years
MINIMUM INITIAL PURCHASE:	$2,500/$1,000 for IRAs
ASSETS UNDER MANAGEMENT ($M):	280.50
PHONE NUMBER:	800-638-5660
TOTAL RETURNS, YEAR BY YEAR, FOR THE PAST FOUR:	1991— 29.21% 1992— 7.19% 1993— 9.42% 1994— 1.01%
BETA (3-Yr):	1.00
ALPHA (3-Yr):	-.37
R2 (3-Yr):	100
STANDARD DEVIATION (3-Yr):	8.02
GROWTH OF $10,000 FROM JAN. 91 TO DEC. 94:	$15,307.75
PORTFOLIO TURNOVER:	1%
EXPENSE RATIO:	.45%

Municipal Bond Funds

A municipal bond is a debt security that is issued by a state or local government, usually an actual municipality. Municipal bonds work in the same fashion as any other bond; the local government, desiring to raise money to fund a new project, will issue bonds to the general public. In general, interest from municipal bonds is free from federal taxation, and residents of the states and cities that are the actual issuing authorities are usually eligible for tax relief from those entities as well. As you might imagine, municipal bonds are especially popular with the heavily tax-burdened; they are also considered good bond investments for retirees in consideration of the tax advantages as well as to their relative safety.

Municipal bond *funds*, then, are mutual funds that are made up of municipal bonds. Prospective muni-bond investors who consider purchasing the securities in the form of a mutual fund do so for the same reasons *any* investor considers mutual funds: to enjoy diversification, professional management, lower cost, and greater liquidity. For example, the *creditworthiness* of a particular governmental entity can be a factor in making a wise muni-bond choice, but many investors are unsure about what to look at to know for sure that the creditworthiness of a local government meets their standards; a professional portfolio manager can do this.

Because there are different types of municipal bonds out there, investors will want to do some homework before making a final decision. Some muni-bond funds offer totally tax-free income to residents of certain states, so prospective investors will want to consider the tax and return merits of those against the tax and return merits of the national versions. Also, consider portfolio maturity length as you would for any other bond fund; the longer the maturity, the greater the interest-rate risk. Finally, understand that some municipal bond funds specialize in muni-bonds that are insured. Muni-bond insurance exists to protect investors against the default of an issuing entity, but you should realize that such bonds (and, consequently, bond *funds*) will charge you for that added protection in the form of a lower yield.

The following set of municipal bond funds represents the five best from the category of National Municipal. Again, muni-bond funds in this category do not offer any additional tax advantages to residents of particular states, but *do* allow investors to remain free from *federal* taxation of their earnings. The funds we considered in this group have average portfolio maturities of fifteen years or less, and the finalists were selected on the basis of short-term (three-year) and long-term (ten-year) returns. Reviewing the fund profiles, you will quickly notice that each of these funds has been awarded a relatively small number of stars for long- and short-term performance. Remember, the total returns of the funds in this book were compared with those of all other funds composed of the same general type of portfolio instrument, and that standard is maintained as well for the muni-bonds. However, it should be understood that muni-bonds are considered by retirement investors primarily for their tax advantages. It is the *combination* of expected tax relief and total return performance with that the prospective investor should be concerned with. The nature of municipal bonds being what it is, the vehicles are not appropriate for long-term growth investors, but should instead be utilized ideally by those who are effectively retired and wish to safely derive a yield that is (in whole or in part) tax-free.

VANGUARD MUNICIPAL HIGH-YIELD
Municipal Bond—National

FUND FAMILY:	Vanguard Group
TICKER SYMBOL:	VWAHX
PORTFOLIO MANAGER:	Ian A. MacKinnon/Jerome J. Jacobs
ADDRESS:	P.O. Box 2600
	Valley Forge, PA 19482
LONG-TERM PERFORMANCE:	★ ★ ★
SHORT-TERM PERFORMANCE:	★
PERFORMANCE AGAINST PEER GROUP:	★ ★ ★ ★ ★
SAFETY:	★ ★
TELEPHONE EXCHANGES:	Yes
BROKERAGE AVAILABILITY:	Yes
MANAGER TENURE:	14 Years
MINIMUM INITIAL PURCHASE:	$3,000/$500 for IRAs
ASSETS UNDER MANAGEMENT ($M):	1770.90
PHONE NUMBER:	800-662-7447
TOTAL RETURNS, YEAR BY YEAR, FOR THE PAST TEN:	1985— 21.65% 1986— 19.67% 1987— -1.57% 1988— 13.81% 1989— 11.07% 1990— 5.91% 1991— 14.75% 1992— 9.88% 1993— 12.66% 1994— -5.07%
BETA (3-Yr):	1.27
ALPHA (3-Yr):	.11
R2 (3-Yr):	53
STANDARD DEVIATION (3-Yr):	7.11
GROWTH OF $10,000 FROM JAN. 85 TO DEC. 94:	$25,869.24
PORTFOLIO TURNOVER:	50%
EXPENSE RATIO:	.20%

VANGUARD MUNICIPAL LONG-TERM
Municipal Bond—National

FUND FAMILY:	Vanguard Group
TICKER SYMBOL:	VWLTX
PORTFOLIO MANAGER:	Ian A. MacKinnon/Jerome J. Jacobs
ADDRESS:	P.O. Box 2600
	Valley Forge, PA 19482
LONG-TERM PERFORMANCE:	★ ★
SHORT-TERM PERFORMANCE:	★
PERFORMANCE AGAINST PEER GROUP:	★ ★ ★ ★ ★
SAFETY:	★ ★
TELEPHONE EXCHANGES:	Yes
BROKERAGE AVAILABILITY:	Yes
MANAGER TENURE:	14 Years
MINIMUM INITIAL PURCHASE:	$3,000/$500 for IRAs
ASSETS UNDER MANAGEMENT ($M):	1,024.90
PHONE NUMBER:	800-662-7447
TOTAL RETURNS, YEAR BY YEAR, FOR THE PAST TEN:	1985— 20.77% 1986— 19.38% 1987— -1.14% 1988— 12.24% 1989— 11.54% 1990- 6.82% 1991- 13.50% 1992- 9.30% 1993- 13.45% 1994- -5.76%
BETA (3-Yr):	1.32
ALPHA (3-Yr):	-.13
R2 (3-Yr):	53
STANDARD DEVIATION (3-Yr):	7.39
GROWTH OF $10,000 FROM JAN. 85 TO DEC. 94:	$25,281.21
PORTFOLIO TURNOVER:	45%
EXPENSE RATIO:	.20%

ELFUN TAX-EXEMPT INCOME
Municipal Bond—National

FUND FAMILY:	Elfun Mutual Funds
TICKER SYMBOL:	ELFTX
PORTFOLIO MANAGER:	Robert R. Kaelin
ADDRESS:	P.O. Box 120074
	Stamford, CT 06912-0074
LONG-TERM PERFORMANCE:	★ ★
SHORT-TERM PERFORMANCE:	★
PERFORMANCE AGAINST PEER GROUP:	★ ★ ★ ★ ★
SAFETY:	★ ★ ★
SALES RESTRICTIONS:	Elfun funds are available only to members of the Elfun Society, an organization affiliated with General Electric Co. For more information, contact General Electric Investment Corp. at the phone number below.
TELEPHONE EXCHANGES:	Yes
BROKERAGE AVAILABILITY:	N/A
MANAGER TENURE:	11 Years
MINIMUM INITIAL PURCHASE:	$100
ASSETS UNDER MANAGEMENT ($M):	1,220.80
PHONE NUMBER:	800-242-0134
TOTAL RETURNS, YEAR BY YEAR, FOR THE PAST TEN:	1985— 23.99% 1986— 17.84% 1987— .34% 1988— 13.07% 1989— 9.21% 1990— 5.98% 1991— 12.08% 1992— 8.51% 1993— 12.11% 1994— -5.77%
BETA (3-Yr):	1.19
ALPHA (3-Yr):	-.68
R2 (3-Yr):	62
STANDARD DEVIATION (3-Yr):	6.18
GROWTH OF $10,000 FROM JAN. 85 TO DEC. 94:	$24,650.10
PORTFOLIO TURNOVER:	24%
EXPENSE RATIO:	.13%

STATE FARM MUNICIPAL BOND
Municipal Bond—National

FUND FAMILY:	State Farm Group
TICKER SYMBOL:	SFBDX
PORTFOLIO MANAGER:	Kurt Moser
ADDRESS:	One State Farm Plaza
	Bloomington, IL 61710
LONG-TERM PERFORMANCE:	★ ★
SHORT-TERM PERFORMANCE:	★
PERFORMANCE AGAINST PEER GROUP:	★ ★ ★ ★ ★
SAFETY:	★ ★ ★ ★
SALES RESTRICTIONS:	State Farm mutual funds are available only to employees of State Farm Insurance Companies and their family members.
TELEPHONE EXCHANGES:	Yes
BROKERAGE AVAILABILITY:	No
MANAGER TENURE:	4 Years
MINIMUM INITIAL PURCHASE:	$1,000
ASSETS UNDER MANAGEMENT ($M):	290.50
PHONE NUMBER:	309-766-2311
TOTAL RETURNS, YEAR BY YEAR, FOR THE PAST TEN:	1985— 20.48% 1986— 18.82% 1987— 3.42% 1988— 9.57% 1989— 10.31% 1990— 7.03% 1991— 11.05% 1992— 7.78% 1993— 9.78% 1994— -2.54%
BETA (3-Yr):	.77
ALPHA (3-Yr):	.31
R2 (3-Yr):	41
STANDARD DEVIATION (3-Yr):	4.95
GROWTH OF $10,000 FROM JAN. 85 TO DEC. 94:	$24,526.04
PORTFOLIO TURNOVER:	8%
EXPENSE RATIO:	.16%

SCUDDER MANAGED MUNICIPAL BONDS
Municipal Bonds—National

FUND FAMILY:	Scudder Funds
TICKER SYMBOL:	SCMBX
PORTFOLIO MANAGER:	Donald M. Carleton/Philip P. Condon
ADDRESS:	P.O. Box 2291
	Boston, MA 02107-2291
LONG-TERM PERFORMANCE:	★ ★
SHORT-TERM PERFORMANCE:	★
PERFORMANCE AGAINST PEER GROUP:	★ ★ ★ ★ ★
SAFETY:	★ ★
TELEPHONE EXCHANGES:	Yes
BROKERAGE AVAILABILITY:	Yes
MANAGER TENURE:	9 Years
MINIMUM INITIAL PURCHASE:	$1,000/$500 for IRAs
ASSETS UNDER MANAGEMENT ($M):	745.40
PHONE NUMBER:	800-225-2470
TOTAL RETURNS, YEAR BY YEAR, FOR THE PAST TEN:	1985— 17.55% 1986— 16.80% 1987— .93% 1988— 12.27% 1989— 11.18% 1990— 6.77% 1991— 12.22% 1992— 8.98% 1993— 13.32% 1994— -6.04%
BETA (3-Yr):	1.28
ALPHA (3-Yr):	-.74
R2 (3-Yr):	57
STANDARD DEVIATION (3-Yr):	6.87
GROWTH OF $10,000 FROM JAN. 85 TO DEC. 94:	$24,048.72
PORTFOLIO TURNOVER:	33%
EXPENSE RATIO:	.63%

CHAPTER FIVE
Selecting Stocks for Retirement

Investors love stocks. They can't really help themselves. As popular as mutual funds have become, as much sense as it makes to utilize them exclusively as long-term investment vehicles, many people are of the opinion that there just seems to be something missing from a portfolio completely devoid of individual stocks. In what has clearly become the age of the mutual fund, stocks have managed to maintain their magnetism for those seeking wealth. There are perhaps a great many reasons for this persistence, but here are a few of the more notable ones:

Stocks Are Sexy

Before the manic popularity of mutual funds took hold, some stockbrokers would try to dissuade investors from considering them by telling them that funds were for cowards or for the unimaginative. As ridiculous as all that sounds, it's clear that many investors do find something rather timid about mutual fund ownership. Let's face it; it does sound a lot cooler to say that you own Ford Motor Company, Xerox, and AT&T than it does to say you own XYZ Mutual Fund. To some, dealing only in mutual funds is philosophically akin to staying in the right-hand lane on the highway, and many of us are, admittedly, averse to such a prospect. This reason for stock purchasing is, obviously, not particularly logical, but it is a reason nonetheless and one that should be acknowledged.

The Lure of the Potential "Quick Hit" Is Always Present with Stocks

One of the more understandable reasons for the popularity of individual stocks has to do with their profit potential. Just as mutual funds can cushion your fall in the event that a portfolio member has a particularly rough time, so can they limit your success if a few stocks in the bunch hit hot streaks. It is not unheard-of for a fortuitous stock selection to achieve returns of 200%, 300%, 400% or more in a given year. Stocks are really the only type of mainstream negotiable security capable of this kind of growth, so it's easy to understand their attractiveness on that basis. Even the more conservative investors who invest in large companies for their relative stability and hefty dividend yield still hope for some spurt in share price that will give them a taste of capital appreciation, and that rise is always a possibility when the investment at hand is an individual stock. As often as we've heard the logical admonitions against investing with the intent of getting rich quickly, it's difficult in practice to exorcise that desire from within ourselves. Individual stocks, then, represent one of the more sensible means by which to satisfy it.

Stocks Are Simply More Enjoyable for Investment Aficionados

The average investor is someone who, among other things, doesn't want to go to a lot of trouble to realize a quality return on his or her money. Lacking a strong desire to keep a close eye on the movement of one's portfolio is one of the main reasons so many opt for mutual funds to begin with. Beyond that, it takes time to both learn about and track investments, and time is a commodity in short supply for most working Americans. What if, however, you happen to *be* one of those who take an active interest in the movement of their portfolio, and even view investing as a hobby of sorts? If this characterization applies to you, there's a good chance that you would just as soon spend your time analyzing stocks as mutual funds; their movement is, overall, less predictable, and there are more fundamentals you must keep your eye on.

Stocks Have the Potential to Appreciate in the Face of Down/Sideways Markets

When you hear that a market index has fallen, does that mean that every stock that comprises that represented market has fallen as well? Hardly. Look at the stock listings in the business section of your newspaper the day after a negative market session and see if you can find any "plus" symbols (+) for any stocks in the "change" column. You'll probably find a lot of them. A good company is a good company, regardless of what the stock market does as a whole. This doesn't mean that good companies won't suffer down days; they'll likely suffer a lot of them in the course of their respective lifetimes. However, unlike your investment in a broad-based stock mutual fund, your investment in an individual company's stock is not nearly as certain to lose value when the overall market registers a poor showing.

ARE INDIVIDUAL STOCKS APPROPRIATE FOR RETIREMENT INVESTORS?

How times have changed. Before the popularity of mutual funds took hold, would we have heard this question? Probably not. Oh, we would have been advised to maintain positions in several stocks for some diversification, but it's not likely that we would have been advised to stay away from stocks as long as we were long-term investors. You see, the phrase *long-term investor* is really the key to determining whether stocks are appropriate for you in the first place. Although retirement planning is the reason you happen to be reading this particular book, the real issue here is whether or not you can be invested for the long term, *regardless* of your particular goal. Whether the subject is retirement planning, funding a child's college education, purchasing a yacht, or anything else, the appropriateness of the investment has more to do with the investor's ability to stay invested in the vehicle being considered than with anything else. Although it would be possible to make a case for solid blue-chip stocks playing a role in a conservative or shorter-term investor's portfolio (and we'll be doing that shortly), the allocation should be kept relatively small. For these people, any quest for growth really should be pursued by means of mutual funds.

CHOOSING THE TYPE OF STOCK THAT'S BEST FOR YOU

There are fundamentally three different types of stocks available to you, and each possesses relative merits that may or may not be of some benefit to your particular situation. We want to take a few minutes to review each and ensure that you are clear how each differs from the others. As you may know, all stocks are *not* created equal, and you will want to be sure that the companies you consider have the kinds of stock features appropriate to your goals and/or limitations. Although this list may differ slightly by form and name depending on who's creating it, the three basic types of individual stocks available for your selection are generally known by the adjectives growth, income, and value. Let's look at each of them now.

Growth Stocks

For the true long-term investor, growth stocks are generally viewed as the way to go. An honest-to-goodness growth stock is characterized by double-digit annualized returns over both shorter and longer time periods. However, the primary growth spurt, the initial long-term upward momentum that can last for years, never continues forever; at some point, growth stocks come back to earth. If you're doing your growth investing by way of mutual funds, it's up to the portfolio manager to replace the tired ex-stars with a fresh batch of rookies. When *you're* the money manager, though, it becomes your responsibility to do so. Perhaps the biggest problem for investors utilizing individual growth stocks in their portfolios lies in the fact that the end of the line for an issue can come rather suddenly, and your portfolio can suffer some real damage by the time you've made the decision to move on. Individual growth stock investing can be the most profitable of all, but it is clearly the riskiest. One of the real problems with a growth stock is the issue of market hypersensitivity. If a stock has enjoyed unobstructed growth for a long period of time, any small bump in the road that slows the pace of growth can cause analysts to recommend against further purchases, and the market (read "big institutional investors") will sell in a flash. Before you know what hit you, your stock is in a "recovery" mode, nursing severe financial wounds.

However, growth stock investing, approached in a prudent, intelligent fashion, may be the best type of investing for the individual stock aficionado. The key for the *average* investor (who by definition may be more passive) is to stick with growth issues that are somewhat predictable and that represent larger companies with a great deal of financial strength. Most investment professionals would tell you that real growth stocks are those that are basically unknown, quite small, and have the potential to return well over 20% per year for the next several years. While we would agree that such a profile does indeed describe the classic growth company, we also recognize the inherent risks associated with such companies and question the wisdom of including them in a retirement account. Again, if you want to truly take a stab at making money in such small-capitalization companies, we can only recommend that you do so within the relatively safe confines of a mutual fund.

Individual growth stock investing within a retirement account should really be limited to less dynamic issues.

Income Stocks

Income stocks, also known as dividend stocks, are not good choices for investors seeking capital appreciation, but can be excellent choices for the more conservative player. Companies that pay high dividends are typically quite large and quite profitable. They have likely reached the end of their primary growth spurt, and are not concerned with reinvesting most or all of their profits back into the company. In general, these companies will distribute a sizable portion (usually at least 50%) of their profits as dividends to shareholders. Actually these stocks can have an advantage over bonds for income investors, in that while the interest a bond pays is fixed, the dividend payout of a quality company will likely rise over time. As an added benefit, the income investor can also expect a modest increase in share price as well, giving him a nice little growth residual to boot. We *do* have to say, though, that a truly conservative investor should consider a very fine balanced or blue-chip mutual fund in lieu of an individual stock play, but those who insist on individual issues should find a lot of big-company quality to choose from.

Value Stocks

Value stocks have become increasingly favored by savvy portfolio managers through the years. Value stocks, simply defined, are those issues that have demonstrated some strength and quality performance in the past, but are currently selling for less than they're worth. How can you tell if a stock is doing just that? Well, there are in fact some excellent measurements that have been developed to allow investors the opportunity to determine if a stock is indeed selling below what it's worth. Chief among them is the *price-to-earnings ratio*, or P/E ratio. The P/E ratio, which is a figure determined by dividing the stock's price by its earnings per share, is actually a representation of how much investors are willing to pay for a company's earnings. If a P/E ratio is high, you may construe that to mean that investors are expecting a high degree of growth in the earnings and are willing to pay a premium to *realize* that earnings growth. By the same token, if a P/E ratio is low, then that means investors in general are *not* expecting much growth in earnings. As a broad rule of thumb, P/Es of 20 and above are considered high, while P/Es in the 10 to 20 range are considered indicative of reasonable growth. A P/E of below 10 is low, indicating that investors are not expecting much growth in the foreseeable future.

The first step, then, to successful value investing is to find stocks with low P/Es. However, a low P/E doesn't mean that a stock is automatically a good buy. Remember, a stock with a P/E measurement suggesting that its forthcoming earnings results will be weak may in fact be a genuinely bad stock and not simply "misunderstood." That's why a low P/E is not the only criterion used for selecting a value stock. Another highly regarded yardstick wielded by value investors is a company's *price-to-book value ratio.* To obtain a price-to-book ratio, you would divide a company's stock price by its book value per share. Book value represents what all of a company's assets are worth. The idea for value investors is to concentrate on issues with low price-to-book ratios so that they may purchase a stock for a price *below* where the company's assets indicate it should be. A company with a price-to-book value ratio of 100% is said to be selling at book value. If the price-to-book is more than 100%, investors are saying that a company is expected to do very well and have thus put a great deal of value on its assets. If the price-to-book is less than 100%, it is felt by investors at large that the company will not do all that well in the foreseeable future and thus they have no reason to pay a premium for its assets. It is the low price-to-book reading that should catch the eye of the value investor.

These are the basics of value investing. Because of the fundamental data that must be analyzed to properly engage in value investing, many stock investors seem to prefer it. These people understand that stock investing can be a risky proposition, and they like the fact that value investing demands an adherence to analysis that will likely mitigate that risk. The *problem* with value investing, however, is that, by definition, value stocks are those that offer only a short-term window of opportunity; once the share price has appreciated to the level at which its appropriate fundamental indicators say it should be, it is no longer a value stock and the profit opportunity is gone. Another problem with value stocks is that, again by definition, there is really no chance of seeing them grow at a significant rate of return for several years in a row; those are simply not the kinds of issues they are. Still another characteristic of the typical value stock that you should be aware of is that few of them represent large, well-known companies with a lot of financial strength behind them. This isn't to say that such companies don't offer value opportunities from time to time; they do. However, the instances are usually few and far between. Finally, value investing takes work. Because value opportunities are opening and closing all the time, the investor who is inclined to utilize these issues must stay on top of the appropriate markets and stock indicators on a daily basis. If you're desirous of doing just that, then value investing may be for you. However, in our experience, most investors don't want to bear that kind of burden.

HOW WE SELECTED THE STOCKS FOR THIS BOOK

All things considered, we believe that retirement investors who are eager to incorporate individual stocks in their portfolios should make use of the growth model. However, as we indicated previously, these people should ensure that their growth selections represent companies with some financial strength behind them, so the ideal growth issues for a retirement account may not be "classic" growth plays in the generally accepted sense. They are, however, growth stocks that are more than suitable for a retirement account.

In order to give investors a solid selection of fine companies, we have chosen to feature thirty different stocks in the next chapter. To isolate our group of thirty issues, we used three simple (but effective) criteria: market capitalization, yield, and average annualized return. It should be noted that there exist a great many criteria by which one can select a list of stocks. A number of fundamental criteria may be regarded as more or less important by each person, so we acknowledge that there is no one perfect list of this sort. Nonetheless, as you read through our explanation of the criteria *we* opted to use here, and as you actually review the list of excellent companies profiled, we are confident that you will agree that the stocks featured here are certainly "top shelf."

To be eligible for our list of finalists, a company had to have at this writing a market capitalization of at least $1 billion. Market capitalization is the value of a corporation as represented by the market price of its stock. Only issued and outstanding stock may be used to determine market capitalization. The actual calculation used to determine market capitalization is easy enough: it is determined by simply multiplying the number of all issued and outstanding shares by the current market price of a share. Many sophisticated investors regard market capitalization as an important factor by which to consider investment in a particular company, as it gives a good picture of financial strength. Many investors are wary of purchasing the stock of a company that, although it may seem to offer the potential for a quality return, does not appear to have a solid financial foundation. We would wholeheartedly agree with that wariness, which is why we decided that our recommended companies should sport a minimum market capitalization of the previously mentioned $1 billion.

Additionally, we felt that a company that could achieve a solid record of growth and pay a solid dividend concurrently would be a welcome candidate. Although we would be the first to admit that the true "slam and jam" growth companies will rarely pay a dividend, we felt that the distribution of at least a 2% yield *along with* an annualized double-digit return would provide further testimony to the strength of a large growth prospect. Furthermore, the payment of significant dividends by companies with good growth records acts as sort of a backup in the event the stock has a less-than-scintillating performance year.

Our final criterion is the simplest to understand, but perhaps the most important. All of the companies featured here had to have a solid level of return in share price over several years. We decided to screen out all companies that could not achieve an annualized rate of return of at least 10% per year for the past ten years.

These, then, are our selection criteria: A minimum market capitalization of $1 billion, an annual yield of at least 2%, and an average annualized rate of return of at least 10% over the past ten years. Below is our final list in no particular order. We think you'll be pleased with what you see, and hope you have a lot of fun building a stock portfolio within your retirement plan. Good luck!

CHAPTER SIX

The 30 Best Growth Stocks to Own for Retirement

FEDERAL NATIONAL MORTGAGE ASSOCIATION
Individual Stock

INDUSTRY:	Thrift
ADDRESS:	3900 Wisconsin Avenue, N.W.
	Washington, D.C. 20016
PHONE NUMBER:	202-752-7115
P/E:	13
BETA:	1.60
% YIELD:	2.4
TICKER SYMBOL:	FNM
PRIMARY MARKET OF EXCHANGE:	New York Stock Exchange
RECENT PRICE:	109
10-YEAR AVERAGE ANNUAL RETURN:	30.5%
STANDARD & POOR'S RATING:	A-
CAPITALIZATION ($ Mil):	2,865.5

Brief Summary

Any casual observer of economic activity within the United
States has probably heard of the Federal National Mortgage
Association, perhaps by its commonly used nickname, "Fannie
Mae." Fannie Mae is, bar none, the largest source of residential
mortgage money in the country. Fannie Mae is involved with
each primary phase of mortgage exchange operations, from
their purchase to their sale, and even to their security. It is the
government's implicit guarantee of Fannie Mae debt (the guarantee by the government is not stated outright) that so
enhances the company's stature, but the bottom line determi-
nant of Fannie Mae's success, plain and simple, is the desire
for mortgage money on the part of consumers. As long as
interest rates cooperate, the demand will be significant and
Fannie Mae will prosper. For the foreseeable future, the economic climate is likely to remain such that the mortgage market will continue to improve and Fannie Mae investors will
remain happy with their choice as a result.

NORWEST CORP.
Individual Stock

INDUSTRY:	Banking
ADDRESS:	6th & Marquette
	Minneapolis, MN 55479
PHONE NUMBER:	612-667-1234
P/E:	13
BETA:	1.30
% YIELD:	2.5
TICKER SYMBOL:	NOB
PRIMARY MARKET OF EXCHANGE:	New York Stock Exchange
RECENT PRICE:	32
10-YEAR AVERAGE ANNUAL RETURN:	20.9%
STANDARD & POOR'S RATING:	A-
CAPITALIZATION ($Mil):	1,044.9

Brief Summary

Norwest Corp. is a banking powerhouse based in the mid-western United States. Norwest maintains over 600 bank offices in fifteen states, while its consumer finance arm, Norwest Financial, can be accessed in over 1,000 offices currently located in forty-six U.S. states and Canada. The well-known Norwest Mortgage, a famous name in the mortgage banking industry, can be found via nearly 700 offices located in all fifty states. Given Norwest's highly proactive approach to realizing sales and its obvious interest in expansion, prospective investors should find Norwest Corp. a welcome portfolio addition for the foreseeable future.

BANKAMERICA CORP.
Individual Stock

INDUSTRY:	Banking
ADDRESS:	Box 37000
	San Francisco, CA 94137
PHONE NUMBER:	812-232-1000
P/E:	11
BETA:	1.60
% YIELD:	2.7
TICKER SYMBOL:	BAC
PRIMARY MARKET OF EXCHANGE:	New York Stock Exchange
RECENT PRICE:	63
10-YEAR AVERAGE ANNUAL RETURN:	19.3%
STANDARD & POOR'S RATING:	B
CAPITALIZATION ($Mil):	2,300.4

Brief Summary

BankAmerica Corp. represents one of the most powerful banking operations in the United States. BankAmerica Corp. is the principal owner of Bank of America, at last count the second-largest bank in the country on the basis of assets. Like many financial institutions, BankAmerica has been in the process of diversifying its interests as well as realizing acquisitions. One of those acquisitions, Continental Bank, will be the recipient of much emphasis by BankAmerica in the near future, which should generate tangible, positive results for shareholders. Although further acquisition plans have been delayed for now, BankAmerica plans to channel its efforts into ensuring that all *current* operations are running as profitably as possible.

PHILIP MORRIS COMPANIES INC.
Individual Stock

INDUSTRY:	Tobacco
ADDRESS:	120 Park Avenue
	New York, NY 10017
PHONE NUMBER:	209-948-6870
P/E:	14
BETA:	1.20
% YIELD:	3.8
TICKER SYMBOL:	MO
PRIMARY MARKET OF EXCHANGE:	New York Stock Exchange
RECENT PRICE:	84
10-YEAR AVERAGE ANNUAL RETURN:	18.5%
STANDARD & POOR'S RATING:	A+
CAPITALIZATION ($Mil):	7,170.0

Brief Summary

Philip Morris is a company that should be no stranger at all to investors; Philip Morris Companies Inc. is a major player in the wide and varied consumer products industry, with interests in four major areas: tobacco, food, beverage alcohol, and financial services (including real estate). Even the most casual observer of the news is well aware of the antismoking climate that exists in the country right now, and one might think that, as a result, an investment in Philip Morris at this point would be a mistake. However, the growth of cigarette smoking *internationally* is quite pronounced, and Morris Companies' astute diversification into areas completely disconnected from the tobacco industry should provide excellent insulation from any problems that may arise in relation to the antismoking crusade taking place now in the United States.

SCHERING-PLOUGH CORP.
Individual Stock

INDUSTRY:	Pharmaceutical
ADDRESS:	One Giralda Farms
	Madison, NJ 07940
PHONE NUMBER:	201-822-7000
P/E:	20
BETA:	.95
% YIELD:	2.0
TICKER SYMBOL:	SGP
PRIMARY MARKET OF EXCHANGE:	New York Stock Exchange
RECENT PRICE:	51
10-YEAR AVERAGE ANNUAL RETURN:	18.0%
STANDARD & POOR'S RATING:	A+
CAPITALIZATION ($Mil):	1,939.2

Brief Summary

Schering-Plough Corp. may not be the most recognizable name in consumer circles, but it is in fact one of the largest manufacturers of prescription and over-the-counter drugs in the world. Schering-Plough is also a force in the biotechnology industry by way of its subsidiary DNAX Research Institute, and it is that aspect of its business that will help keep Schering a strong revenue-generator well into the future—but it is the company's straight-up consumer drug business that continues to be the most currently successful part of its business. Schering is the company that has brought such products as *Afrin, Scholl's,* and *Coppertone* to the marketplace, and the demand for its recently introduced antihistamine *Claritin* continues to be strong. Schering's strong product base, along with its push into emerging markets territories, should keep this company a winner for the long term.

MERCK & CO., INC.
Individual Stock

INDUSTRY:	Pharmaceutical
ADDRESS:	P.O. Box 100
	Whitehouse Station, NJ 08889-0100
PHONE NUMBER:	908-423-1000
P/E:	24
BETA:	1.10 %
YIELD:	2.0
TICKER SYMBOL:	MRK
PRIMARY MARKET OF EXCHANGE:	New York Stock Exchange
RECENT PRICE:	59
10-YEAR AVERAGE ANNUAL RETURN:	16.0
STANDARD & POOR'S RATING:	A+
CAPITALIZATION ($Mil):	7,234.7

Brief Summary

Merck & Co. sports one of the best-known names in American industry. Merck is one of the leading manufacturers of pharmaceutical products for both humans and animals, and has been responsible for bringing some of the most important health care products to market: *Mevacor* is a well-known drug used to help lower cholesterol, and *Pepcid*, an ulcer-fighting product that has seen a milder version of its brew heavily promoted recently as an over-the-counter solution to sour stomach, is also a cornerstone product from the folks at Merck. Recently, Merck has received approval to sell a drug called *Fosamax*, which is designed to fight osteoporosis in older women, so it's likely that Merck's winning ways will continue to benefit investors in the future as they have up to this point.

CAMPBELL SOUP COMPANY
Individual Stock

INDUSTRY:	Food
ADDRESS:	Campbell Place
	Camden, NJ 08103
PHONE NUMBER:	609-342-4800
P/E:	18
BETA:	.95
% YIELD:	2.3
TICKER SYMBOL:	CPB
PRIMARY MARKET OF EXCHANGE:	New York Stock Exchange
RECENT PRICE:	51
10-YEAR AVERAGE ANNUAL RETURN:	16.2%
STANDARD & POOR'S RATING:	B
CAPITALIZATION ($Mil):	1,288.5

Brief Summary

Campbell Soup Company is responsible for creating one of the most recognizable food products known to consumers, but in truth the Campbell Soup Company sells a lot more than just soup. Campbell Soup Company is the parent company of famous food manufacturers like Pepperidge Farm, Vlasic, Franco-American, and Prego, and the wide and varied tastes that these (and other) names cater to is an indication that Campbell is determined to be a force in the food manufacturing industry now and for years to come. Investors should expect the international expansion of this company (and its subsidiaries) in the near future to be the linchpin of continued growth for some years to come.

SARA LEE CORPORATION
Individual Stock

INDUSTRY:	Food
ADDRESS:	Three First National Plaza
	Chicago, IL 60602
PHONE NUMBER:	312-726-2600
P/E:	18
BETA:	1.00
% YIELD:	2.2
TICKER SYMBOL:	SLE
PRIMARY MARKET OF EXCHANGE:	New York Stock Exchange
RECENT PRICE:	29
10-YEAR AVERAGE ANNUAL RETURN:	16.2%
STANDARD & POOR'S RATING:	A
CAPITALIZATION ($Mil):	1,426.9

Brief Summary

The name Sara Lee is usually associated with those delicious, ready-made baked goods found in the frozen foods section of your supermarket, but in point of fact the Sara Lee Corporation is involved in a lot more than just the baking of cakes. Sara Lee maintains a sizable stake in so-called specialty meats, owning such big names as Hillshire Farms, Jimmy Dean, and Kahn's. Furthermore, Sara Lee's interests stretch well beyond the food industry, a fact to which the company's ownership of Hanes, L'eggs, and Playtex will attest. Although it may be tough for many people to think of Sara Lee as being intrinsically involved in the development of hosiery, investors will probably come to appreciate this unique diversification of consumer product bases for years to come.

COLGATE-PALMOLIVE COMPANY
Individual Stock

INDUSTRY:	Household Products
ADDRESS:	300 Park Avenue
	New York, NY 10022
	PHONE NUMBER: 212-310-2000
P/E:	17
BETA:	1.20
% YIELD:	2.5
TICKER SYMBOL:	CL
PRIMARY MARKET OF EXCHANGE:	New York Stock Exchange
RECENT PRICE:	67
10-YEAR AVERAGE ANNUAL RETURN:	16.5%
STANDARD & POOR'S RATING:	B+
CAPITALIZATION ($Mil):	985.6

Brief Summary

Colgate-Palmolive is indeed one company, but the names "Colgate" and "Palmolive" are easily recognized separately by consumers as the sources of many well-known personal and household products. In fact, Colgate-Palmolive Company is the home to many popular brand names of such products, including *Ajax, Fab,* and *Irish Spring.* Additionally, Colgate-Palmolive acquired the popular Mennen Company back in 1992, further strengthening its already notable status in the area of toiletry products. Many investors might be surprised to learn that the company has garnered well over 50% of its operating profit each year for the last several years from *outside* the United States—and that emphasis on foreign exposure, along with a renewed commitment to domestic success, should bolster Colgate-Palmolive over the next several years.

GENERAL MILLS, INC.
Individual Stock

INDUSTRY:	Food
ADDRESS:	P.O. Box 1113
	Minneapolis, MN 55440
PHONE NUMBER:	612-540-2444
P/E:	33
BETA:	N/A
% YIELD:	3.3
TICKER SYMBOL:	GIS
PRIMARY MARKET OF EXCHANGE:	New York Stock Exchange
RECENT PRICE:	57
10-YEAR AVERAGE ANNUAL RETURN:	15.7%
STANDARD & POOR'S RATING:	A
CAPITALIZATION ($Mil):	1,076.4

Brief Summary

General Mills has long been a mainstay in the food industry, and has remained so by virtue of its strong desire for intra-industry diversification. General Mills is the company that brings consumers popular breakfast fare like *Cheerios* and *Wheaties*, baking mixes bearing the renowned Betty Crocker name, and an assortment of other well-known food products. General Mills was even a force in the restaurant industry until very recently, but sold off those ventures to focus purely on its consumer foods interests. The shoring up of those interests, accomplished in part with help from a new international emphasis realized from joint ventures with Nestle and PepsiCo, is expected to provide investors with a healthy diet of returns for some time to come.

BROKEN HILL PROPRIETARY CO. LTD.
Individual Stock (American Depository Receipt)

INDUSTRY:	Oil & Gas/Mining
ADDRESS (U.S.):	550 California Street
	San Francisco, CA 94104
PHONE NUMBER:	415-774-2030
P/E:	15
BETA:	.70
% YIELD:	2.7
TICKER SYMBOL:	BHP
PRIMARY MARKET OF EXCHANGE:	New York Stock Exchange
RECENT PRICE:	54
10-YEAR AVERAGE ANNUAL RETURN:	14.8%
STANDARD & POOR'S RATING:	N/R
CAPITALIZATION ($Mil):	2,551.4

Brief Summary

Broken Hill Proprietary Co. Ltd. is one of a few companies making our list that is based outside of the United States. That fact should not be a source of any concern for you; the truth is, over 50% of all so-called "blue-chip" companies are located in countries other than the United States. Broken Hill is the largest company to be found in Australia, with its primary interests being those related to the production and refinement of oil, minerals, and similar resources. Additionally, Broken Hill maintains a near-40% interest in the famous Australian beer manufacturer Foster's Brewing Group. Profits from the company's mineral and steel operations have been the key to its success as of late, and it appears that newly realized opportunities in the Far East will help to continue that record into the future.

GLAXO WELLCOME PLC
Individual Stock (American Depository Receipt)

INDUSTRY:	Pharmaceutical
ADDRESS (U.S.):	499 Park Avenue
	New York, NY 10022
PHONE NUMBER:	212-308-5186
P/E:	18
BETA:	1.10
% YIELD:	4.5
TICKER SYMBOL:	GLX
PRIMARY MARKET OF EXCHANGE:	New York Stock Exchange
RECENT PRICE:	24
10-YEAR AVERAGE ANNUAL RETURN:	14.4%
STANDARD & POOR'S RATING:	N/R
CAPITALIZATION ($Mil):	3,706.7

Brief Summary

In the world of the supercompetitive and highly capitalized pharmaceutical companies, British-based Glaxo Wellcome is king. Glaxo is another excellent example of a foreign company that represents a fine long-term opportunity for U.S. investors. Glaxo has built a reputation for being very nonspecific in scope, meaning that the company has succeeded in developing a number of different drugs to relieve a vast array of medical symptoms and problems. Although it's likely that Glaxo may experience some shorter-term turbulence as a result of some slowing in the sales rates of its more currently popular entries (notably the antiviral agent *Zovirax*), the broad horizons embraced by Glaxo overall will serve as the catalyst for its continued good fortune well into the future.

UNILEVER PLC
Individual Stock (American Depository Receipt)

INDUSTRY:	Food
ADDRESS (U.S.):	390 Park Avenue
	New York, NY 10022
PHONE NUMBER:	212-906-3398
P/E:	15
BETA:	.70
% YIELD:	2.6
TICKER SYMBOL:	UL
PRIMARY MARKET OF EXCHANGE:	New York Stock Exchange
RECENT PRICE:	79
10-YEAR AVERAGE ANNUAL RETURN:	14.6%
STANDARD & POOR'S RATING:	NR
CAPITALIZATION ($Mil):	1,613.7

Brief Summary

The Unilever Group, a huge conglomeration of companies that produce and market a variety of consumer goods throughout the world, is made up of two different but not-so-separate holding companies: Unilever PLC, which is incorporated in Great Britain, and Unilever N.V., which is a corporation based in The Netherlands. Although the numerous holdings of the Unilever Group are, for the most part, divided between Unilever PLC and Unilever N.V., the companies are really one and the same for all practical purposes. The boards of directors of each company are the same, and the two entities are inextricably intertwined in ways too numerous to mention. Unilever, which is ultimately responsible for the development and marketing of products like ice cream, soup, margarine, tea, detergent, and a host of personal hygiene products, is a textbook example of a multinational corporation. Unilever is currently operational in eighty countries, and can buy and sell notable companies the way some people trade baseball cards. Unilever's continued success will depend largely on its aggressive approach to making additional smart acquisitions and on the degree to which it embraces the Pacific Rim and other emerging markets. So far, there's no sign that the corporate giant is going to let up in either area.

UNILEVER N.V.
Individual Stock

INDUSTRY:	Food
ADDRESS:	390 Park Avenue
	New York, NY 10022
PHONE NUMBER:	212-906-3398
P/E:	15
BETA:	.80
% YIELD:	2.9
TICKER SYMBOL:	UN
PRIMARY MARKET OF EXCHANGE:	New York Stock Exchange
RECENT PRICE:	131
10-YEAR AVERAGE ANNUAL RETURN:	13.5%
STANDARD & POOR'S RATING:	A
CAPITALIZATION ($Mil):	2,092.5

Brief Summary
See Unilever PLC.

CPC INTERNATIONAL, INC.
Individual Stock

INDUSTRY:	Food
ADDRESS:	International Plaza
	Englewood Cliffs, NJ 07632
PHONE NUMBER:	201-894-4000
P/E:	20
BETA:	1.00
% YIELD:	2.0
TICKER SYMBOL:	CPC
PRIMARY MARKET OF EXCHANGE:	New York Stock Exchange
RECENT PRICE:	69
10-YEAR AVERAGE ANNUAL RETURN:	14.1%
STANDARD & POOR'S RATING:	A+
CAPITALIZATION ($Mil):	1,002.0

Brief Summary

CPC International is a top-level producer of food products. Although the company is responsible for bringing to market some consumer foods whose names you are probably familiar with (*Skippy* peanut butter and *Golden Griddle* pancakes, to name just two), it has chosen to specialize in the area of refined corn products. *Mazola* corn oil and margarine and *Karo* corn syrup are examples of two such products that CPC International makes available to the public, and there are others. Nonetheless, CPC International's fortunes, like those of *any* company aspiring to maintain its truly big-time status, will depend on the totality of the results it realizes on many different fronts. The company has recently acquired a company that does a thriving business in the "instant hot snacks" arena over in Europe, and CPC recently landed a deal that will give it the bakery portion of Kraft Foods. Such aggressive opportunity-seeking on the part of CPC International can only bode well for investors in the coming years.

DE BEERS CONSOLIDATED MINES LIMITED
Individual Stock

INDUSTRY:	Mining
ADDRESS:	36 Stockdale Street
	Kimberley 8300
	South Africa
P/E:	17
BETA:	.95
% YIELD:	2.9
TICKER SYMBOL:	DBRSY
PRIMARY MARKET OF EXCHANGE:	NASDAQ Small Capitalization
RECENT PRICE:	28
10-YEAR AVERAGE ANNUAL RETURN:	13.6%
STANDARD & POOR'S RATING:	N/R
CAPITALIZATION ($Mil):	1,069.1

Brief Summary

Although De Beers is a legendary name in the diamond industry, there's lots more going on at the company besides diamond production. De Beers maintains strong interests in such metals as copper, platinum, and gold, and is involved as well in other areas such as general industry and real estate. However, it is De Beers' dominance of the diamond market that has propelled it to its current stature; the company has ownership, to one degree or another, of a plethora of diamond mines in the diamond-rich country of South Africa, and there doesn't appear to be another diamond producer in the Western world that can come close to De Beers in terms of industry dominance. Although demand for diamonds fell off a bit recently with the macroeconomic turmoil evidenced in the normally diamond-hungry Japan and the United States, the slow but sure recoveries each of those economies is currently experiencing will surely increase demand for the gems, and, as a result, investor profits, over the next several years.

KIMBERLY-CLARK CORPORATION
Individual Stock

INDUSTRY:	Household Products
ADDRESS:	P.O. Box 619100
	Dallas, TX 75261-9100
PHONE NUMBER:	214-830-1200
P/E:	21
BETA:	1.10
% YIELD:	2.6
TICKER SYMBOL:	KMB
PRIMARY MARKET OF EXCHANGE:	New York Stock Exchange
RECENT PRICE:	67
10-YEAR AVERAGE ANNUAL RETURN:	12.7%
STANDARD & POOR'S RATING:	A+
CAPITALIZATION ($Mil):	1,075.8

Brief Summary

Kimberly-Clark is the soft-sounding name of a company that deals in the lion's share of personal products that have softness as one of their hallmarks. Kimberly-Clark manufactures facial tissues, bathroom tissues, paper towels, disposable diapers, and similar items under a variety of popular brand names that include *Kleenex* and *Huggies.* Kimberly-Clark is currently in the midst of a massive cost-cutting/streamlining trend, and the resulting "leanness and meanness" can only help the company's bottom line. Kimberly-Clark's chief rival in the same personal hygiene products market is Procter & Gamble. Actually, Procter & Gamble has been more the dominant force in these businesses than a true rival; however, Kimberly-Clark's current cost-cutting measures, combined with a possible merger with Scott Paper (with K-C emerging as the survivor), should give investors plenty to crow about in the coming years.

GENERAL ELECTRIC CO.
Individual Stock

INDUSTRY:	Electrical Equipment
ADDRESS:	3135 Easton Turnpike
	Fairfield, CT 06431
PHONE NUMBER:	203-373-2211
P/E:	17
BETA:	1.10
% YIELD:	2.5
TICKER SYMBOL:	GE
PRIMARY MARKET OF EXCHANGE:	New York Stock Exchange
RECENT PRICE:	62
10-YEAR AVERAGE ANNUAL RETURN:	12.5%
STANDARD & POOR'S RATING:	A+
CAPITALIZATION ($Mil):	10,649.4

Brief Summary

General Electric is truly nothing less than one of the largest industrial companies in the world. The name General Electric, including the oft-used initials "GE," is one of the most recognizable in the consumer world. General Electric Company is actually a conglomeration of twelve different businesses, including aircraft engines, broadcasting, plastics, power generation, and transportation, to name five. One of the most interesting aspects of a company as large and as widely diversified as General Electric is that even if some of its interests falter due to economic slowdown (or for *any* reason, really), the overall company can still be successful on the strength of its other businesses. For investors, that fact alone should make General Electric stock a top-notch consideration at almost any time.

WARNER-LAMBERT COMPANY
Individual Stock

INDUSTRY:	Pharmaceuticals/Food (Confections)
ADDRESS:	201 Tabor Rd.
	Morris Plains, NJ 07950-2693
PHONE NUMBER:	201-540-2000
P/E:	17
BETA:	1.05
% YIELD:	2.7
TICKER SYMBOL:	WLA
PRIMARY MARKET OF EXCHANGE:	New York Stock Exchange
RECENT PRICE:	89
10-YEAR AVERAGE ANNUAL RETURN:	12.6%
STANDARD & POOR'S RATING:	A-
CAPITALIZATION ($Mil):	1,218.4

Brief Summary

Warner-Lambert is another company that has brought a variety of brand name consumer products to the fore. Warner's involvement in the development and sales of personal products is the reason we can enjoy the benefits of *Listerine, Benadryl,* and the numerous products bearing the *Schick* name, to mention just a few of Warner's offerings. Warner-Lambert is also the parent to a number of well-known gum and mint offspring like *Chiclets, Dentyne, Trident,* and *Certs.* However, as with any company that has pharmaceutical development as a part of its business, it is the drugs produced by Warner-Lambert which represent the most reliable source of revenue over the long term. Warner-Lambert is involved with Glaxo in bringing *Zantac* to the over-the-counter market as an antacid, and the company will also enjoy a significant measure of revenue from pharmaceutical offerings that are designed to treat epilepsy and Alzheimer's. For investors, then, Warner-Lambert represents a terrific haven for long-term, growth-minded monies.

SBC COMMUNICATIONS, INC.
Individual Stock

INDUSTRY:	Telecommunications
ADDRESS:	175 E. Houston
	P.O. Box 2933
	San Antonio, TX 78299
PHONE NUMBER:	210-351-2044
P/E:	19
BETA:	.85
% YIELD:	2.9
TICKER SYMBOL:	SBC
PRIMARY MARKET OF EXCHANGE:	New York Stock Exchange
RECENT PRICE:	54
10-YEAR AVERAGE ANNUAL RETURN:	12.4%
STANDARD & POOR'S RATING:	A
CAPITALIZATION ($Mil):	3,373.0

Brief Summary

SBC Communications, Inc., is one of seven children left on their own by the breakup of telecommunications giant AT&T. SBC Communications is, specifically, a holding company that provides telecommunications services to five states located in Middle America: Arkansas, Kansas, Missouri, Oklahoma, and Texas. In a nutshell, SBC prospects are looking good primarily because of bold deregulation moves within the telecommunications industry, both already taken and soon-to-be taken by state governments, as well as by the federal government. The best news for the company (and for investors) comes out of Texas (where SBC maintains almost 60% of its access lines): Governor Bush recently signed into law a bill that will dramatically improve the company's ability to compete with the big boys, in part by permitting SBC to determine its rates by way of a different, more beneficial (to the company) formula.

BANC ONE CORPORATION
Individual Stock

INDUSTRY:	Banking
ADDRESS:	100 E. Broad St.
	Columbus, OH 43271
PHONE NUMBER:	614-248-5944
P/E:	16
BETA:	1.40
% YIELD:	3.4
TICKER SYMBOL:	ONE
PRIMARY MARKET OF EXCHANGE:	New York Stock Exchange
RECENT PRICE:	37
10-YEAR AVERAGE ANNUAL RETURN:	12.1%
STANDARD & POOR'S RATING:	A+
CAPITALIZATION ($Mil):	1,479.6

Brief Summary

Banc One Corporation is one of the largest banking institutions in the country, and it is seeking to become even larger. Recently, Banc One agreed to terms regarding its prospective purchase of Premier Bancorp, a banking powerhouse within the state of Louisiana. Banc One Corporation has successfully built a small empire by staying away from the regions of the country already dominated by financial services giants and by instead centering its activity in states like West Virginia, Kentucky, Utah, and Arizona, to name just a few. Although an immediate surge in share price is unlikely, due primarily to the stagnant economic recovery taking place within the U.S. currently, Banc One's attention to the improvement of current operations as well as to the acquisition of new banking institutions only bodes well for investors in this company in the future.

ROYAL DUTCH PETROLEUM
Individual Stock

INDUSTRY:	Petroleum
ADDRESS:	30 Carel Van Bylandtlaan
	2596 HR The Hague
	The Netherlands
PHONE NUMBER (U.S.):	212-261-5660
P/E:	14
BETA:	.70
% YIELD:	3.8
TICKER SYMBOL:	RD
PRIMARY MARKET OF EXCHANGE:	New York Stock Exchange
RECENT PRICE:	123
10-YEAR AVERAGE ANNUAL RETURN:	11.5%
STANDARD & POOR'S RATING:	A
CAPITALIZATION ($Mil):	6694.0

Brief Summary

Royal Dutch Petroleum is actually one half of an interesting corporate entity: The Royal Dutch/Shell Transport Group. Royal Dutch/Shell is the largest international oil company in the world, a company structured in the form of a union of two separate parent holding companies: the Royal Dutch Petroleum Company, incorporated in The Netherlands, and the Shell Transport and Trading Company, P.L.C., incorporated in Great Britain. Royal Dutch owns 60% of the assets of the Group, while Shell owns the remaining 40%. The Group, and therefore both holding companies, should continue their winning ways, due in no small way to aggressive marketing efforts being undertaken in the Pacific Rim and Eastern Europe, and to aggressive production efforts being made in Romania and Russia. Both parent holding companies of the Group should make solid investments for those seeking an energy play in the next several years.

J. C. PENNEY COMPANY
Individual Stock

INDUSTRY:	Retail
ADDRESS:	14841 North Dallas Parkway
	P.O. Box 659000
	Dallas, TX 75265-9000
PHONE NUMBER:	214-591-1000
P/E:	12
BETA:	1.10
% YIELD:	3.8
TICKER SYMBOL:	JCP
PRIMARY MARKET OF EXCHANGE:	New York Stock Exchange
RECENT PRICE:	48
10-YEAR AVERAGE ANNUAL RETURN:	11.1%
STANDARD & POOR'S RATING:	A-
CAPITALIZATION ($Mil):	1,062.7

Brief Summary

J. C. Penney is a name that is about as old and as respected as any you'll find in the annals of American commerce. Although recent U.S. economic history has not been too kind to retailers like Penney, the company's longevity and dedication to finding the right formula have been able to keep the department store and catalog giant among the top five U.S. retailers (on the basis of size). In order to stay attractive within the changing consumer climate, Penney has stressed more private-label brands and has sought to be more competitive for the "average" consumer's dollar. It should not be lost on investors, either, that Penney's financial strength is excellent, an always-important factor and one that carries even more significance in this period of economic uncertainty.

SHELL TRANSPORT
Individual Stock (American Depository Receipt)

INDUSTRY:	Petroleum
ADDRESS (U.S.):	30 Carel Van Bylandtlaan
	2596 HR The Hague
	The Netherlands
PHONE NUMBER (U.S.):	212-261-5660
P/E:	16
BETA:	.75
% YIELD:	4.0
TICKER SYMBOL:	SC
PRIMARY MARKET OF EXCHANGE:	New York Stock Exchange
RECENT PRICE:	71
10-YEAR AVERAGE ANNUAL RETURN:	10.8%
STANDARD & POOR'S RATING:	A-
CAPITALIZATION ($Mil):	3,997.8

Brief Summary
See Royal Dutch Petroleum.

MOBIL CORP.
Individual Stock

INDUSTRY:	Petroleum
ADDRESS:	3225 Gallows Rd.
	Fairfax, VA 22037
	Oshkosh, WI 54903
PHONE NUMBER:	703-846-3000
P/E:	22
BETA:	.70
% YIELD:	3.4
TICKER SYMBOL:	MOB
PRIMARY MARKET OF EXCHANGE:	New York Stock Exchange
RECENT PRICE:	99
10-YEAR AVERAGE ANNUAL RETURN:	10.7%
STANDARD & POOR'S RATING:	B+
CAPITALIZATION ($Mil):	3,951.8

Brief Summary

Is there anyone living in modern society who has not heard of Mobil Corp.? Mobil Corp. is one of the largest petroleum companies in the world. Many consumers are familiar with the combination gas station/mini mart retail stores that bear Mobil's name, and it's likely that if you either drive a car or ride as a regular passenger in one, you've visited and helped fill the coffers of a Mobil station. The number of Mobil retail outlets in operation currently is nearly 20,000, and the company produced well over 800,000 barrels of oil a day in 1994. What does the future hold? Worldwide oil and gas production is expected to rise significantly at Mobil over the next several years, thanks to new and/or accelerated operations in varied locations like Qatar, Indonesia, and the coast of Canada. Investors should take note.

SPRINT CORPORATION
Individual Stock

INDUSTRY:	Telecommunications
ADDRESS:	P.O. Box 11315
	Plaza Station
	Kansas City, MO 64112
PHONE NUMBER:	913-624-3000
P/E:	14
BETA:	1.00
% YIELD:	2.8
TICKER SYMBOL:	FON
PRIMARY MARKET OF EXCHANGE:	New York Stock Exchange
RECENT PRICE:	35
1-YEAR RETURN:	10.8%
STANDARD & POOR'S RATING:	B
CAPITALIZATION ($Mil):	1,206.5

Brief Summary

Sprint Corporation is a huge operator in the independent telephone system industry, and its current size is due in no small measure to the 1993 merger with Centel. Sprint is a comprehensive provider of telecommunications services, intrinsically involved in the local and long distance business and also a major player in the cellular phone industry. What does the future hold for Sprint? The company is actively seeking to bring to fruition a plan with overseas-based telecommunications services providers to create a truly worldwide telecommunications service from which all desired associated services could be obtained by individuals and corporations. Success of this venture, in one form or another, will surely provide investors with glorious rewards well into the next century.

MAY DEPARTMENT STORES COMPANY
Individual Stock

INDUSTRY:	Retail
ADDRESS:	611 Olive Street
	St. Louis, MO 63101
PHONE NUMBER:	314-342-6300
P/E:	14
BETA:	1.30
% YIELD:	2.4
TICKER SYMBOL:	MA
PRIMARY MARKET OF EXCHANGE:	New York Stock Exchange
RECENT PRICE:	43
10-YEAR AVERAGE ANNUAL RETURN:	10.7%
STANDARD & POOR'S RATING:	A+
CAPITALIZATION ($Mil):	1,072.3

Brief Summary

May Department Stores Company is actually the parent company to a host of well-known retailers with names like Lord & Taylor, Filene's, and Robinsons-May. May Department Stores is also the operator of Payless Shoe Source outlets, the largest self-service shoe store chain in the country. The outlook for May is excellent, chiefly because the company is so obviously acquisition-oriented. This aggressive approach to increasing its store base bodes well for the future, and the company is also in the process of setting up a separate Payless operation catering exclusively to children's footwear needs. As long as May maintains a proactive posture in the acquisition and rejuvenation of popular regional department stores like the recently obtained Wanamaker (based in Philadelphia), company revenues should continue to be excellent.

EMERSON ELECTRIC CO.
Individual Stock

INDUSTRY:	Electrical Equipment
ADDRESS:	8000 West Florissant Ave.
	St. Louis, MO 63136
PHONE NUMBER:	314-553-2000
P/E:	17
BETA:	1.10
% YIELD:	2.4
TICKER SYMBOL:	EMR
PRIMARY MARKET OF EXCHANGE:	New York Stock Exchange
RECENT PRICE:	70
10-YEAR AVERAGE ANNUAL RETURN:	10.4%
STANDARD & POOR'S RATING:	A+
CAPITALIZATION ($Mil):	1,558.2

Brief Summary

Emerson Electric Co. may not be a name that is immediately recognizable to many consumers, but the fact is that Emerson Electric is quite well known within industrial sectors. Emerson is in the business of manufacturing a variety of electrical and electronic products, from appliance components to computer support products to industrial motors, and everything in between. Like any smart company seeking to increase profit opportunities into the next century, Emerson has undertaken a number of proactive steps to enhance its exposure, including the development of new products and expansion into foreign markets. Newly accessible Eastern Europe has become a fresh source of low-cost manufacturing to the company, and the growth of emerging markets in the Far East will also provide a wealth of opportunity for the company and its investors for some time to come.

AT&T CORP.
Individual Stock

INDUSTRY:	Telecommunications
ADDRESS:	32 Avenue of the Americas
	New York, NY 10013-2412
PHONE NUMBER:	212-387-5400
P/E:	20
BETA:	.85
% YIELD:	2.0
TICKER SYMBOL:	T
PRIMARY MARKET OF EXCHANGE:	New York Stock Exchange
RECENT PRICE:	63
10-YEAR AVERAGE ANNUAL RETURN:	10.2%
STANDARD & POOR'S RATING:	A-
CAPITALIZATION ($Mil):	10,105.8

Brief Summary

AT&T is a company that has done some evolving over the years to get to its present form. Most important, the AT&T we all know and love today was created by the famous (or infamous, depending on your perspective) court-ordered decimation of the Bell System in the early eighties. The current version of AT&T received about one quarter of the former entity's assets at the time of the breakup, and has done quite well with them since. AT&T is clearly interested in staying on the cutting edge of the so-called "global information" trend, and such interest is evidenced by a variety of steps taken by the telecommunications giant, including the recent acquisition of a popular cellular company, a move into the financial services industry, and a commitment to seeing their voice/data/video technology dreams become a reality. It's full speed ahead for AT&T into the year 2000.

MONSANTO COMPANY
Individual Stock

INDUSTRY:	Chemical
ADDRESS:	800 North Lindbergh Boulevard
	St. Louis, MO 63167
PHONE NUMBER:	314-694-1000
P/E:	17
BETA:	1.15
% YIELD:	2.6
TICKER SYMBOL:	MTC
PRIMARY MARKET OF EXCHANGE:	New York Stock Exchange
RECENT PRICE:	100
10-YEAR AVERAGE ANNUAL RETURN:	10.2%
STANDARD & POOR'S RATING:	A-
CAPITALIZATION ($Mil):	1,135.4

Brief Summary

Monsanto Company is nothing short of a comprehensive chemical-manufacturing giant—comprehensive in that Monsanto is in the business of producing a huge variety of products, including herbicides, fibers, plastics, detergents, pharmaceuticals, and a number of other chemically based offerings. One of the best pieces of news to come down the pike recently for Monsanto is that more and more professional farmers are turning to its well-known *Roundup* herbicide for the purpose of killing weeds and other unwanted growths in their fields. Beyond that, Monsanto is in the process of developing a host of other agricultural products that will help the company increase its hold on that marketplace for many years to come.

CHAPTER SEVEN
Why Annuities Are Excellent Retirement Vehicles

We have chosen to include in this book a selection of the five best variable annuities you can purchase to help you achieve your retirement goals. Before we actually profile the particular variable annuities we like best, let's spend some time talking about annuities in general. You may recall that we touched on them briefly in Chapter 1, but it is appropriate to discuss them again, and more fully, at this time.

The idea behind an annuity of *any* type is that you make some sort of arrangement whereby you receive a regularly distributed payout. Annuities are usually thought of in connection with retirement, in an arrangement whereby the retired person (the "annuitant") receives a monthly distribution from an insurance company after having invested money in a product offered by the company. For the longest time, annuities came in just one form—fixed. With a *fixed annuity,* the investor places his or her money into a vehicle that is similar to a bank CD and that offers rates that are only slightly more competitive. It wasn't too long, however, before someone came up with the bright idea of creating an annuity that offered

investors a great deal more growth potential than that which
existed with the fixed product. That someone was economist
William Greenough, whose work on behalf of the Teachers
Insurance and Annuity Association brought about the first variable products in 1952. With the *variable* annuity, the investor
places his money into any number of the *mutual funds* offered
by the insurance company. In either case, once the investor
"annuitizes" the account, he then receives a payout that is
based on its value at annuitization, as well as on the precise
type of payout option selected. You may even withdraw the
entire amount of the account before you actually annuitize,
which can be a wise move considering that the payout sched-
ules initiated by annuitization will be weighted in favor of the
insurance companies.

The chief advantage to investing in an annuity is, of
course, the benefits associated with tax-deferred growth. In
that regard annuities are very similar to other types of retirement plan "umbrellas" like IRAs, 401(k)s, and so on, except
that because annuities are purchased with after-tax dollars, the
contributions *to* them are not tax-deductible. However, you'll
find that it is possible to house an annuity within a retirement
plan that offers tax-deductible benefits, but beware: you do not
enjoy any sort of *double* tax deferral by placing an already tax-
deferred account inside of another, but that's not even the *most*
significant disadvantage to structuring an annuity within an
IRA or other similarly tax-preferred plan. The most significant
disadvantage, in our opinion, lies in the fact that annuities, on
the whole, are more expensive and offer fewer investment
options than other types of vehicles. Therefore, if you make
your annuity an IRA, you are now making your IRA more
expensive and more inflexible than it should be. Many brokers,
lured by the higher commissions annuities can typically pay,
will sometimes skillfully talk investors into buying annuities
for their IRAs. Resist doing so. The best way to utilize an
annuity in conjunction with another "umbrella" like an IRA is

to keep the two separate, placing money into the annuity only when you've "maxed out" your other plan's annual contribution limits (annuities have no such limits). There are just too many excellent no-load options available for IRAs for you to seriously consider an annuity for yours.

FIXED VERSUS VARIABLE ANNUITIES

We can tell you right off the bat that we don't think much of fixed annuities for long-term investors. The reason for that is no different from the reason we don't think very much of money markets or bank CDs for long-term players: poor total return. We're not saying that investors with a *shorter* time frame or those who consider themselves to be very conservative should avoid them (they are, after all, tax deferred), but if you *do* wish to consider a fixed annuity for your portfolio, pay close attention to the insurance company's ratings. Insurance companies can be rated by any of several independent ratings services (A. M. Best and Moody's are two of the better-known services), and these ratings pertain chiefly to the financial stability and soundness of the companies. The reason this is important is probably obvious, but let's take this opportunity to relate it, as well as to show why a company's ratings should be less of a concern for *variable* annuity investors.

When you place your money in a fixed annuity, that investment becomes part of the assets of the life insurance company itself. Accordingly, if the insurance company is beset with some kind of financial trouble, it can have a direct effect on the safety of your investment. If that trouble is serious enough, it could potentially result in the loss of a portion, or perhaps all, of your money. Do not, then, simply be a "yield-chaser." Sure, shop for the most competitive yield you can find, but not if it means rejecting an insurance company that sports an outstanding rating.

When you place your money in a *variable* annuity, the money must be kept separate from the insurance company's assets. Remember, variable annuity subaccounts are made up of mutual funds, so there's no reason for the money to be infused into the insurance company anyway. Do not miss the importance of this distinction; if the sponsoring insurance company of a variable annuity should encounter financial difficulty, investors will not have to fear that they will lose their money, although they may have to wait a bit in order to retrieve their investment should trouble actually strike. What should you take from this? Just that while it would be nice for the sponsoring insurance company to have as high a rating as possible, you should not be *overly* concerned with the rating, at least not if it causes you to reject an annuity that offers a solid selection of mutual funds.

ARE ANNUITIES REALLY INSURANCE PRODUCTS AT ALL?

A frequent observation made by those who become familiar with annuities is, "These don't seem to have a lot to do with insurance, do they?" The reason for that thinking is not difficult to understand; annuities, both fixed and variable, resemble investments a lot more than they do traditional insurance products that pay a benefit as the result of an obvious and distinct loss. On closer inspection, though, the broad mechanism of an annuity *does* fit into the classic definition of insurance, since your invested dollars (called premiums) are paid to the insurance company so that the insurance company will one day be able to pay you a benefit designed to support you during the years you are no longer working. Your "loss" in this case is a loss of income. However, others have noticed that the line between *insurance product* and *investment product* has become somewhat blurred over the years, especially with the advent of the variable product in which the premiums are invested in mutual funds and kept separate from the assets of the insurance company altogether. Accordingly, a challenge to the insurance industry was made that resulted in a Supreme Court ruling that annuities are actually investment products and thus can be sold by other kinds of financial institutions (such as banks). For the time being, however, annuities are still sold primarily by insurance companies, and probably will be for the foreseeable future.

HOW WE PICKED THE ANNUITIES FOR THIS BOOK

First of all, we only consider variable annuities. We've already spoken about our relative distaste for the fixed version, and besides, their less-complicated structure makes it fairly easy for anyone to consider them on the basis of two easy-to-find pieces of data: yield (which always changes, anyway) and the rating of the insurer. Sifting through variable annuities, however, is considerably more challenging. The first order of business is to decide which features of a variable annuity are important.

There are publications in existence that rate annuities by actually rating all of the different subaccounts (mutual funds) available from all of the different variable annuities out there on the basis of fund objective. You end up looking at a list of best growth funds, best bond funds, best international funds, and so on, which is fine, except that you may well have to purchase four or five different annuities in order to have access to the various top annuity mutual funds (also called "subaccounts") available. That's crazy. Our philosophy is different. It was our intent to screen each annuity in its entirety and make evaluations on the basis of what each whole annuity offers, and that's just what we did. Remember, it is generally understood that annuities are more limited in scope to begin with, which is one of the reasons we tell you to maximize your other retirement plans *before* you seek to purchase an annuity.

In our opinion, there are three features of a variable annuity that exceed all others in terms of importance. These are: number of mutual fund options available, range of options available, and quality of management available. We do not believe that size of the surrender charge is significant, because if you pick an annuity wisely you should never have to leave it for another. We do not rate the annuity on the basis of the insurance company's rating, because the rating is not terribly relevant to the variable product. We do not even gauge the annuities on the basis of sub-account performance, for the reason outlined above. It is our belief that, when it comes to annuities, if the quality of fund management is high enough, and the number and range of fund options available is sizable, long-term performance will take care of itself.

Let's talk more about the three categories we *do* feel are relevant. First of all, we believe it's important for an annuity to provide investors with a large number of mutual funds from which to choose. Even if the *range* of options (we'll talk more about that in a minute) is not wide, we think that, given the choice, it's always better to have two different growth funds (taking "different" to mean different advisory companies) to choose from than to have just one growth fund. Second, we also believe that it's important for a variable annuity to provide investors with a wide range of fund options. By range of options, we are referring to the various broad fund type categories of mutual fund, such as growth, growth and income, international stock, corporate bond, and so on; the greater the range, the more competitive the annuity. The final category we examined had to do with the quality of the fund management. Basically, we asked the question, "Are the mutual funds within a given annuity managed by an unknown or mediocre advisory group, or are they managed by one of the better-known and performance-proven money management firms in the industry?" We do not look at individual portfolio managers here, but rather at the firms for which they work. We will be the first to admit that there is more room for subjectivity in this last category, and that not everyone would necessarily agree with our perception of which firm is a good money manager and which is a not-so-good money manager. However, we believe that our many collective years of experience managing money for clients in and out of great numbers of mutual funds has given us a large amount of insight regarding this subject, as well as a commensurate degree of credibility.

You should also be advised that each annuity we examined was evaluated on the basis of these three pieces of criteria *together*. This means that if an annuity has both a large number and very wide range of fund options, but lacks a high-quality advisory firm to *guide* those funds, it would not make our list of finalists. Similarly, if a variable annuity boasts great management, but offers only four funds, it too would not show up on our list.

In addition to the three ratings categories mentioned, the annuity profiles that follow include added information such as address, phone number, and availability of certain key features in order to help you define your choices.

CHAPTER EIGHT

The 5 Best Annuities to Own for Retirement

KEYPORT PREFERRED ADVISOR
Variable Annuity

INSURANCE COMPANY:	Keyport Life Insurance Company
INSURANCE COMPANY RATINGS:	A+ (A.M. Best)
	AA- (Standard & Poor's)
ADDRESS:	125 High Street
	Boston, MA 02110-2712
NUMBER OF SUBACCOUNT OPTIONS:	★ ★ ★ ★
RANGE OF SUBACCOUNT OPTIONS:	★ ★ ★ ★ ★
QUALITY OF SUBACCOUNT MANAGEMENT:	★ ★ ★ ★ ★
TELEPHONE EXCHANGES:	Yes
NUMBER OF EXCHANGES ALLOWED PER YEAR:	12
MINIMUM INITIAL INVESTMENT:	$5,000
SALES CHARGES:	Declining seven-year surrender charge, beginning at 7%
DOLLAR COST AVERAGING:	Yes
SYSTEMATIC WITHDRAWAL PLAN:	Yes
GUARANTEED DEATH BENEFIT:	Yes; minimum of total purchase payments
ACCOUNT STATEMENTS:	Issued quarterly
AVAILABILITY:	All states except New York
MAXIMUM ISSUE AGE:	80
TELEPHONE NUMBER:	800-367-3653

Summary

Keyport Preferred Advisor emerged from our screening process as one of the clearly-superior variable annuity options out there today. Preferred Advisor currently makes eleven different mutual fund subaccounts available to retirement investors (excluding fixed accounts), which is not the highest number you'll see here but is significant nonetheless. Furthermore, the range of subaccount options is excellent. Investors may choose from an array of funds that includes several seeking long-term growth, a mortgage-backed fund, an S&P 500 index fund, a high-yield bond fund, an international stock fund, and a utilities fund, as well as a new addition to the portfolio that specializes in long-term growth of Asian-based securities. Perhaps most impressively, Keyport Preferred Advisor offers to investors the chance to have their money managed by Stein Roe & Farnham, Inc., of the renowned SteinRoe mutual funds and one of the most prestigious money management firms to be found anywhere. Specifically, the Stein Roe-managed funds within this annuity are the Capital Appreciation Fund, the Managed Growth Stock Fund, the Managed Assets Fund, the Mortgage Securities Income Fund, and the Cash Income Fund. The remaining subaccounts within the Preferred Advisors annuity are managed by the highly respected Colonial Management Associates, Inc., which also has as one of its main functions the supervision of the mutual funds of the Colonial family.

While prospective annuity investors will likely find that each annuity may have various features designed to make it more competitive, all serious variable annuity seekers would do well to give Keyport a close examination.

AMERICAN SKANDIA ADVISORS PLAN II
Variable Annuity

INSURANCE COMPANY:	American Skandia Life Assurance Corporation
INSURANCE COMPANY RATINGS:	A- (A.M. Best)
	BBB+ (Standard & Poor's)
ADDRESS:	One Corporate Drive
	Shelton, CT 06484-0883
NUMBER OF SUBACCOUNT OPTIONS:	★ ★ ★ ★ ★
RANGE OF SUBACCOUNT OPTIONS:	★ ★ ★ ★ ★
QUALITY OF SUBACCOUNT MANAGEMENT:	★ ★ ★ ★ ★
TELEPHONE EXCHANGES:	Yes
NUMBER OF EXCHANGES ALLOWED PER YEAR:	12 free; $10 per switch after 12
MINIMUM INITIAL INVESTMENT:	$1,000
SALES CHARGES:	Declining seven-year surrender charge, beginning at 7.5%
DOLLAR COST AVERAGING:	Yes ($10,000 min. account value required)
SYSTEMATIC WITHDRAWAL PLAN:	Yes
GUARANTEED DEATH BENEFIT:	Yes; minimum of total purchase payments
ACCOUNT STATEMENTS:	Quarterly
AVAILABILITY:	All states except New York
MAXIMUM ISSUE AGE:	No maximum age restriction except where required by law
TELEPHONE NUMBER:	800-752-6342

Summary

As the star ratings should indicate, American Skandia Advisors Plan II may be one of the very best variable annuities available today, if not *the* best. Currently, Advisors Plan sports a whopping twenty-two investment options, and in fact it appears that this number may continue to grow. As you might imagine, with twenty-two different subaccounts, it is difficult for any prospective investor to complain about a lack of choice. Beyond the sheer numbers, the *variety* of funds covered is equally impressive. There are a plethora of growth funds from which to choose, as well as a utility fund, a high-yield bond fund, an international bond fund, a natural resources fund, a total return bond fund, and several other equity income and asset allocation offerings. Both the number of choices and their breadth would seem to make this annuity unbeatable on this basis alone, but would you believe it gets better? American Skandia has seen fit to tap a number of the most respected money managers available today for their expertise in piloting many of these funds. In fact, a quick look at the list of available managers reads like a Most Wanted list of mutual fund companies and portfolio captains: Berger Associates, Inc.; Founders Asset Management, Inc.; Fred Alger Management, Inc.; Janus Capital Corporation; and T. Rowe Price Associates, Inc., to name just five of the fourteen different money management firms available for you to choose from within this wonderful variable product.

American Skandia should be applauded for offering retirement investors such a progressive annuity package, although we suspect that the copious number of investors who will undoubtedly flock to this product in the coming years will be all the applause they're looking for.

THE BEST OF AMERICA IV
Variable Annuity

INSURANCE COMPANY:	Nationwide Life Insurance Company
INSURANCE COMPANY RATINGS:	A+ (A.M. Best)
	AAA (Standard & Poor's)
ADDRESS:	P.O. Box 16609
	Columbus, OH 43216-6609
NUMBER OF SUBACCOUNT OPTIONS:	★ ★ ★ ★ ★
RANGE OF SUBACCOUNT OPTIONS:	★ ★ ★ ★ ★
QUALITY OF SUBACCOUNT MANAGEMENT:	★ ★ ★ ★ ★
TELEPHONE EXCHANGES:	Yes
NUMBER OF EXCHANGES ALLOWED PER YEAR:	One exchange allowed each day
MINIMUM INITIAL INVESTMENT:	None
SALES CHARGES:	Declining seven-year surrender charge, beginning at 7%
DOLLAR COST AVERAGING:	Yes
SYSTEMATIC WITHDRAWAL PLAN:	Yes
GUARANTEED DEATH BENEFIT:	Yes; minimum of total purchase payments
ACCOUNT STATEMENTS:	Issued quarterly
AVAILABILITY:	All states
MAXIMUM ISSUE AGE:	No maximum age restriction except where required by law
TELEPHONE NUMBER:	800-848-6331

Summary

The Best of America IV annuity from Nationwide Insurance Company has long enjoyed the stature associated with being one of the best annuities in the country. Before it became fashionable for insurance companies to develop competitive variable products containing several high-quality mutual funds, Nationwide's Best of America made such a selection available to prospective investors thirsting for a more sophisticated private retirement plan. The number of different subaccount options that investors may choose is a mind-boggling twenty-eight, clearly superior to the vast majority of variable annuities out there. As you might guess, it's difficult to leave a category of mutual fund untouched when you're offering twenty-eight of them to investors. Within The Best of America IV investors will find a range of fund selection that includes an S&P 500 index fund, a socially responsible fund, a gold fund, several international stock funds, a global bond fund, a real estate fund, four bond funds, as well as an array of conservative and aggressive growth funds and bond funds. Further strengthening the number and range of these fund options are the ten different money management firms that have been retained to guide them. A sample list of the big guns to be found here includes Dreyfus Corporation, Fidelity Investments, Oppenheimer Management Corporation, Twentieth Century Companies, and Warburg Pincus. Investors who prioritize quality money management in their search for a variable annuity would have to include Best of America IV on their "short list."

It is surely clear to you by now that The Best of America IV is, at this time, one of the truly great annuities available, especially from the standpoint of the professional investor. To this end, we believe it is worth mentioning Best of America's very liberal policy toward subaccount exchanging (one switch per day is allowable), which all serious investors will greatly appreciate.

INVESTOR'S SELECT
Variable Annuity

INSURANCE COMPANY:	Lincoln Benefit Life Company
INSURANCE COMPANY RATINGS:	A+ (A.M. Best)
	AA+ (Standard & Poor's)
ADDRESS:	206 South 13th St.
	Lincoln, NE 68508
NUMBER OF SUBACCOUNT OPTIONS:	★ ★ ★ ★ ★
RANGE OF SUBACCOUNT OPTIONS:	★ ★ ★ ★ ★
QUALITY OF SUBACCOUNT MANAGEMENT:	★ ★ ★ ★ ★
TELEPHONE EXCHANGES:	Yes
NUMBER OF EXCHANGES ALLOWED PER YEAR:	One free switch per month; $25 per switch thereafter
MINIMUM INITIAL INVESTMENT:	$1,200
SALES CHARGES:	Declining seven-year surrender charge, beginning at 7%
DOLLAR COST AVERAGING:	Yes
SYSTEMATIC WITHDRAWAL PLAN:	Yes
GUARANTEED DEATH BENEFIT:	Yes; minimum of total purchase payments compounded at 4% per year
ACCOUNT STATEMENTS:	Issued quarterly
AVAILABILITY:	All states except New York
MAXIMUM ISSUE AGE:	80
TELEPHONE NUMBER:	800-865-5237

Summary

The Investor's Select variable annuity available from Lincoln Benefit is another one of those variable products that was clearly developed with the serious investor in mind. There are eighteen different subaccounts available, which is not as numerous as some but still excellent nevertheless and worthy of a five-star rating in this category. As far as the breadth, or range, of the options is concerned, it too is superior. Retirement investors who choose the Investor's Select to be a cornerstone of their planning will have the opportunity to access a marvelous selection of mutual funds that includes several growth funds, an equity-income fund, a couple of international funds, a utility

fund, three bond funds, and various balanced/total return portfolios. As far as the management of these funds is concerned,
Lincoln Benefit has obtained the services of such champion
fund pilots as Janus, Fidelity, IAI, Federated, and Scudder. It's
difficult to overemphasize the importance of accessing the
highest-quality portfolio management possible. Names like
Fidelity, Janus, and Scudder should jump out at you if you are
at all acquainted with living legends among mutual funds, and
to have such management firms available to you within a variable annuity is a distinct advantage. The fact is, all variable
annuities are *not* the same, and you should strive to find one
such as Investor's Select that offers a distinctively better quality
of management than that typically found within most variable
products.

Although there are other variable annuities that offer a
slightly wider breadth of fund options, Investor's Select is still
among the best in that department. Furthermore, some
investors who would like to have a good fund selection but
don't want to be burdened with sorting through an almost-
manic array of different fund types might actually be happier
in an annuity like Investor's Select. Either way, give this one a
close look before you make that all-important final decision.

COMMONWEALTH
Variable Annuity

INSURANCE COMPANY:	The Life Insurance Company of Virginia
INSURANCE COMPANY RATINGS:	A+ (A.M. Best)
	AA (Standard & Poor's)
ADDRESS:	6610 West Broad St.
	Richmond, VA 23230
NUMBER OF SUBACCOUNT OPTIONS:	★ ★ ★ ★ ★
RANGE OF SUBACCOUNT OPTIONS:	★ ★ ★ ★ ★
QUALITY OF SUBACCOUNT MANAGEMENT:	★ ★ ★ ★ ★
TELEPHONE EXCHANGES:	Yes
NUMBER OF EXCHANGES ALLOWED PER YEAR:	One free switch per month; $10 per switch thereafter
MINIMUM INITIAL INVESTMENT:	$5,000
SALES CHARGES:	Declining six-year surrender charge, beginning at 6%
DOLLAR COST AVERAGING:	Yes
SYSTEMATIC WITHDRAWAL PLAN:	Yes
GUARANTEED DEATH BENEFIT:	Yes; minimum of total purchase payments
ACCOUNT STATEMENTS:	Issued biannually
AVAILABILITY:	All states except Maine, New York, and Washington
MAXIMUM ISSUE AGE:	75
TELEPHONE NUMBER:	800-521-8884

Summary

The Commonwealth annuity from Life of Virginia is another candidate that appeared to be headed for finalist status right from the start of our screening process. At a time when so many insurance companies are slow to respond to the needs of investors in search of a quality subaccount selection within their variable annuities, Life of Virginia clearly serves those investors well by providing them with twenty-eight different fund options, a formidable number. Although it is likely that, in the interest of competition, you'll soon see a plethora of annuities offering umpteen numbers of fund options to investors, the fact remains that only a handful of annuities like Commonwealth are doing so at this time, and so it is annuities like Commonwealth on which you should be focused. Beyond the sheer *number* of options is a range that is equally stellar. Among the choices are four asset allocation funds, three money markets, six bond funds of varying maturity lengths and portfolio qualities, a real estate fund, a utilities fund, three international funds, and a host of growth funds representing various levels of aggressiveness. For us, and hopefully for you as well, quality of fund management is extremely important. Here, too, Life of Virginia doesn't fail investors. In fact, the list of portfolio management companies reads like a *Who's Who* of money managers: Fidelity, Janus, Federated, Oppenheimer, and Neuberger & Berman are five names even the most passive mutual fund investor should recognize, with Aon Advisors, a fine advisory affiliate of Life of Virginia itself, rounding out the group of six fund managers found here.

The Commonwealth annuity is top-notch, plain and simple. With a number and range of fund options second to none, as well as a group of managers that includes some of the most renowned firms in the world, Life of Virginia gives investors the opportunity to get the very best from their retirement monies. We would suggest, without reservation, that you compare Life of Virginia's Commonwealth with any annuities you're considering *before* you place your investment.

CHAPTER NINE
Treasury Securities for a Secure Retirement

Treasury vehicles are regarded as the conservative staple of American investing. If you are a highly conservative investor, you probably own, have owned, or would *like* to own some sort of Treasury vehicle at some point in your investment life. As you might expect, Treasuries are popular with the very conservative because of their safety, *not* because of their yield. Treasury vehicles are *debt securities,* which is a fancy way of saying that they are bonds. However, rather than lending your money to XYZ Company to use, you lend your money to the U.S. government. *That's* why Treasuries are so highly regarded by superconservative investors; they are backed by the full faith and credit of the U.S. government. After all, if you can't trust your own Uncle Sam, who *can* you trust? In all seriousness, "full faith and credit" really means that if the government starts to run short of money and suspects that it will have a hard time honoring its obligations, it can (and *will*) always print *more* money. The point is, Treasury investors know that there is virtually no chance that they will lose any money that is invested in this type of security, as long as they hold the bond(s) to maturity. This, however, can be an important point that we'll discuss a bit later.

After reading the first paragraph of this chapter, you probably have a pretty good idea that Treasuries are not the *highest-yielding* securities to be found. You're right. On the risk/reward scale so often referred to in discussions of appropriate portfolio selections, Treasuries are at the top of the risk heading for safety, and at close to the bottom for reward, of all vehicles that can legitimately be referred to as "investments." Accordingly, Treasuries are highly inappropriate for any investors who are seeking growth from their portfolios. You just cannot earn a competitive return (overall) on Treasury securities. This isn't simply in comparison with stocks; other types of bonds will trounce Treasuries on a regular basis in a contest of returns.

WHO SHOULD INVEST IN TREASURIES?

Treasury securities should really be considered heavily by no one but the most conservative investor. An ideal investor in Treasuries is someone who has hopefully amassed a sizable sum for retirement and does not wish to further subject his monies to the whims of the stock market. He is probably within ten to fifteen years of the event of his death, and wishes to keep his risk exposure as low as possible while still earning some semblance of a current quality return. In *our* terminology, Preservationists would be the likeliest candidates for Treasuries, although Preservation—Accumulators might have some use for them as well. Anyone other than a Preservationist who elects to include Treasuries in his portfolio should be doing so with an eye to perhaps stabilizing the more-volatile items he already owns, *not* with the intention of realizing a solid rate of return from the vehicles themselves. Again, *safety* is the watchword of Treasuries, not *growth*.

"Treasuries" is actually a broad term that's used to describe all types of Treasury securities. There are basically three different types of Treasury securities out there, and it's important to understand the differences if you're considering purchasing these things for your portfolio. The word "Treasuries" can refer to either *Treasury bills, Treasury notes,* or *Treasury bonds.* Let's take a brief look at each.

Treasury Bills

Treasury bills, or T-bills, have the shortest maturities of all Treasury securities. Treasury bills are the safest of the already-safe Treasuries *because* their maturities are so short: one year or less. Treasury bills that mature in less than a year are either three-month or six-month maturities. Treasury bills are sold in minimum denominations of $10,000 at a discount to face value. This means that you will actually pay less than $10,000 for your T-bill, and the differential between what you pay and $10,000 is your interest. For example, if you purchase a one-year T-bill for $9,600, the $400 difference represents what you make on the investment. Furthermore, you can determine your *rate* of interest with these numbers, by dividing the amount of the discount by what you actually paid for the T-bill. So, if you in fact purchased a one-year T-bill for $9,600, your investment yield is calculated as follows:

$400 (amount of discount) divided by $9,600 (actual purchase price) = 4.16%

Let's talk a bit more about the sales process of T-bills so that you're absolutely clear on how it works. Treasury bills are auctioned to the public every week (except for one-year T-bills, which are auctioned monthly). Most people who purchase T-bills do so in the form of a *noncompetitive bid*, which means that they fork over $10,000 with the understanding that they will receive the yield that is settled on at the Treasury auction. So, once that yield is determined, you will receive a check for the amount of the discount. Referring to the above example, if the yield that results from the Treasury auction at which *you* are bidding on one-year T-bills is 4.16%, you will receive what amounts to a refund check in the amount of $400.

As you might have guessed, T-bills are the lowest-yielding of the Treasuries. This is because their maturities are shortest; in other words, you receive less of a rate because you are giving the government less time to use your money. In reality, T-bills don't offer a significantly better return than money market vehicles, and in fact their yields are generally poorer than those found in money market mutual funds because they offer the greatest amount of safety; always remember the risk/reward trade-off.

Treasury Notes and Bonds

We've decided to lump Treasury notes and Treasury bonds together because they work in exactly the same fashion. The only difference between the two lies in the length of the maturities: Treasury notes come in varying maturities of one to ten years, and Treasury bonds have maturities of ten years and longer. Right away, you should be able to figure out that T-notes will offer a bit less in yield than T-bonds because, as we learned in the discussion of T-bills, T-note investors are giving the government less time to use their money than are T-bond investors.

T-notes and T-bonds are generally available in denominations of $1,000, $5,000, $10,000, $100,000, and $1 million. The auctions for these securities are held every one to three months, depending on the maturity length. The interest on these instruments is paid every six months, but those insistent on receiving monthly income can arrange to have the maturities staggered so that they receive an interest check each month.

T-notes and T-bonds are regarded as more "honest to goodness" investments than are T-bills. The reason for this is that T-bills' maturities are just too short to offer an even halfway-serious investor much enticement. Most T-bill investors utilize the instruments for money-market–type purposes, and opt for the Treasuries with the longer maturities when they want to realize a return that is at least "chewable."

THE CASE FOR TREASURIES

In addition to the rock-solid safety and stability of Treasury notes and bonds, these vehicles are also popular because they are liquid. You are not locked in to a specific minimum period of time in which you have to hold the securities. There is no penalty for early withdrawal, which is a selling point for Treasuries and against CDs. Furthermore, Treasury securities are not subject to state and local taxes. This is another selling point for Treasuries in comparison with other investments with similar degrees of risk, and investors with severe tax liabilities would be wise to closely examine Treasuries for this reason. Finally, Treasury securities are one of the very few types of bonds in existence that are *noncallable*. This means that the issuer (in this case the government) cannot redeem the bonds before maturity if broad-market interest rates fall. This is a big advantage over corporate issues and especially municipal bonds, which ostensibly offer their own unique benefits to conservative investors.

THE CASE AGAINST TREASURIES

There are essentially two disadvantages to Treasuries. First, and most obvious, is the fact that these instruments provide little to no real growth for investors. However, the extent to which this is a real disadvantage is a relative determination. That is, most who will opt for Treasuries to begin with will probably be past the point where capital accumulation will be a high priority.

The second disadvantage to Treasuries, though, is one that has the potential to affect all who place their money in them: interest rate risk. Interest rate risk has the potential to affect *all* bondholders, and it is the risk associated with having interest rates move against you once you've purchased a bond. Briefly, when interest rates drop, bonds gain in value because new issues will now pay a lower rate, adding value to the current issues. By the same token, when interest rates rise, outstanding bonds lose value because the new issues offer a better rate to prospective investors. It is when rates rise, then, that they "move against" bondholders. The longer the bond's maturity, the greater the risk. Your best defense against interest rate risk is to become familiar with where rates at large are at and where they seem to be headed. Additionally, it should be mentioned that if you purchase a bond and hold it to maturity, you won't have to be concerned with losing any of your principal. Understanding interest rate risk and intently familiarizing yourself with your own investment outlook, therefore, is the best defense against rate risk.

TREASURIES AS MUTUAL FUNDS

It is possible to purchase U.S. Treasuries in the form of mutual funds, and there can be distinct advantages to doing so. Most important, your bonds are under the guidance of a professional investment manager who can help to negotiate interest risk on your behalf. Also, when you set up an account at a mutual fund company or discount brokerage that makes many different types of investments available to you simultaneously, it becomes easier to make Treasuries a flexible part of your overall portfolio rather than put yourself in the position of having to be a slave to the vehicles.

HOW TO BUY TREASURIES

If you wish to purchase some Treasuries for your portfolio, there are several ways to go about it. First, as discussed above, you can buy Treasuries in the form of mutual funds, and many no-load fund families make them available for very modest minimum investment requirements. If you consider adding Treasuries in this way, be sure to review just what types of Treasuries are contained in the fund's portfolio. Are they notes? Bonds? Some of both? Make sure you know.

You may also purchase Treasury securities from a bank or brokerage firm. Many people like to go this route, as it's quite convenient and the fee assessed by the financial institution is quite nominal, usually much less than $100.

If you wish to buy Treasury securities directly, a method that is becoming more heavily favored by consumers who are increasingly cost-conscious, you may do so from a Federal Reserve bank or bank branch. Banks and branches are located in just about every major city in the United States. You may also purchase Treasuries from the Bureau of Public Debt, which is located at 1300 C St., S.W., Washington, D.C. 20239. If you simply want more information about Treasuries, a great resource is the Consumer Information Center, Pueblo, CO 81009. Write and ask for their pamphlet *Information about Marketable Treasury Securities.*

Index

American AAdvantage Balanced
   Institutional, 144-146
American Skandia Advisors Plan II, 251
annuities
   advantages of, 242
   American Skandia Advisors Plan II,
      251
   best, 249-258
   Commonwealth, 257
   defined, 18, 241
   fixed, 19, 241, 243
   guarantees and, 19
   insurance companies and, 18
   Keyport Preferred Advisor, 249
   The Best of America IV, 253
   variable, 19, 242, 249-258
AT&T Corp., 238

Babson Bond L, 154-156
Babson-Stewart Ivory International, 94-
   96
Babson Value, 72-74
balanced funds
   American AAdvantage Balanced
      Institutional, 144-146
   best, 128-153
   CGM Mutual, 133-135
   Dodge & Cox Balanced, 136-138
   Eclipse Financial Asset Balanced,
      141-143
   Evergreen Foundation Y, 128-130
   FBP Contrarian Balanced, 151-153
   State Farm Balanced, 130-133

   T. Rowe Price Balanced, 138-140
   Vanguard STAR, 149-151
   Vanguard/Wellington, 146-168
Banc One Corporation, 230
BankAmerica Corp., 212
bond funds
   Babson Bond L, 154-156
   best, 154-177
   Bond Portfolio for Endowments, 156-
      158
   Dreyfus A Bonds Plus, 161-163
   Columbia Fixed-Income Securities,
      158-160
   Elfun Income, 163-165
   Fidelity Advisor Institutional Limited
      Term Bond, 166-168
   Fidelity Intermediate Bond, 168-170
   Fidelity Investment Grade bond, 170-
      172
   MAS Fixed-Income, 173-175
   Scudder Income, 175-177
Bond Portfolio for Endowments, 156-
   158
Broken Hill Proprietary Co. Ltd., 220

Campbell Soup Company, 216
Certificates of Deposit, 19
CGM Mutual, 133-135
Clipper Fund, 102-104
Colgate-Palmolive Company, 218
Columbia Fixed-Income Securities, 158-
   160
Columbia Growth, 104-106

Commonwealth, 257
contributions
    defined contributions, 15
    IRA, 13
    Keogh plans, 15
    tax-deductible, 13
CPC International, Inc., 224

De Beers Consolidated Mines Limited, 225
Dodge & Cox Balanced, 136-138
Dodge & Cox Stock Fund, 49-51
Dreyfus A Bonds Plus, 161-163

Eclipse Financial Asset Balanced, 141-143
Elfun Global, 80-82
Elfun Income, 163-165
Elfun Trusts, 107-109
Emerson Electric Co., 237
Evergreen Foundation Y, 128-130

FBP Contrarian Balanced, 151-153
Federal National Mortgage Association, 210
Fidelity Advisor Institutional Equity Growth, 110-112
Fidelity Advisor Institutional Limited Term Bond, 166-168
Fidelity Fund, 70-72
Fidelity Intermediate Bond, 168-170
Fidelity Investment Grade Bond, 170-172
Fidelity Retirement Growth, 112-114
Fidelity Select specialty funds, 180-183
fixed annuities, 19
401(k) plans
    defined, 17
    flexibility in, 18
403(b) plans. See 401(k) plans
457 plans. See 401(k) plans

General Electric Co., 227
General Mills, Inc., 219
Glaxo Wellcome PLC, 221
growth and income funds
    Babson Value, 72-74
    best, 49-74
    Dodge & Cox Stock Fund, 49-51
    Fidelity Fund, 70-72
    MAS Value, 52-54
    Mutual Beacon, 54-56
    Mutual Qualified, 57-58
    Mutual Shares, 59-61
    Neuberger and Berman Guardian Fund, 61-64
    SAFECO Equity Fund, 64-66
    Vanguard/Windsor Fund, 67-69
growth funds
    best, 102-127
    Clipper Fund, 102-104
    Columbia Growth, 104-106
    Elfun Trusts, 107-109
    Fidelity Advisor Institutional Equity Growth, 110-112
    Fidelity Retirement Growth, 112-114
    Mairs and Power Growth Fund, 115-117
    Managers Capital Appreciation, 117-119
    Omni Investment, 120-122
    Steinroe Special, 122-125
    Vanguard/Primecap Fund, 125-127

Harbor International, 75-77

income
    earned, 12
    fixed percentage contributions, 15
    See also salary reduction plans
index funds
    best, 185-190
    defined, 185
    Dreyfus Peoples Index Fund, Inc., 189
    Fidelity Market Index, 187
    SEI S&P 500 Index, 188
    T. Rowe Price Equity Index, 190
    Vanguard Index 500, 186
Individual Retirement Accounts. See IRAs
insurance companies
    annuities and, 18, 244
    variable annuities and, 20
Internal Revenue Service. See IRS
international funds
    Babson-Stewart Ivory International, 94-96
    best, 75-101

Elfun Global, 80-82
Harbor International, 75-77
Lexington Worldwide Emerging
    Markets Fund, 83-85
Managers International Equity, 99-101
Morgan Stanley Institutional
    International Equity Fund, 78-80
Scudder Global, 86-88
T. Rowe Price Foreign Fund, 88-90
T. Rowe Price International Stock, 91-
    93
Warburg Pincus International Equity
    Fund—Common Shares, 96-99
investments
    active, 34
    aggressive-growth, 28
    annuities, 241-258
    asset allocation models, 27
    balanced funds, 128-153
    bond funds, 154-177
    buy and hold types of, 34
    conservative, 29
    constructing portfolios, 29
    financial calculators and, 30
    fundamental analysts and, 35
    growth, 28, 102-127
    growth and income funds, 49-74
    index funds, 185-190
    international funds, 75-101
    municipal bond funds, 191-197
    mutual funds, 37-197
    passive, 33
    sector/specialty funds, 178-184
    selecting retirement, 23-35
    specialty funds, 178-184
    stocks, 199-239
    technical analysts and, 34
    Treasury securities, 259-265
investors
    conservative, 19, 259
    fundamental analysts, 35
    late starters as, 32
    long-term, 19
    retirement goals for, 23
    retiring in less than five to ten years,
        26
    retiring in less than ten years, 25
    retiring in ten or more years, 25

selecting stock for retirement, 199-239
    technical analysts, 34
Investor's Select, 255
IRAs
    annual fees for, 14
    banks and, 13
    contributions to, 13
    defined, 13
    mutual fund companies and, 14
    opening, 13
    penalties for early withdrawal, 14
IRS
    annuities and tax penalties, 20
    deducting contributions and, 21
    IRAs and tax penalties, 14

J.C. Penney Company, 232

Keogh plans
    defined benefit plans, 16
    defined contributions, 15
    money purchase plans, 15
    profit-sharing plans, 16
    self-employment and, 15-17
    types of, 15-17
Keyport Preferred Advisor, 249
Kimberly-Clark Corporation, 226

Lexington Worldwide Emerging Markets
    Fund, 83-85

Mairs and Power Growth Fund, 115-117
Managers Capital Appreciation, 117-119
Managers International Equity, 99-101
MAS Fixed-Income, 173-175
MAS Value, 52-54
May Department Stores Company, 236
Merck & Co., Inc., 215
Mobil Corp., 234
money purchase plans
    contributions to, 15
    Keogh plans and, 15
Monsanto Company, 239
Morgan Stanley Institutional
    International Equity Fund, 78-80
municipal bond funds
    defined, 191
    Elfun Tax-Exempt Income, 195

Scudder Managed Municipal Bonds, 197
State Farm Municipal Bond, 196
Vanguard Municipal High-Yield, 193
Vanguard Municipal Long-Term, 194
Mutual Beacon, 54-56
mutual funds
  advantages of, 38
  American AAdvantage Balanced Institutional, 144-146
  Babson Bond L, 154-156
  Babson-Stewart Ivory International, 94-96
  Babson Value, 72-74
  balanced, 47, 128-153
  best, 49-197
  bond funds, 154-177
  Bond Portfolio for Endowments, 156-158
  Dreyfus A Bonds Plus, 161-163
  CGM Mutual, 133-135
  Clipper Fund, 102-104
  Columbia Fixed-Income Securities, 158-160
  Columbia Growth, 104-106
  costs of investing in, 40
  defined, 28, 37
  Dodge & Cox Balanced, 136-138
  Dodge & Cox Stock Fund, 49-51
  Dreyfus Peoples Index Fund, Inc., 189
  Eclipse Financial Asset Balanced, 141-143
  Elfun Global, 80-82
  Elfun Income, 163-165
  Elfun Tax-Exempt Income, 195
  Elfun Trusts, 107-109
  Evergreen Foundation Y, 128-130
  FBP Contrarian Balanced, 151-153
  Fidelity Advisor Institutional Equity Growth, 110-112
  Fidelity Advisor Institutional Limited Term Bond, 166-168
  Fidelity Fund, 70-72
  Fidelity Intermediate Bond, 168-170
  Fidelity Investment Grade Bond, 170-172
  Fidelity Market Index, 187
  Fidelity Retirement Growth, 112-114

Fidelity Select Computers, 180
Fidelity Select Electronics, 181
Fidelity Select Home Finance, 182
Fidelity Select Software and Computers, 183
growth and income, 44, 47, 49-75
growth investments and, 28, 102-127
Harbor International, 75-77
index funds, 185-190
international, 44, 75-101
introduction to best, 42
investing in, 37-48
IRAs and, 13
Lexington Worldwide Emerging Markets Fund, 83-85
load funds, 40
Mairs and Power Growth Fund, 115-117
managers and, 38
Managers Capital Appreciation, 117-119
Managers International Equity, 99-101
MAS Fixed-Income, 173-175
MAS Value, 52-54
Morgan Stanley Institutional International Equity Fund, 78-80
Municipal bond funds, 191-197
Mutual Beacon, 54-56
Mutual Qualified, 57-58
Mutual Shares, 59-61
Neuberger and Berman Guardian Fund, 61-64
no-load funds, 41
Omni Investment, 120-122
SAFECO Equity Fund, 64-66
Scudder Global, 86-88
Scudder Income, 175-177
Scudder Managed Municipal Bonds, 197
sector/specialty funds, 178-184
SEI S&P 500 Index, 188
specialty funds, 178-184
State Farm Balanced, 130-133
State Farm Municipal bond, 196
Steinroe Special, 122-125
Treasuries as, 264
T. Rowe Price Balanced, 138-140
T. Rowe Price Equity Index, 190

T. Rowe Price Foreign Fund, 88-90
T. Rowe Price International Stock, 91-93
T. Rowe Price Science and Technology, 184
Vanguard Index 500, 186
Vanguard Municipal High-Yield, 193
Vanguard Municipal Long-Term, 194
Vanguard/Primecap Fund, 125-127
Vanguard STAR, 149-151
Vanguard/Wellington, 146-168
Vanguard/Windsor Fund, 67-69
volatility measurements, 45
Warburg Pincus International Equity Fund—Common Shares, 96-99
Mutual Qualified, 57-58
Mutual Shares, 59-61

Neuberger and Berman Guardian Fund, 61-64
Norwest Corp., 211

Omni Investment, 120-122, 122-125

Philip Morris Companies, Inc., 213
portfolios
   checking periodically, 34
profit-sharing plans
   contributions to, 16
   Keogh plans and, 16

retirement
   annuities and, 241
   selecting stock for, 199-239
   Treasury securities, 259
retirement accounts
   defined, 11
   earned income and, 12
   IRAs, 12-14
   Keogh plans, 15-17
   overview, 11-22
   plans v. investments, 12
   SEP-IRAs, 14-15
retirement phases
   accumulation, 25
   accumulation-preservation, 25
   preservation, 27
   preservation-accumulation, 26

retirement plans
   401(k) plans, 17
   accumulation phase, 25
   accumulation-preservation phase, 25
   annuities, 18-20
   checking your portfolio, 34
   company-sponsored, 17-22
   fixed annuities, 19
   planning phases, 25-27
   preservation-accumulation phase, 26
   preservation phase, 27
   selecting investments, 22
   social security and, 31
   tax-deferred growth and, 21
   variable annuities, 19, 249-258
Royal Dutch Petroleum, 231

SAFECO Equity Fund, 64-66
salary reduction plans, 17-22
Sara Lee Corporation, 217
SBC Communications, Inc., 229
Schering-Plough Corp., 214
Scudder Global, 86-88
Scudder Income, 175-177
sector/specialty funds
   defined, 178
   Fidelity Select Computers, 180
   Fidelity Select Electronics, 181
   Fidelity Select Home Finance, 182
   Fidelity Select Software and Computers, 183
   T. Rowe Price Science and Technology, 184
   types of, 180-184
securities. See Treasury securities
self-employment
   Keogh plans and, 15-17
   SEP-IRAs and, 15
SEP-IRAs
   contributions to, 15
   defined, 14
   self-employment and, 15
   small businesses and, 15
Shell Transport, 233
Simplified Employee Pension Plan. See SEP-IRA
specialty funds. See sector/specialty funds

Sprint Corporation, 235
State Farm Balanced, 130-133
Steinroe Special, 122-125
stocks
    AT&T Corp., 238
    Banc One Corporation, 230
    BankAmerica Corp., 212
    best, 209-239
    Broken Hill Proprietary Co. Ltd., 220
    Campbell Soup Company, 216
    choosing, 202
    Colgate-Palmolive Company, 218
    CPC International, Inc., 224
    De Beers Consolidated Mines
        Limited, 225
    defined, 199
    Emerson Electric Co., 237
    Federal National Mortgage
        Association, 210
    General Electric Co., 227
    General Mills, Inc., 219
    Glaxo Wellcome PLC, 221
    growth, 202
    income, 204
    J.C. Penney Company, 232
    Kimberly-Clark Corporation, 226
    May Department Stores Company, 236
    Merck & Co., Inc., 215
    Mobil Corp., 234
    Monsanto Company, 239
    Norwest Corp., 211
    Philip Morris Companies, Inc., 214
    Royal Dutch Petroleum, 231
    Sara Lee Corporation, 217
    SBC Communications, Inc., 229
    Schering-Plough Corp., 214
    selecting for retirement, 199-239
    Shell Transport, 233
    Sprint Corporation, 235
    Unilever N.V., 223

Unilever PLC, 222
value, 204
Warner-Lambert Company, 228

The Best of America IV, 253
Treasury securities, 259-265
    advantages of, 263
    bills, 261
    defined, 259
    how to buy, 264
    notes and bonds, 262
T. Rowe Price Balanced, 138-140
T. Rowe Price Foreign Fund, 88-90
T. Rowe Price International Stock, 91-93
T. Rowe Price Science and Technology,
    184

Unilever N.V., 223
Unilever PLC, 222

Vanguard/Primecap Fund, 125-127
Vanguard STAR, 149-151
Vanguard/Wellington, 146-148
Vanguard/Windsor Fund, 67-69
variable annuities
    best, 249-258
    defined, 9
    insurance companies and , 20
volatility measurements
    alpha, 45
    balanced, 47
    beta, 46
    bond funds, 48
    growth, 47
    R2 and R2 squared, 46
    standard deviation, 46

Warburg Pincus International Equity
    Fund—Common Shares, 96-98
Warner-Lambert Company, 228

About the Authors

J. W. Dicks is the editor of the *Mutual Fund Advisor*, a monthly newsletter devoted to mutual fund investment strategies. The newsletter features model portfolios any investor can use to design his own successful investment plan. For a complementary issue, please call 1-800-333-3700.

Charles C. Smith, Jr., is the founder of Delta Advisory Services, a registered investment advisory firm that specializes in the management of no-load mutual funds. For a free list of current recommendations, call 1-800-333-3700.

James L. Paris is a Certified Financial Planner and professional money manager. He is president of James L. Paris Securities, a broker-dealer that specializes in variable annuities. For a free review of your portfolio holdings and to receive a free report on variable annuity strategies for the '90s, call 1-800-950-PLAN. James L. Paris Securities is a member of NASD. The firm's services are not available in all states.